The
Reference Shelf®

Policing in 2020

The Reference Shelf
Volume 93 • Number 1
H.W. Wilson
A Division of EBSCO Information Services, Inc.

Published by
GREY HOUSE PUBLISHING
Amenia, New York
2021

The Reference Shelf

The books in this series contain reprints of articles, excerpts from books, addresses on current issues, and studies of social trends in the United States and other countries. There are six separately bound numbers in each volume, all of which are usually published in the same calendar year. Numbers one through five are each devoted to a single subject, providing background information and discussion from various points of view and concluding with an index and comprehensive bibliography that lists books, pamphlets, and articles on the subject. The final number of each volume is a collection of recent speeches. Books in the series may be purchased individually or on subscription.

Publisher's Cataloging-In-Publication Data
(Prepared by The Donohue Group, Inc.)

Names: Grey House Publishing, Inc., compiler.
Title: Policing in 2020 / [compiled by Grey House Publishing].
Other Titles: Reference shelf ; v. 93, no. 1.
Description: Amenia, New York : Grey House Publishing, 2021. | Includes bibliographical references and index.
Identifiers: ISBN 9781642657890 (v. 93, no. 1) | ISBN 9781642655995 (volume set)
Subjects: LCSH: Police--United States--Sources. | Police brutality--United States--Sources. | Police--United States--Finance--Sources. | Police--United States--Public opinion--Sources. | LCGFT: Reference works.
Classification: LCC HV8139 .P65 2021 | DDC 363.20973--dc23

Printed in Canada

Contents

Preface: Policing America   ix

1

The Police Force

Understanding Police Brutality   3
The Long, Painful History of Police Brutality in the U.S.   9
Katie Nodjimbadem, *Smithsonian*, July 27, 2017

What the Police Really Believe   13
Zack Beauchamp, *Vox*, July 7, 2020

George Floyd and the History of Police Brutality in America   23
Kadijatou Diallo and John Shattuck, *The Boston Globe*, June 1, 2020

10 Things We Know about Race and Policing in the U.S.   26
Drew DeSilver, Michael Lipka, and Dalia Fahmy, *Pew Research Center*, June 3, 2020

Why Statistics Don't Capture the Full Extent of the Systemic Bias in Policing   37
Laura Bronner, *FiveThirtyEight*, June 25, 2020

2

Policing in Place

Community Policing and the Role of Police   43
Polling Finds a Divide in How Americans View Police and Protestors   49
Timothy Rich, et al., *The Hill*, August 11, 2020

The Negative Consequences of Entangling Local Policing and Immigration Enforcement   53
Danyelle Solomon, Tom Jawetz, and Sanam Malik, Center for American Progress, March 21, 2017

Has ICE Found a Way to Get around Sanctuary Policies?   64
Jack Herrera, *PacificStandard*, May 7, 2019

Calls for Reform Bring Renewed Focus to Community Policing, but Does It Work?   67
Candice Norwood, *PBS NewsHour*, September 18, 2020

3

Plague Policing

Policing in the Age of COVID-19   75

Policing during the Coronavirus Pandemic   81
Ed Chung, Betsy Pearl, and Lea Hunter, Center for American Progress, April 14, 2020

Explainer: Why Police Will Be Crucial Players in the Battle
    against Coronavirus   85
Terry Goldsworthy and Robyn Lincoln, *The Conversation*, March 26, 2020

Do We Really Need the COVID-19 Police?   88
Marc Siegel, *The Hill*, December 1, 2020

U.S. Policing after Wave One of COVID-19   91
Vanda Felbab-Brown, *Lawfare*, May 20, 2020

COVID-19 Curbs Community Policing at a Time of Diminishing Trust   98
By David Montgomery, The Pew Charitable Trusts, October 1, 2020

4

Training Days

Police Education and Policy   105

Police Reformers Push for De-escalation Training, but the Jury Is Out on Its
    Effectiveness   111
Erin Schumaker, *ABC News*, July 5, 2020

Private Company Moves to Profit from New York's Police Reforms   117
Alice Speri, *The Intercept*, August 9, 2020

Police Reforms Stall around the Country, Despite New Wave of Activism   124
Nolan D. McCaskill, *Politico*, September 23, 2020

Could "Insight Policing" Have Saved Sandra Bland, Freddie
    Gray and Others?   128
Megan Price, *The Conversation*, July 22, 2015

5

Steps Toward Reform

Solving Problems for a Better Policing System 133
"Perfect Storm": Defund the Police, COVID-19 Lead to Biggest Police Budget
Cuts in Decade 137
Kevin Johnson and Kristine Phillips, *USA Today*, July 31, 2020

Los Angeles Cuts LAPD Spending, Taking Police Staffing to Its Lowest Level in
12 Years 141
By David Zahniser, Dakota Smith, Emily Alpert Reyes, *Los Angeles Times*, July 1, 2020

What Exactly Does It Mean to Defund the Police? 145
Amanda Arnold, *The Cut*, June 12, 2020

The Defunding Debate 150
Jack Herrera, *Columbia Journalism Review*, Summer 2020

6

Policing the Digital Citizen

Technology in Policing 159
The Microsoft Police State: Mass Surveillance, Facial Recognition, and the
Azure Cloud 165
Michael Kwet, *The Intercept*, July 14, 2020

Cops in Miami, NYC Arrest Protesters from Facial Recognition Matches 174
Kate Cox, *Ars Technica*, August 19, 2020

Police Are Using Facial Recognition for Minor Crimes Because They Can 177
Alfred Ng, *CNET*, October 24, 2020

Body Cameras Are Seen as Key to Police Reform: But Do They Increase
Accountability? 180
Candice Norwood, *PBS NewsHour*, June 25, 2020

Body Cameras May Not Be the Easy Answer Everyone Was Looking For 185
Lindsey Van Ness, The Pew Charitable Trusts, January 14, 2020

Amazon's Doorbell Camera Ring Is Working with Police—and Controlling
What They Say 190
Kari Paul, *The Guardian*, August 30, 2019

How to Reform Police Monitoring of Social Media 195
Rachel Levinson-Waldman and Angel Diaz, Brookings Institution, July 9, 2020

Bibliography 203
Websites 207
Index 209

Policing America

The State of Policing in America

American policing has never been more controversial than it is in 2021. In 2020, with the world in the midst of a global pandemic that disrupted daily life and shocked economies around the world, repeated incidents involving the controversial police treatment of African Americans gave new impetus to the Black Lives Matter movement, which emerged in 2014 to protest racial bias in policing. By the end of the year, many municipalities were considering dramatic changes to the way that tax revenues are allocated, reducing budgets for police departments and expanding funding for alternatives to policing. The national "Defund the Police" movement had begun to gain steam and, for the first time in American history, a majority of Americans agreed that police engaged in discriminatory violence targeting minority Americans disproportionately. Polling organizations found that, across America, faith and trust in police had fallen. This, coupled with budgetary problems related to the COVID-19 pandemic, placed police departments in a precarious position, with many facing potential funding and personnel shortages.[1]

Across the nation, there was widespread disagreement about the state of policing. Donald Trump and many of his allies alleged that calls for reform had been overstated and even suggested that the rise of militant leftist organizations was connected to this controversy, a claim that has been disproven. Many Americans likewise embraced the idea that police were being unfairly criticized, and there were counter movements to express support for police. Thanks to the political rhetoric and divisiveness that characterized American political life in 2020, the debate became increasingly hyperbolic. However, there is sufficient evidence to suggest that calls for police reform are justified. The question is, can police and activists work together to find a path to reform that addresses the criticisms of the public without sacrificing the welfare of police?

A Tough Job

To be certain, working in a police department can be a difficult and demanding job. Police are called upon to intercede in conflicts and thus are sometimes asked to place themselves in harm's way. Even when not confronting danger directly, police frequently face workplace pressure and stress and, because they are charged with enforcing laws that are frequently unpopular, they are more likely than persons in many other professions to encounter hostility from citizens. The stress of police life is one of the reasons that police suffer from a higher rate of burnout than those in many other fields, and early retirement is also more common.[2]

Each day in America police officers effectively help citizens with a wide variety of problems. From handling domestic disturbances to investigating crimes, there are thousands of earnest police officers and administrators who put forth an honest effort to help those in need and endeavor to live up to the oaths that police take, to serve the public trust. Further, being a police officer in America is a task that has become more difficult over time. Police in 2020 faced shrinking budgets, problems attracting new officers and trained specialists, and increasing danger on the job not because of rising crime rates but because their duties brought the risk of exposure to COVID-19. Meanwhile, widely circulated instances of police misconduct brought entire departments, including officers who attempted to perform their duties fairly, under increasing scrutiny, exposing them to vehement anger from the public. There has perhaps never been a more stressful time to be a police officer. However, the fact that there are "good cops" trying to perform well in their jobs in no way delegitimizes the very real problems within the policing system.

The Structural Problems

The essential argument among those calling for reform is that police departments have not done enough to combat racial prejudice, to punish officer misconduct, or to prevent officers from using excessive and unnecessary force. Further, critics allege that police departments actively discourage officers and staff from reporting misconduct and, in many cases, shield members of police departments accused of misconduct from punishment or scrutiny. The reform movement is not about targeting police but about instigating significant changes in the structure and administration of policing that can address these long-standing problems.

Contrary to popular belief, racial prejudice among police and the misuse of force is not primarily a matter of individual bad actors engaging in misconduct. It is a signifier of a deeper problem. Research indicates that prejudicial treatment and the excessive use of force are the result of structural prejudices that have been incorporated into police culture. Over the decades, police have become increasingly militaristic, in part because of political influence shaped by misconceptions about the relationship between crime, race, and economic class. Violent crime rates in America have been falling since the 1960s, and yet violent interactions between police and citizens have increased over this same period.[3] Over the decades, police have adopted increasingly militant tactics even as violent crime has plummeted. The primary reason for this is political. For centuries, politicians in America have utilized the fear of crime to gain support. By threatening an increasing risk of violence and crime, even if the threat is not realistic, politicians attempt to frighten citizens into giving their support by promising to "clean up" society. Politicians in this vein often offer solutions that involve increasingly punitive "crime fighting" laws and policies, and among these has been the incorporation of military-style equipment (firearms, protective gear, the use of tear gas) and militant tactics into domestic police departments. The American "SWAT Team" is essentially a domestic security unit that was modeled after military strike teams.

The use of military equipment and tactics has been controversial for decades, and there are many Americans who object to police officers treating crime fighting as a "war." Many believe crime is better viewed as the result of complex social and economic factors that cannot be solved without equally comprehensive strategies. Another problem is that much of the emphasis in fighting crime has been directed toward poor African American communities. The primary reason for this is also political. Prejudicial attitudes about race and crime have pervaded American popular culture since before the earliest days of the republic, and these attitudes continue to motivate how cities, counties, and police departments allocate resources and on how they design their efforts to address crimes in various communities. Over the years, overt racism has become less obvious, but ingrained, structural attitudes about race continue to overemphasize crime and the potential threat of minorities in America, especially of African Americans.[4]

Ultimately, the militarization of American policing has made policing much more difficult, because such tactics increase the potential for escalation and violence. Studies have repeatedly shown that the adoption of military-grade weapons and tactics has failed to keep police safe and that, in fact, police are more likely to be injured on the job when utilizing aggressive tactics and the threat of violence. Studies have also shown that the adoption of military-style weapons and tactics has not reduced crime rates. At the same time, militant tactics increase the potential for negative interactions with members of the public and create negative public perceptions of police.[5]

Addressing prejudicial treatment, the use of excessive force, and other problems is therefore not only about protecting the interest of the citizens whom police are sworn to protect and serve but also about protecting police officers or other representatives of the state. Reforming police tactics and methods, focusing on de-escalation, and deemphasizing the use of militant tactics are goals that would, if successful, not only protect citizens from police but might also reduce officer stress and keep officers safer.[6]

A Problem of Perception and Performance

Numerous public opinion polls and widespread national protests have shown that support for police has dropped to the lowest level in history. In the summer of 2020, after police in many cities violently responded to civil rights protests against police brutality and prejudicial treatment, the United Nations council on racial prejudice issued a statement criticizing America for failing to address the prejudicial abuse of power by American police.[7] This unprecedented criticism from the United Nations is but one facet in the growing pool of evidence suggesting that police have an increasingly severe public-image problem.

Racial bias and use of excessive force in policing are only two of numerous criticisms that have been directed at the American policing system. Critics have also questioned the way that police have utilized digital technology, such as drones and facial recognition systems, and have accused police and other state agencies of violating civil liberties in their increasing use of mass surveillance. These are the latest issues in more than 20 years of controversy over how and when police are allowed to access digital data and whether or not individuals should be entitled to privacy regarding their digital data. Likewise, recent evidence suggests that police training leaves officers ill equipped to address specialized problems like dealing with citizens suffering from drug addiction and/or mental illness. Though this criticism is not new, questions about the effectiveness of police interventions in nonviolent disturbances have come to the forefront again as the Defund the Police movement initiated a new debate about the allocation of community resources.

Police and all other representatives of state and local governments are servants of the people. Citizens fund police departments with the expectation that police will faithfully uphold and enforce laws in keeping with the welfare of the citizenry. Police are not expected to enforce governmental or political will; their role is to "serve and protect." It is therefore a betrayal of constitutional, federal, and state law as well as the underlying social contract between citizens and their government for police to abuse their power. Thus, when police officers perform their roles with racial prejudice, or when they abuse their power for personal gain, or when they fail to address corruption and misconduct within their ranks, they are committing a crime. Allegations of police misconduct must always be taken seriously, and police must protect rather than trammel the rights of citizens. This is a two-way street. The support of citizens and communities is not only beneficial for the welfare of police officers but is essential to the success of efforts to combat crime. While many Americans may disagree that police misconduct is widespread or that there is any justification for the kind of wide-reaching reforms that have been proposed, there is no denying the loss of public support and trust. Without this trust, police are ineffective.

Ultimately, if reforms are handled in a way that meets the challenges of police as well as the needs of citizens, reforms could help to make the lives of police safer and less stressful while also creating a system that better reflects the needs and rights of citizens. The police debate, like many other American political debates, has been too often clouded by political rhetoric and assignations of blame, but it is useful to remember that the ultimate goal of any society is to create a functioning system where the greatest number of people possible can live the best and most productive lives. In a perfect world, this would mean that those who serve the public would enjoy the support and trust of the people because the people would feel supported by the state. Given the heightened political tensions of 2020 and the increasingly contentious debate over governmental reform, it remains to be seen whether reformers and administrators can find common ground and can institute the kinds of changes needed to heal the relationship between America's police and the American people.

Works Used

Andrew, Scottie. "There's a Growing Call to Defund the Police: Here's What It Means." *CNN*. Jun 17, 2020. https://www.cnn.com/2020/06/06/us/what-is-defund-police-trnd/index.html.

Gross, Terry. "Militarization of Police Means U.S. Protesters Face Weapons Designed for War." *NPR*. Jul 1, 2020. https://www.npr.org/2020/07/01/885942130/militarization-of-police-means-u-s-protesters-face-weapons-designed-for-war.

"Impact of Stress on Police Officers' Physical and Mental Health." *Science Daily*. Sep 29, 2008. https://www.sciencedaily.com/releases/2008/09/080926105029. htm.

Ingraham, Christopher. "White People Are More Likely to Deal Drugs, but Black People Are More Likely to Get Arrested for It." *Washington Post*. Sep 30, 2014. https://www.washingtonpost.com/news/wonk/wp/2014/09/30/white-people-are-more-likely-to-deal-drugs-but-black-people-are-more-likely-to-get-arrested-for-it/.

Koerth, Maggie, and Amelia Thomson-DeVeaux. "Many Americans Are Convinced Crime Is Rising in the U.S.: They're Wrong." *FiveThirtyEight*. Aug 3, 2020. https://fivethirtyeight.com/features/many-americans-are-convinced-crime-is-rising-in-the-u-s-theyre-wrong/.

Mummolo, Jonathan. "Militarization Fails to Enhance Police Safety or Reduce Crime but May Harm Police Reputation." *PNAS*. Sep 11, 2018. https://www.pnas.org/content/115/37/9181.

"U.S. Criticized for Police Brutality, Racism at U.N. Rights Review." *NBC News*. Nov 10, 2020. https://www.nbcnews.com/news/nbcblk/u-s-criticized-police-brutality-racism-u-n-rights-review-n1247256.

Notes

1. Andrew, "There's a Growing Call to Defund the Police: Here's What It Means."
2. "Impact of Stress on Police Officers' Physical and Mental Health," *Science Daily*.
3. Koerth and Thomson-DeVeaux, "Many Americans Are Convinced Crime Is Rising in the U.S.: They're Wrong."
4. Ingraham, "White People Are More Likely to Deal Drugs, but Black People Are More Likely to Get Arrested for It."
5. Mummolo, "Militarization Fails to Enhance Police Safety or Reduce Crime but May Harm Police Reputation."
6. Gross, "Militarization of Police Means U.S. Protestors Face Weapons Designed for War."
7. "U.S. Criticized for Police Brutality, Racism at U.N. Rights Review," *NBC News*.

1
The Police Force

By Rickmouser45, via Wikimedia.

A mural in honor of George Floyd in Portland, Oregon. Floyd's death at the hands of police sparked nationwide protests.

Understanding Police Brutality

Police brutality and the use of excessive force is one of the most controversial issues in America, and with good reason. Police are granted authority, through municipal, regional, state, and federal law, to curtail the civil liberties of citizens and to utilize force and even violence to uphold the law. Citizens in democratic societies place their faith in the state and its agents, and when these individuals abuse their authority, it is a violation of this trust and of democracy itself, which depends on mutual trust between the citizenry and the state.

The proliferation of social media and private digital technologies has greatly changed the debate over police misconduct. Citizens utilizing digital cameras have documented and distributed evidence of police misconduct, changing the debate over police reform. In addition, research and analysis stretching back for decades has shown, without question, that African Americans and minority Americans are more likely to be subjected to abuse by police officers. The combination of increased documentation and research indicating widespread racial bias among police has made the issue of police reform one of the most controversial political issues as America enters the 2020s.

Bad Apples or a Rotten Tree

Each year, around 1,000 American civilians are killed by police. Data indicates that as many as 2,000 more are shot by police but do not die from those injuries. Thousands more are injured each year in incidents not involving a gun.[1] On the surface, these statistics mean very little, because evaluating the use of force by police must take into account whether that force was justified or necessary. Police are charged with intervening in dangerous situations and, in some cases, with confronting potentially dangerous individuals. For this reason, police are authorized to utilize force (even lethal force) when required. Thus, the fact that police shoot more than 3,000 Americans each year does not, in itself, indicate that they are engaging in misconduct. What must be ascertained is whether the use of force by police is justified and is being handled in a fair manner.

One of the data points that raises concern among public safety advocates is that the use of force by police is far more common than the use of force by citizens against police. Each year in America, around forty to fifty officers are shot in the line of duty, while police shoot more than 3,000 people. This means that it is at least sixty times more likely for a police officer to shoot a civilian than for a civilian to shoot a police officer.[2] Again, this statistic does not independently indicate a high level of police misconduct, because it is impossible to ascertain whether this level of police violence can be justified. However, there is sufficient data to suggest that police in the United States have a tendency to utilize confrontational and potentially violent methods excessively.

Interestingly, data from around the world suggests that it is not entirely necessary to utilize force to the extent that U.S. police officers do. Studies show, for instance, that U.S. officers kill more suspects in a single year than officers in the United Kingdom do in more than a decade. While one might argue that the United States has more crime or more dangerous criminals than the United Kingdom, this is not the case. UK crime rates are similar to those in the United States, and UK police appear to be as, if not more, effective as U.S. police in preventing crime and apprehending criminals.[3] Different policing strategies are not the only difference between the two nations, however. The United Kingdom has far more stringent laws on gun ownership, and research indicates that higher levels of gun ownership are equated with higher levels of violent crime.

Those who argue that U.S. police are always or very often justified in using force must also contend with decades of research suggesting that police in the United States are more likely to use force when confronting African American or minority suspects then when confronting white suspects suspected of the same crimes. Though many Americans do not believe that racial bias is prevalent in U.S. policing, there are many independent studies going back to the 1970s that collectively prove that African Americans are more likely to be stopped, investigated, arrested, imprisoned, subjected to force, or killed by police.[4] A 2018 study conducted in Chicago, for instance, indicates that Chicago police were fourteen times more likely to use force when engaging an African American citizen than a white citizen.[5] Studies indicate that 1 out of every 1,000 black men will be killed by police, making police violence the sixth-highest cause of death for black males in America.[6] Some have argued that black men are more likely to be involved in crime, but this is not the case. White Americans commit more crimes, in every category of crime, than African Americans. The perception of high rates of criminality among African American populations is an artifact of a long-standing pattern in which police target predominantly African American communities.

Studies indicate that white officers are more likely than minority officers to use force, including lethal force, and that white officers are more likely to use force against African American suspects as opposed to white suspects.[7] Statistics in this vein would seem to indicate that the use of excessive violence against minorities might be the result of individual racism among officers who apply their own racial prejudice to their work. However, studies also indicate that minority offices are also more likely to use force against minority suspects, and this indicates that the problem is more complex. Research indicates that the use of violence by police, and racial disparities in police treatment of citizens, is institutional in nature. While there are individual bad actors within police departments who harbor racial prejudice and demonstrate racial bias in their handling of situations, the culture of policing in America encourages and exacerbates racism and the use of violence and further results in officers being pressured to utilize or to accept the use of violence and differential treatment of suspects based on race and class.

While the notion that racial prejudice and the use of violence are structural problems within American policing is controversial, the research on the issue is robust. Over the years, dozens of studies have found evidence of structural racism in many arenas of American society, from the media to political institutions, and studies have likewise shown that structural and institutionalized racism play a significant role in police behavior. In contrast to individual racism, structural racism occurs because of the way that racial prejudice has been integrated into cultural norms. In terms of policing, what this means is that police departments have evolved to embrace the perception of higher levels of criminality and potential for violence among black suspects. Police then preemptively utilize violent tactics when engaging with African American citizens. Individuals embedded in this culture may not fully realize that their behavior is being shaped by institutionalized prejudice or that their behavior is furthering racist perceptions.[8]

Structural racism is difficult to combat because it is based on the often-unconscious embrace of preconceptions about race. Historical reviews of policing in the United States indicate that the institutionalized perception that African Americans are more dangerous and must be treated as such has a long history in America, reaching back to when some of the earliest law enforcement organizations in the country were founded specifically to capture and punish escaped slaves. Over the years, individual racism has played a role, and administrators and politicians have encouraged police departments to overemphasize minority criminality. Police therefore spend more time searching for criminal behavior among African American communities, and the crime uncovered during these investigations creates a skewed perception that crime is more common among African Americans. This misconception then spreads through society.

To provide one of many examples, in the 1980s it was widely believed that African Americans were responsible for the so-called "crack cocaine" epidemic in America. Popular culture reinforced this idea with films, television shows, and other media highlighting the role of predominantly black inner-city gangs and communities in the crisis. In reality, white individuals sold and used cocaine at a higher rate than African Americans, and the individuals responsible for bringing cocaine into the United States were predominantly white. The perception that the drug trade is a predominantly urban and African American is an example of structural racism. Contrast this with the recent opioid epidemic, which the media portrays as predominantly impacting white Americans. In this case, opioid users have been portrayed as victims rather than criminals, and blame has been focused on the role of nonwhite Hispanic individuals in fueling the supply of illegal opioids on the American market.[9]

Approaching Reform

To be certain, each day around the United States police officers genuinely and effectively help citizens. Most Americans agree that some kind of policing is occasionally necessary, and during times of crisis the bravery and effort of many police officers has been frequently noted. There is a perception among some Americans that recent calls for police reform and protests against racism and the use of force by police constitute an attack against the institution of policing itself. This has led to the growth of movements supporting the police across the United States. The issue has become increasingly polarized, as many U.S. politicians have misleadingly depicted the issue as a threat to law and order. The politicization of the issue has unfortunately obscured the underlying goals of police reform movements.

For many years, calls for police reform have been limited by assertions that the key strategy should be to identify and penalize "bad apples" within police departments. Research, however, indicates that addressing misbehaving officers is ineffective unless other steps are taken to reduce or reverse the insidious effect of institutionalized and structural racism and overemphasis on the use of force. This research indicates that the basic culture and strategy of policing must be altered to limit violent police encounters.

Recently, police reform committees and politicians interested in reform have focused on strategies designed to address police culture. For instance, one of the most talked-about police reform efforts of the 2010s is the use of "de-escalation training," which are programs aimed at teaching police officers to more effectively defuse conflicts to avoid violence. A number of police departments around the nation have invested in de-escalation training, and some studies have shown that, when officers embrace the principals involved, the strategy can effectively reduce violent encounters. However, research into the effectiveness of de-escalation training has been mixed, and it is unclear, as of 2020, whether or not de-escalation training can reduce violent police encounters. Some studies have indicated that de-escalation training has had limited impact on reducing the use of force, but this does not necessarily mean that such training is a waste of time or resources. De-escalation training can only be effective when officers perceive the benefits and actively utilize it as a strategy.

While Americans frequently disagree about the need for and nature of police reform, there is one level at which the need for some kind of change is undeniable. In 2020, polling organizations found that trust in police had hit an all-time low among the American public. Though studies differed in their findings, overall under 60 percent of white Americans and less than 40 percent of minority Americans reported a "great deal" or "quite a lot" of confidence in police. This level of skepticism in American policing is a serious problem. For many reasons, police departments are totally dependent on public support to be effective. Without this support, police are more likely to be hurt or killed on the job and they are less likely to effectively prevent crimes. Whatever form reform takes, the goal of restoring public trust is one that can positively impact all Americans.

Works Used

Clark, Caitlin. "Texas A&M Study: White Police Officers Use Force More Often Than Non-White Colleges." *Texas A&M Today*. Jun 24, 2020. https://today.tamu.edu/2020/06/24/texas-am-study-white-police-officers-use-force-more-often-than-non-white-colleagues/.

Fan, Andrew. "Chicago Police Are 14 Times More Likely to Use Force Against Young Black Men Than Against Whites." *The Intercept*. Aug 16, 2018. https://theintercept.com/2018/08/16/chicago-police-misconduct-racial-disparity/.

Lally, Robin. "Police Use of Fatal Force Identified as a Leading Cause of Death in Young Men." *Rutgers*. Aug 8, 2019. https://www.rutgers.edu/news/police-use-fatal-force-identified-leading-cause-death-young-men.

Lartey, Jamiles. "By the Numbers: US Police Kill More in Days Than Other Countries Do in Years." *The Guardian*. Jun 9, 2015. https://www.theguardian.com/us-news/2015/jun/09/the-counted-police-killings-us-vs-other-countries.

Netherland, Julie, and Helena B. Hansen. "The War on Drugs That Wasn't: Wasted Whiteness, 'Dirty Doctors,' and Race in Media Coverage of Prescription Opioid Misuse." *Culture, Medicine, and Psychiatry*, vol. 40, no. 4, 2016.

Peeples, Lynne. "What the Data Say about Police Shootings." *Nature*. Sep 4, 2019. https://www.nature.com/articles/d41586-019-02601-9.

Sauter, Michael B., and Charles Stockdale. "The Most Dangerous Jobs in the US Include Electricians, Firefighters and Police Officers." *USA Today*. Jan 8, 2019. https://www.usatoday.com/story/money/2019/01/08/most-dangerous-jobs-us-where-fatal-injuries-happen-most-often/38832907/.

Siegel, Michael. "Racial Disparities in Fatal Police Shootings: An Empirical Analysis Informed by Critical Race Theory." *Boston University Law Review*, vol. 100, no. 1069. https://www.bu.edu/bulawreview/files/2020/05/10-SIEGEL.pdf.

Williams, Timothy. "Study Supports Suspicion That Police Are More Likely to Use Force on Blacks." *New York Times*. Jul 7, 2016. https://www.nytimes.com/2016/07/08/us/study-supports-suspicion-that-police-use-of-force-is-more-likely-for-blacks.html.

Notes

1. Peeples, "What the Data Say about Police Shootings."
2. Sauter and Stockdale, "The Most Dangerous Jobs in the US Include Electricians, Firefighters, and Police Officers."
3. Lartey, "By the Numbers: US Police Kill More in Days Than Other Countries Do in Years."
4. Williams, "Study Supports Suspicion That Police Are More Likely to Use Force on Blacks."
5. Fan, "Chicago Police Are 14 Times More Likely to Use Force Against Young Black Men Than Against Whites."
6. Lally, "Police Use of Fatal Force Identified as a Leading Cause of Death in Young Men."

7. Clark, "Texas A&M Study: White Police Offices Use Force More Often Than Non-White Colleagues."

8. Siegel, "Racial Disparities in Fatal Police Shootings: An Empirical Analysis Informed by Critical Race Theory."

9. Netherland and Hansen, "The War on Drugs That Wasn't."

The Long, Painful History of Police Brutality in the U.S.

By Katie Nodjimbadem
Smithsonian, July 27, 2017

Editor's Note, May 29, 2020: In 2017, *Smithsonian* covered the history of police brutality upon the protests over the verdict in the Philando Castile murder case. With the Twin Cities once again under the national spotlight after the killing of George Floyd, we revisit the subject matter below.

Last month, hours after a jury acquitted former police officer Jeronimo Yanez of manslaughter in the shooting death of 32-year-old Philando Castile, protesters in St. Paul, Minnesota, shutdown Interstate 94. With signs that read: "Black Lives Matter" and "No Justice, No Peace," the chant of "Philando, Philando" rang out as they marched down the highway in the dark of night.

The scene was familiar. A year earlier, massive protests had erupted when Yanez killed Castile, after pulling him over for a broken taillight. Dashcam footage shows Yanez firing through the open window of Castile's car, seconds after Castile disclosed that he owned and was licensed to carry a concealed weapon.

A respected school nutritionist, Castile was one of 233 African-Americans shot and killed by police in 2016, a startling number when demographics are considered. African-Americans make up 13 percent of the U.S. population but account for 24 percent of people fatally shot by police. According to the *Washington Post*, blacks are "2.5 times as likely as white Americans to be shot and killed by police officers."

Today's stories are anything but a recent phenomenon. A cardboard placard in the collections of the Smithsonian's National Museum of African American History and Culture and on view in the new exhibition "More Than a Picture," underscores that reality.

The yellowing sign is a reminder of the continuous oppression and violence that has disproportionately shaken black communities for generations—"We Demand an End to Police Brutality Now!"—is painted in red and white letters.

"The message after 50 years is still unresolved," remarks Samuel Egerton, a college professor, who donated the poster to the museum. He carried it in protest during the 1963 March on Washington. Five decades later, the poster's message rings alarmingly timely. Were it not for the yellowed edges, the placard could almost be mistaken for a sign from any of the Black Lives Matter marches of the past three years.

"There are those who are asking the devotees of civil rights, 'When will you be satisfied?'" said Martin Luther King, Jr. in his iconic "I Have a Dream" speech at the 1963 march. His words continue to resonate today after a long history of violent confrontations between African-American citizens and the police. "We can never be satisfied as long as the Negro is the victim of the unspeakable horrors of police brutality."

"This idea of police brutality was very much on people's minds in 1963, following on the years, decades really, of police abuse of power and then centuries of oppression of African-Americans," says William Pretzer, senior history curator at the museum.

Modern policing did not evolve into an organized institution until the 1830s and '40s when northern cities decided they needed better control over quickly growing populations. The first American police department was established in Boston in 1838. The communities most targeted by harsh tactics were recent European immigrants. But, as African-Americans fled the horrors of the Jim Crow south, they too became the victims of brutal and punitive policing in the northern cities where they sought refuge.

In 1929, the Illinois Association for Criminal Justice published the Illinois Crime Survey. Conducted between 1927 and 1928, the survey sought to analyze causes of high crime rates in Chicago and Cook County, especially among criminals associated with Al Capone. But also the survey provided data on police activity—although African-Americans made up just five percent of the area's population, they constituted 30 percent of the victims of police killings, the survey revealed.

"There was a lot of one-on-one conflict between police and citizens and a lot of it was initiated by the police," says Malcolm D. Holmes, a sociology professor at the University of Wyoming, who has researched and written about the topic of police brutality extensively.

That same year, President Herbert Hoover established the National Commission on Law Observance and Enforcement to investigate crime related to prohibition in addition to policing tactics. Between 1931 and 1932, the commission published the findings of its investigation in 14 volumes, one of which was titled "Report on Lawlessness in Law Enforcement." The realities of police brutality came to light, even though the commission did not address racial disparities outright.

During the Civil Rights Era, though many of the movement's leaders advocated for peaceful protests, the 1960s were fraught with violent and destructive riots.

Aggressive dispersion tactics, such as police dogs and fire hoses, against individuals in peaceful protests and sit-ins were the most widely publicized examples of police brutality in that era. But it was the pervasive violent policing in communities of color that built distrust at a local, everyday level.

One of the deadliest riots occurred in Newark in 1967 after police officers severely beat black cab driver John Smith during a traffic stop. Twenty-six people died and many others were injured during the four days of unrest. In 1968, President

Lyndon B. Johnson organized the National Advisory Commission on Civil Disorders to investigate the causes of these major riots.

The origins of the unrest in Newark weren't unique in a police versus citizen incident. The commission concluded "police actions were 'final' incidents before the outbreak of violence in 12 of the 24 surveyed disorders."

Today, live streaming, tweets, and Facebook posts have blasted the incidents of police brutality beyond the black community and into the mainstream media.

The commission identified segregation and poverty as indicators and published recommendations for reducing social inequalities, recommending an "expansion and reorientation of the urban renewal program to give priority to projects directly assisting low-income households to obtain adequate housing." Johnson, however, rejected the commission's recommendations.

Black newspapers reported incidents of police brutality throughout the early and mid-20th century and the popularization of radio storytelling spread those stories even further. In 1991, following the beating of cab driver Rodney King, video footage vividly told the story of police brutality on television to a much wider audience. The police officers, who were acquitted of the crime, had hit King more than 50 times with their batons.

Today, live streaming, tweets and Facebook posts have blasted the incidents of police brutality, beyond the black community and into the mainstream media. Philando Castile's fiancée, Diamond Reynolds, who was in the car with her daughter when he was shot, streamed the immediate aftermath of the shooting on her phone using Facebook live.

"Modern technology allows, indeed insists, that the white community take notice of these kinds of situations and incidents," says Pretzer.

And as technology has evolved, so has the equipment of law enforcement. Police departments with military-grade equipment have become the norm in American cities. Images of police officers in helmets and body armor riding through neighborhoods in tanks accompany stories of protests whenever one of these incidents occurs.

"What we see is a continuation of an unequal relationship that has been exacerbated, made worse if you will, by the militarization and the increase in fire power of police forces around the country," says Pretzer.

The resolution to the problem, according to Pretzer, lies not only in improving these unbalanced police-community relationships, but, more importantly, in eradicating the social inequalities that perpetuate these relationships that sustain distrust and frustration on both sides.

'There's a tendency to stereotype people as being more or less dangerous. There's a reliance upon force that goes beyond what is necessary to accomplish police duty," says Holmes. "There's a lot of this embedded in the police departments that helps foster this problem."

Print Citations

CMS: Nodjimbadem, Katie. "The Long, Painful History of Police Brutality in the U.S." In *The Reference Shelf: Policing in 2020,* edited by Micah L. Issitt, 9-12. Amenia, NY: Grey House Publishing, 2021.

MLA: Nodjimbadem, Katie. "The Long, Painful History of Police Brutality in the U.S." *The Reference Shelf: Policing in 2020,* edited by Micah L. Issitt, Grey Housing Publishing, 2021, pp. 9-12.

APA: Nodjimbadem, K. (2021). The long, painful history of police brutality in the U.S. In Micah L. Issitt (Ed.), *The reference shelf: Policing in 2020* (pp. 9-12). Amenia, NY: Grey Housing Publishing.

What the Police Really Believe

By Zack Beauchamp
Vox, July 7, 2020

Arthur Rizer is a former police officer and 21-year veteran of the US Army, where he served as a military policeman. Today, he heads the criminal justice program at the R Street Institute, a center-right think tank in DC. And he wants you to know that American policing is even more broken than you think.

"That whole thing about the bad apple? I hate when people say that," Rizer tells me. "The bad apple rots the barrel. And until we do something about the rotten barrel, it doesn't matter how many good f****** apples you put in."

To illustrate the problem, Rizer tells a story about a time he observed a patrol by some officers in Montgomery, Alabama. They were called in to deal with a woman they knew had mental illness; she was flailing around and had cut someone with a broken plant pick. To subdue her, one of the officers body-slammed her against a door. Hard.

Rizer recalls that Montgomery officers were nervous about being watched during such a violent arrest—until they found out he had once been a cop. They didn't actually have any problem with what one of them had just done to the woman; in fact, they started laughing about it.

"It's one thing to use force and violence to affect an arrest. It's another thing to find it funny," he tells me. "It's just pervasive throughout policing. When I was a police officer and doing these kind of ride-alongs [as a researcher], you see the underbelly of it. And it's ... gross."

America's epidemic of police violence is not limited to what's on the news. For every high-profile story of a police officer killing an unarmed Black person or tear-gassing peaceful protesters, there are many, many allegations of police misconduct you don't hear about—abuses ranging from excessive use of force to mistreatment of prisoners to planting evidence. African Americans are arrested and roughed up by cops at wildly disproportionate rates, relative to both their overall share of the population and the percentage of crimes they commit.

Something about the way police relate to the communities they're tasked with protecting has gone wrong. Officers aren't just regularly treating people badly; a deep dive into the motivations and beliefs of police reveals that too many believe they are justified in doing so.

To understand how the police think about themselves and their job, I interviewed more than a dozen former officers and experts on policing. These sources, ranging from conservatives to police abolitionists, painted a deeply disturbing picture of the internal culture of policing.

Police officers across America have adopted a set of beliefs about their work and its role in our society. The tenets of police ideology are not codified or written down, but are nonetheless widely shared in departments around the country.

The ideology holds that the world is a profoundly dangerous place: Officers are conditioned to see themselves as constantly in danger and that the only way to guarantee survival is to dominate the citizens they're supposed to protect. The police believe they're alone in this fight; police ideology holds that officers are under siege by criminals and are not understood or respected by the broader citizenry. These beliefs, combined with widely held racial stereotypes, push officers toward violent and racist behavior during intense and stressful street interactions.

In that sense, police ideology can help us understand the persistence of officer-involved shootings and the recent brutal suppression of peaceful protests. In a culture where Black people are stereotyped as more threatening, Black communities are terrorized by aggressive policing, with officers acting less like community protectors and more like an occupying army.

The beliefs that define police ideology are neither universally shared among officers nor evenly distributed across departments. There are more than 600,000 local police officers across the country and more than 12,000 local police agencies. The officer corps has gotten more diverse over the years, with women, people of color, and LGBTQ officers making up a growing share of the profession. Speaking about such a group in blanket terms would do a disservice to the many officers who try to serve with care and kindness.

However, the officer corps remains overwhelmingly white, male, and straight. Federal Election Commission data from the 2020 cycle suggests that police heavily favor Republicans. And it is indisputable that there are commonly held beliefs among officers.

"The fact that not every department is the same doesn't undermine the point that there are common factors that people can reasonably identify as a police culture," says Tracey Meares, the founding director of Yale University's Justice Collaboratory.

The Danger Imperative

In 1998, Georgia sheriff's deputy Kyle Dinkheller pulled over a middle-aged white man named Andrew Howard Brannan for speeding. Brannan, a Vietnam veteran with PTSD, refused to comply with Dinkheller's instructions. He got out of the car and started dancing in the middle of the road, singing "Here I am, shoot me" over and over again.

In the encounter, recorded by the deputy's dashcam, things then escalate: Brannan charges at Dinkheller; Dinkheller tells him to "get back." Brannan heads back to the car—only to reemerge with a rifle pointed at Dinkheller. The officer fires first, and misses; Brannan shoots back. In the ensuing firefight, both men are wounded, but Dinkheller far more severely. It ends with Brannan standing over Dinkheller,

> **"Maintaining the edge" is a vital reason why officers seem so willing to employ force that appears obviously excessive when captured by body cams and cell phones.**

pointing the rifle at the deputy's eye. He yells—"Die, f*****!"—and pulls the trigger.

The dashcam footage of Dinkheller's killing, widely known among cops as the "Dinkheller video," is burned into the minds of many American police officers. It is screened in police academies around the country; one training turns it into a video game-style simulation in which officers can change the ending by killing Brannan. Jeronimo Yanez, the officer who killed Philando Castile during a 2016 traffic stop, was shown the Dinkheller video during his training.

"Every cop knows the name 'Dinkheller'—and no one else does," says Peter Moskos, a former Baltimore police officer who currently teaches at the John Jay College of Criminal Justice.

The purpose of the Dinkheller video, and many others like it shown at police academies, is to teach officers that any situation could escalate to violence. Cop killers lurk around every corner.

It's true that policing is a relatively dangerous job. But contrary to the impression the Dinkheller video might give trainees, murders of police are not the omnipresent threat they are made out to be. The number of police killings across the country has been falling for decades; there's been a 90 percent drop in ambush killings of officers since 1970. According to Bureau of Labor Statistics data, about 13 per 100,000 police officers died on the job in 2017. Compare that to farmers (24 deaths per 100,000), truck drivers (26.9 per 100,000), and trash collectors (34.9 per 100,000). But police academies and field training officers hammer home the risk of violent death to officers again and again.

It's not just training and socialization, though: The very nature of the job reinforces the sense of fear and threat. Law enforcement isn't called to people's homes and streets when things are going well. Officers constantly find themselves thrown into situations where a seemingly normal interaction has gone haywire—a marital argument devolving into domestic violence, for example.

"For them, any scene can turn into a potential danger," says Eugene Paoline III, a criminologist at the University of Central Florida. "They're taught, through their experiences, that very routine events can go bad."

Michael Sierra-Arévalo, a professor at UT-Austin, calls the police obsession with violent death "the danger imperative." After conducting 1,000 hours of fieldwork and interviews with 94 police officers, he found that the risk of violent death occupies an extraordinary amount of mental space for many officers—far more so than it should, given the objective risks.

Here's what I mean: According to the past 20 years of FBI data on officer fatalities, 1,001 officers have been killed by firearms while 760 have died in car crashes.

For this reason, police officers are, like the rest of us, required to wear seat belts at all times.

In reality, many choose not to wear them even when speeding through city streets. Sierra-Arévalo rode along with one police officer, whom he calls officer Doyle, during a car chase where Doyle was going around 100 miles per hour—and still not wearing a seat belt. Sierra-Arévalo asked him why he did things like this. Here's what Doyle said:

There's times where I'll be driving and the next thing you know I'll be like, 'Oh s***, that dude's got a f****** gun!' I'll stop [mimics tires screeching], try to get out—f***. Stuck on the seat belt ... I'd rather just be able to jump out on people, you know. If I have to, be able to jump out of this deathtrap of a car.

Despite the fact that fatal car accidents are a risk for police, officers like Doyle prioritize their ability to respond to one specific shooting scenario over the clear and consistent benefits of wearing a seat belt.

"Knowing officers consistently claim safety is their primary concern, multiple drivers not wearing a seatbelt and speeding towards the same call should be interpreted as an unacceptable danger; it is not," Sierra-Arévalo writes. "The danger imperative—the preoccupation with violence and the provision of officer safety—contributes to officer behaviors that, though perceived as keeping them safe, in fact put them in great physical danger."

This outsized attention to violence doesn't just make officers a threat to themselves. It's also part of what makes them a threat to citizens.

Because officers are hyper-attuned to the risks of attacks, they tend to believe that they must always be prepared to use force against the—sometimes even disproportionate force. Many officers believe that, if they are humiliated or undermined by a civilian, that civilian might be more willing to physically threaten them.

Scholars of policing call this concept "maintaining the edge," and it's a vital reason why officers seem so willing to employ force that appears obviously excessive when captured by body cams and cellphones.

"To let down that edge is perceived as inviting chaos, and thus danger," Moskos says.

This mindset helps explain why so many instances of police violence—like George Floyd's killing by officer Derek Chauvin in Minneapolis—happen during struggles related to arrest.

In these situations, the officers aren't always threatened with a deadly weapon: Floyd, for example, was unarmed. But when the officer decides the suspect is disrespecting them or resisting their commands, they feel the need to use force to reestablish the edge.

They need to make the suspect submit to their authority.

A Siege Mentality

Police officers today tend to see themselves as engaged in a lonely, armed struggle against the criminal element. They are judged by their effectiveness at that task, measured by internal data such as arrest numbers and crime rates in the areas they patrol. Officers believe these efforts are underappreciated by the general public; according to a 2017 Pew report, 86 percent of police believe the public doesn't really understand the "risks and challenges" involved in their job.

Rizer, the former officer and R Street researcher, recently conducted a separate large-scale survey of American police officers. One of the questions he asked was whether they would want their children to become police officers. A majority, around 60 percent, said no—for reasons that, in Rizer's words, "blew me away."

"The vast majority of people that said 'no, I don't want them to become a police officer' was because they felt like the public no longer supported them—and that they were 'at war' with the public," he tells me. "There's a 'me versus them' kind of worldview, that we're not part of this community that we're patrolling."

You can see this mentality on display in the widespread police adoption of an emblem called the "thin blue line." In one version of the symbol, two black rectangles are separated by a dark blue horizontal line. The rectangles represent the public and criminals, respectively; the blue line separating them is the police.

In another, the blue line replaces the central white stripe in a black-and-white American flag, separating the stars from the stripes below. During the recent anti-police violence protests in Cincinnati, Ohio, officers raised this modified banner outside their station.

In the "thin blue line" mindset, loyalty to the badge is paramount; reporting excessive force or the use of racial slurs by a colleague is an act of treason. This emphasis on loyalty can create conditions for abuses, even systematic ones, to take place: Officers at one station in Chicago, Illinois, tortured at least 125 Black suspects between 1972 and 1991. These crimes were uncovered by the dogged work of an investigative journalist rather than a police whistleblower.

"Officers, when they get wind that something might be wrong, either participate in it themselves when they're commanded to—or they actively ignore it, find ways to look the other way," says Laurence Ralph, a Princeton professor and the author of *The Torture Letters*, a recent book on the abuses in Chicago.

This insularity and siege mentality is not universal among American police. Worldviews vary from person to person and department to department; many officers are decent people who work hard to get to know citizens and address their concerns.

But it is powerful enough, experts say, to distort departments across the country. It has seriously undermined some recent efforts to reorient the police toward working more closely with local communities, generally pushing departments away from deep engagement with citizens and toward a more militarized and aggressive model.

"The police have been in the midst of an epic ideological battle. It's been taking place ever since the supposed community policing revolution started back in the 1980s," says Peter Kraska, a professor at Eastern Kentucky University's School of Justice Studies. "In the last 10 to 15 years, the more toxic elements have been far more influential."

Since the George Floyd protests began, police have tear-gassed protesters in 100 different US cities. This is not an accident or the result of behaviors by a few bad apples. Instead, it reflects the fact that officers see themselves as at war—and the protesters as the enemies.

A 2017 study by Heidi Reynolds-Stenson, a sociologist at Colorado State University-Pueblo, examined data on 7,000 protests from 1960 to 1995. She found that "police are much more likely to try to quell protests that criticize police conduct."

"Recent scholarship argues that, over the last twenty years, protest policing [has gotten] more aggressive and less impartial," Reynolds-Stenson concludes. "The pattern of disproportionate repression of police brutality protests found in this study may be even more pronounced today."

There's a reason that, after New York Police Department Lt. Robert Cattani kneeled alongside Black Lives Matter protesters on May 31, he sent an email to his precinct apologizing for the "horrible decision to give into a crowd of protesters' demands." In his mind, the decision to work with the crowd amounted to collaboration with the enemy.

"The cop in me," Cattani wrote, "wants to kick my own ass."

Anti-Blackness

Policing in the United States has always been bound up with the color line. In the South, police departments emerged out of 18th century slave patrols—bands of men working to discipline slaves, facilitate their transfer between plantations, and catch runaways. In the North, professional police departments came about as a response to a series of mid-19th century urban upheavals—many of which, like the 1834 New York anti-abolition riot, had their origins in racial strife.

While policing has changed dramatically since then, there's clear evidence of continued structural racism in American policing. The *Washington Post*'s Radley Balko has compiled an extensive list of academic studies documenting this fact, covering everything from traffic stops to use of deadly force. Research has confirmed that this is a nationwide problem, involving a significant percentage of officers.

When talking about race in policing and the way it relates to police ideology, there are two related phenomena to think about.

The first is overt racism. In some police departments, the culture permits a minority of racists on the force to commit brutal acts of racial violence with impunity.

Examples of explicit racism abound in police officer conduct. The following three incidents were reported in the past month alone:

- In leaked audio, Wilmington, North Carolina, officer Kevin Piner said, "we are just going to go out and start slaughtering [Blacks]," adding that he "can't wait" for a new civil war so whites could "wipe them off the f****** map." Piner was dismissed from the force, as were two other officers involved in the conversation.

- Joey Lawn, a 10-year veteran of the Meridian, Mississippi, force, was fired for using an unspecified racial slur against a Black colleague during a 2018 exercise. Lawn's boss, John Griffith, was demoted from captain to lieutenant for failing to punish Lawn at the time.

- Four officers in San Jose, California, were put on administrative leave amid an investigation into their membership in a secret Facebook group. In a public post, officer Mark Pimentel wrote that "black lives don't really matter"; in another private one, retired officer Michael Nagel wrote about female Muslim prisoners: "i say we repurpose the hijabs into nooses."

In all of these cases, superiors punished officers for their offensive comments and actions—but only after they came to light. It's safe to say a lot more go unreported.

Last April, a human resources manager in San Francisco's city government quit after spending two years conducting anti-bias training for the city's police force. In an exit email sent to his boss and the city's police chief, he wrote that "the degree of anti-black sentiment throughout SFPD is extreme," adding that "while there are some at SFPD who possess somewhat of a balanced view of racism and anti-blackness, there are an equal number (if not more)—who possess and exude deeply rooted anti-black sentiments."

Psychological research suggests that white officers are disproportionately likely to demonstrate a personality trait called "social dominance orientation." Individuals with high levels of this trait tend to believe that existing social hierarchies are not only necessary, but morally justified—that inequalities reflect the way that things actually should be. The concept was originally formulated in the 1990s as a way of explaining why some people are more likely to accept what a group of researchers termed "ideologies that promote or maintain group inequality," including "the ideology of anti-Black racism."

This helps us understand why some officers are more likely to use force against Black suspects, even unarmed ones. Phillip Atiba Goff, a psychologist at John Jay and the CEO of the Center for Policing Equity think tank, has done forthcoming research on the distribution of social dominance orientation among officers in three different cities. Goff and his co-authors found that white officers who score very highly in this trait tend to use force more frequently than those who don't.

"If you think the social hierarchy is good, then maybe you're more willing to use violence from the state's perspective to enforce that hierarchy—and you think that's your job," he tells me.

But while the problem of overt racism and explicit commitment to racial hierarchy is a serious one, it's not necessarily the central problem in modern policing.

The second manifestation of anti-Blackness is more subtle. The very nature of policing, in which officers perform a dizzying array of stressful tasks for long hours, brings out the worst in people. The psychological stressors combine with police ideology and widespread cultural stereotypes to push officers, even ones who don't hold overtly racist beliefs, to treat Black people as more suspect and more dangerous. It's not just the officers who are the problem; it's the society they come from, and the things that society asks them to do.

While overt racists may be overrepresented on police forces, the average white officer's beliefs are not all that different from those of the average white person in their local community. According to Goff, tests of racial bias reveal somewhat higher rates of prejudice among officers than the general population, but the effect size tends to be swamped by demographic and regional effects.

"If you live in a racist city, that's going to matter more for how racist your law enforcement is ... than looking at the difference between law enforcement and your neighbors," he told me.

In this sense, the rising diversity of America's officer corps should make a real difference. If you draw from a demographically different pool of recruits, one with overall lower levels of racial bias, then there should be less of a problem with racism on the force.

There's some data to back this up. Pew's 2017 survey of officers found that Black officers and female officers were considerably more sympathetic to anti-police brutality protesters than white ones. A 2016 paper on officer-involved killings of Black people, from Yale's Joscha Legewie and Columbia's Jeffrey Fagan, found that departments with a larger percentage of Black officers had lower rates of killings of Black people.

But scholars caution that diversity will not, on its own, solve policing's problems. In Pew's survey, 60 percent of Hispanic and white officers said their departments had "excellent" or "good" relations with the local Black community, while only 32 percent of Black officers said the same. The hierarchy of policing remains extremely white—across cities, departmental brass and police unions tend to be disproportionately white relative to the rank-and-file. And the existing culture in many departments pushes nonwhite officers to try and fit in with what's been established by the white hierarchy.

"We have seen that officers of color actually face increased pressure to fit into the existing culture of policing and may go out of their way to align themselves with traditional police tactics," says Shannon Portillo, a scholar of bureaucratic culture at the University of Kansas-Edwards.

There's a deeper problem than mere representation. The very nature of policing, both police ideology and the nuts-and-bolts nature of the job, can bring out the worst in people—especially when it comes to deep-seated racial prejudices and stereotypes.

The intersection of commonly held stereotypes with police ideology can prime officers for abusive behavior, especially when they're patrolling majority-Black neighborhoods where residents have long-standing grievances against the cops. Some kind of incident with a Black citizen is certain to set off a confrontation; officers will eventually feel the need to escalate well beyond what seems necessary or even acceptable from the outside to protect themselves.

"The drug dealer—if he says 'f*** you' one day, it's like getting punked on the playground. You have to go through that every day," says Moskos, the former Baltimore officer. "You're not allowed to get punked as a cop, not just because of your ego but because of the danger of it."

The problems with ideology and prejudice are dramatically intensified by the demanding nature of the policing profession. Officers work a difficult job for long hours, called upon to handle responsibilities ranging from mental health intervention to spousal dispute resolution. While on shift, they are constantly anxious, searching for the next threat or potential arrest.

Stress gets to them even off the job; PTSD and marital strife are common problems. It's a kind of negative feedback loop: The job makes them stressed and nervous, which damages their mental health and personal relationships, which raises their overall level of stress and makes the job even more taxing.

According to Goff, it's hard to overstate how much more likely people are to be racist under these circumstances. When you put people under stress, they tend to make snap judgments rooted in their basic instincts. For police officers, raised in a racist society and socialized in a violent work atmosphere, that makes racist behavior inevitable.

"The mission and practice of policing is not aligned with what we know about how to keep people from acting on the kinds of implicit biases and mental shortcuts," he says. "You could design a job where that's not how it works. We have not chosen to do that for policing."

Across the United States, we have created a system that makes disproportionate police targeting of Black citizens an inevitability. Officers don't need to be especially racist as compared to the general population for discrimination to recur over and over; it's the nature of the police profession, the beliefs that permeate it, and the situations in which officers find themselves that lead them to act in racist ways.

This reality helps us understand why the current protests have been so forceful: they are an expression of long-held rage against an institution that Black communities experience less as a protection force and more as a sort of military occupation.

In one landmark project, a team including Yale's Meares and Hopkins's Vesla Weaver facilitated more than 850 conversations about policing among residents of six different cities, finding a pervasive sense of police lawlessness among residents of highly policed Black communities.

Residents believe that police see them as subhuman or animal, that interactions with officers invariably end with arrests and/or physical assaults, and that the Constitution's protections against police abuse don't apply to Black people.

"[It's often said that] if you don't have anything on you, just agree to a search and everything will be okay. Let me tell you, that's not what happens," Weaver tells me, summarizing the beliefs of her research subjects. "What actually happens is that you're bound to get beat up, you're bound to get dragged to the station. The police can search you for whatever. We don't get due process, we don't get restitution—this is what we live by."

Police don't treat whole communities like this because they're born worse or more evil than civilians. It's better to understand the majority of officers as ordinary Americans who are thrown into a system that conditions them to be violent and to treat Black people, in particular, as the enemy. While some departments are better than others at ameliorating this problem, there's not a city in the country that appears to have solved it entirely.

Rizer summarizes the problem by telling me about one new officer's experience in Baltimore.

"This was a great young man," Rizer says. "He joined the Baltimore Police Department because he wanted to make a difference."

Six months after this man graduated from the academy, Rizer checked in on him to see how he was doing. It wasn't good.

"They're animals. All of them," Rizer recalls the young officer telling him. "The cops, the people I patrol, everybody. They're just f****** animals."

This man was, in Rizer's mind, "the embodiment of what a good police officer should have been." Some time after their conversation, he quit the force—pushed out by a system that takes people in and breaks them, on both sides of the law.

Print Citations

CMS: Beauchamp, Zack. "What the Police Really Believe." In *The Reference Shelf: Policing in 2020*, edited by Micah L. Issitt, 13-22. Amenia, NY: Grey House Publishing, 2021.

MLA: Beauchamp, Zack. "What the Police Really Believe." *The Reference Shelf: Policing in 2020*, edited by Micah L. Issitt, Grey Housing Publishing, 2021, pp. 13-22.

APA: Beauchamp, Z. (2021). What the police really believe. In Micah L. Issitt (Ed.), *The reference shelf: Policing in 2020* (pp. 13-22). Amenia, NY: Grey Housing Publishing.

George Floyd and the History of Police Brutality in America

By Kadijatou Diallo and John Shattuck
The Boston Globe, June 1, 2020

The horrific death, captured on video, of George Floyd, a 46-year-old black man who died after a white Minneapolis police officer kneeled on his neck, spotlights the longstanding crisis of racism in policing.

To understand the protests that have erupted across the United States, one needs to understand the deeply troubled history of policing and race. Police brutality, racial discrimination, and violence against minorities are intertwined and rooted throughout US history. Technology has made it possible for the level and extent of the problem finally to be publicly documented. The anger expressed in the wake of Floyd's killing reflects the searing reality that Black people in the United States continue to be dehumanized and treated unjustly.

Law enforcement officers have long used their authority to control the behavior and movement of Blacks. Before the Civil War, slave patrols were tasked with tracking runaway slaves throughout the United States. After abolition, Blacks were detained and punished for infractions that would otherwise have been considered trivial had they been committed by whites. Policing was tied to the use of force by a justice system aimed at maintaining a social hierarchy based on a belief in the racial superiority of whites. For more than a century after the Civil War, police officials were often secret members of white supremacist groups like the Ku Klux Klan.

Police relations with minority communities today reflect this deep legacy of racism.

In 2019, data compiled by the National Academy of Sciences showed that Blacks are 2.5 times more likely to be killed by police than whites. Police tend to target Blacks on suspected infractions more than white suspects. This is especially evident in drug-related offenses. Despite having similar rates of drug use as white Americans, Blacks are disproportionately arrested and convicted on drug offenses. Between 1995 and 2005, Blacks constituted 13 percent of drug users but accounted for 46 percent of drug convictions.

Racial profiling is an indicator of continuing racism in the criminal justice system. Research shows that police rely on the relationship between neighborhood demographics and suspects to identify "out-of-place" individuals in predominately nonminority areas. As Shytierra Gaston of Northeastern University concludes,

"Race serves as a marker of where people 'belong', and racial incongruity as a marker of suspicion."

The 1980s "Broken Windows" theory of policing posited that cracking down on small-scale infractions like vandalism, public drinking, and loitering prevented more serious crime from occurring in neighborhoods. This resulted in discretionary enforcement, with minority communities targeted most often, leading to controversial tactics like stop-and-frisk, which disproportionately impacted Black and Latino men.

Racial profiling is an indicator of continuing racism in the criminal justice system.

Implicit bias on the part of officials within the criminal justice system and society at large remains a consistent pattern. A 2004 study by researchers at the American Psychological Association found that Blacks are often associated with descriptive adjectives such as "dangerous," "aggressive," "violent," and "criminal." These negative stereotypes affect policing decisions.

Through our work on the Renewing Rights and Responsibilities Project at the Harvard Kennedy School's Carr Center for Human Rights Policy, we highlight the historical roots of racial discrimination and their current impact on American society. By recognizing the long history of racism in the justice system, Americans can grasp why deaths like George Floyd's are symptomatic of a larger failure of American justice.

As horrendous as watching George Floyd's murder was, we found, as a Black woman and a white man, that the most hurtful aspect was watching commentators, public officials, and some of our fellow Americans attempting to invalidate or outright dismiss the grievances against systemic racial discrimination that have cost so many lives in our country.

Like clockwork, the public narrative changed from focusing on the deadly actions of a police officer and the system that so often shields miscreant officers like him from accountability, to scrutinizing the victim's past and demonizing the protestors. It was as if this justified the murder and absolved the country of centuries-long racial injustice. The current protests are a glimmer of hope for change, but if history is any guide and change does not occur, the nation may soon be talking about another unarmed Black victim of police violence.

Print Citations

CMS: Diallo, Kadijatou, and John Shattuck. "George Floyd and the History of Police Brutality in America." In *The Reference Shelf: Policing in 2020,* edited by Micah L. Issitt, 23-25. Amenia, NY: Grey House Publishing, 2021.

MLA: Diallo, Kadijatou, and John Shattuck. "George Floyd and the History of Police Brutality in America." *The Reference Shelf: Policing in 2020,* edited by Micah L. Issitt, Grey Housing Publishing, 2021, pp. 23-25.

APA: Diallo, K., & Shattuck, J. (2021). George Floyd and the history of police brutality in America. In Micah L. Issitt (Ed.), *The reference shelf: Policing in 2020* (pp. 23-25). Amenia, NY: Grey Housing Publishing.

10 Things We Know about Race and Policing in the U.S.

By Drew DeSilver, Michael Lipka, and Dalia Fahmy
Pew Research Center, June 3, 2020

Days of protests across the United States in the wake of George Floyd's death in the custody of Minneapolis police have brought new attention to questions about police officers' attitudes toward black Americans, protesters and others. The public's views of the police, in turn, are also in the spotlight. Here's a roundup of Pew Research Center survey findings from the past few years about the intersection of race and law enforcement.

1. Majorities of both black and white Americans say black people are treated less fairly than whites in dealing with the police and by the criminal justice system as a whole. In a 2019 Center survey, 84% of black adults said that, in dealing with police, blacks are generally treated less fairly than whites; 63% of whites said the same. Similarly, 87% of blacks and 61% of whites said the U.S. criminal justice system treats black people less fairly.

More than eight-in-ten black adults say blacks are treated less fairly than whites by police, criminal justice system

% who say, in general in our country these days, blacks are treated less fairly than whites ...

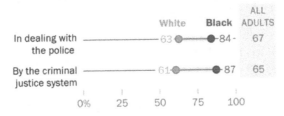

Note: White and black adults include those who report being only one race and are non-Hispanic.
Source: Survey of U.S. adults conducted Jan. 22-Feb. 5, 2019.

PEW RESEARCH CENTER

2. Black adults are about five times as likely as whites to say they've been unfairly stopped by police because of their race or ethnicity (44% vs. 9%), according to the same survey. Black men are especially likely to say this: 59% say they've been unfairly stopped, versus 31% of black women.

Black men are far more likely than black women to say they've been unfairly stopped by the police

% of black adults, by gender, who say each of the following has happened to them because of their race or ethnicity

● Women   ● Men

	Women	Men
People acted like they were suspicious of them	59	73
People acted as if they were not smart	59	61
Been subject to slurs or jokes	49	57
Been treated unfairly in hiring, pay or promotion	48	50
Feared for their personal safety	40	46
Been unfairly stopped by police	31	59
People assumed they were racist or prejudiced	20	31

Note: Blacks include those who only report being one race and are non-Hispanic.
Source: Survey of U.S. adults conducted Jan. 22-Feb. 5, 2019.

PEW RESEARCH CENTER

3. White Democrats and white Republicans have vastly different views of how black people are treated by police and the wider justice system. Overwhelming majorities of white Democrats say black people are treated less fairly than whites by the police (88%) and the criminal justice system (86%), according to the 2019 poll. About four-in-ten white Republicans agree (43% and 39%, respectively).

Vast gaps between white Republicans, Democrats on views of treatment of blacks

*Among whites, % of **Republicans** and **Democrats** saying, in general in our country these days, blacks are treated less fairly than whites in each of the following situations*

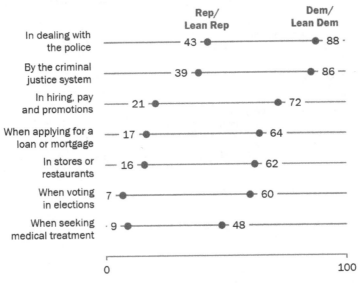

Note: "In dealing with the police" and "By the criminal justice system" were asked of separate random subsamples of respondents.
Source: Survey of U.S. adults conducted Jan. 22-Feb. 5, 2019.
"Race in America 2019"

PEW RESEARCH CENTER

4. Nearly two-thirds of black adults (65%) say they've been in situations where people acted as if they were suspicious of them because of their race or ethnicity, while only a quarter of white adults say that's happened to them. Roughly a third of both Asian and Hispanic adults (34% and 37%, respectively) say they've been in such situations, the 2019 survey found.

Most blacks say someone has acted suspicious of them or as if they weren't smart

% of each group saying each of the following has happened to them because of their race or ethnicity

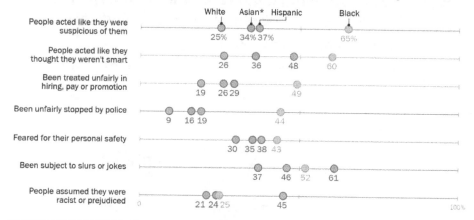

*Asians were interviewed in English only.
Note: Whites, blacks and Asians include those who report being only one race and are non-Hispanic. Hispanics are of any race.
Source: Survey of U.S. adults conducted Jan. 22-Feb. 5, 2019.
"Race in America 2019"

PEW RESEARCH CENTER

5. Black Americans are far less likely than whites to give police high marks for the way they do their jobs. In a 2016 survey, only about a third of black adults said that police in their community did an "excellent" or "good" job in using the right amount of force (33%, compared with 75% of whites), treating racial and ethnic groups equally (35% vs. 75%), and holding officers accountable for misconduct (31% vs. 70%).

Blacks are about half as likely as whites to have a positive view of police treatment of racial and ethnic groups or officers' use of force

% saying the police in their community do an excellent or good job when it comes to ...

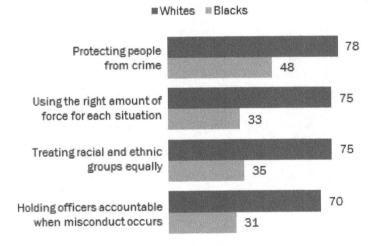

Note: Whites and blacks include only non-Hispanics.
Source: Survey of U.S. adults conducted Aug. 16-Sept. 12, 2016.
"The Racial Confidence Gap in Police Performance"

PEW RESEARCH CENTER

6. In the past, police officers and the general public have tended to view fatal encounters between black people and police very differently. In a 2016 survey of nearly 8,000 policemen and women from departments with at least 100 officers, two-thirds said most such encounters are isolated incidents and not signs of broader problems between police and the black community. In a companion survey of more than 4,500 U.S. adults, 60% of the public called such incidents signs of broader problems between police and black people. But the views given by police themselves were sharply differentiated by race: A majority of black officers (57%) said that such incidents were evidence of a broader problem, but only 27% of white officers and 26% of Hispanic officers said so.

Most white, Latino officers say fatal encounters between blacks and police are isolated incidents; majority of black officers disagree

% of officers saying the deaths of blacks during encounters with police in recent years are ...

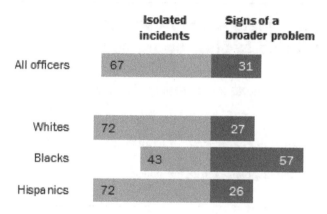

Note: No answer category not shown. Whites and blacks include only non-Hispanics. Hispanics are of any race.
Source: Survey of law enforcement officers conducted May 19-Aug. 14, 2016.
"Behind the Badge"

PEW RESEARCH CENTER

7. Around two-thirds of police officers (68%) said in 2016 that the demonstrations over the deaths of black people during encounters with law enforcement were motivated to a great extent by anti-police bias; only 10% said (in a separate question) that protesters were primarily motivated by a genuine desire to hold police accountable for their actions. Here as elsewhere, police officers' views differed by race: Only about a quarter of white officers (27%) but around six-in-ten of their black colleagues (57%) said such protests were motivated at least to some extent by a genuine desire to hold police accountable.

Most officers say protests mainly motivated by bias toward police

% of officers saying protests over deaths of blacks who died during encounters with the police are motivated ___ by ...

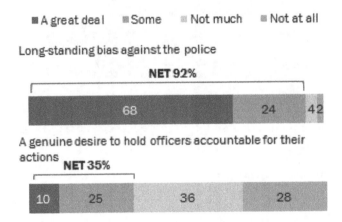

Note: No answer category not shown. NETs calculated before rounding.
Source: Survey of law enforcement officers conducted May 19-Aug. 14, 2016.
"Behind the Badge"

PEW RESEARCH CENTER

8. White police officers and their black colleagues have starkly different views on fundamental questions regarding the situation of blacks in American society, the 2016 survey found. For example, nearly all white officers (92%)—but only 29% of their black colleagues—said the U.S. had made the changes needed to assure equal rights for blacks.

Police, public divided by race over whether attaining equality requires more changes

% saying that ...

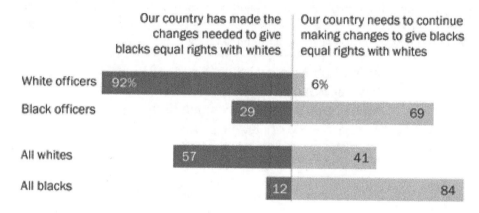

	Our country has made the changes needed to give blacks equal rights with whites	Our country needs to continue making changes to give blacks equal rights with whites
White officers	92%	6%
Black officers	29	69
All whites	57	41
All blacks	12	84

Note: No answer category not shown.
Source: Survey of law enforcement officers conducted May 19-Aug. 14, 2016; survey of U.S. adults conducted Aug. 16-Sept. 12, 2016.
"Behind the Badge"

PEW RESEARCH CENTER

9. A majority of officers said in 2016 that relations between the police in their department and black people in the community they serve were "excellent" (8%) or "good" (47%). However, far higher shares saw excellent or good community relations with whites (91%), Asians (88%) and Hispanics (70%). About a quarter of police officers (26%) said relations between police and black people in their community were "only fair," while nearly one-in-five (18%) said they were "poor"—with black officers far more likely than others to say so. (These percentages are based on only those officers who offered a rating.)

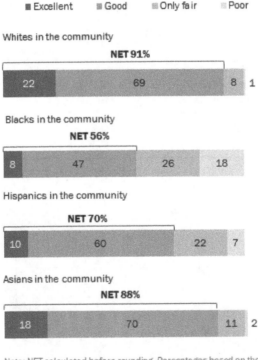

About half or more officers say police have positive relations with the racial, ethnic groups in their communities

% of officers saying they would rate relations between the police in their department and the following groups in the community they serve ...

■ Excellent ▨ Good ▨ Only fair ▨ Poor

Whites in the community

NET 91%

| 22 | 69 | 8 | 1 |

Blacks in the community

NET 56%

| 8 | 47 | 26 | 18 |

Hispanics in the community

NET 70%

| 10 | 60 | 22 | 7 |

Asians in the community

NET 88%

| 18 | 70 | 11 | 2 |

Note: NET calculated before rounding. Percentages based on those officers who rated relations with each group. A total of 15% of all officers report they could not rate relations with Asians because there are too few in the community where they worked; 2% say there are too few blacks and 3% say there are too few Hispanics or whites.
Source: Survey of law enforcement officers conducted May 19-Aug. 14, 2016.
"Behind the Badge"

PEW RESEARCH CENTER

10. An overwhelming majority of police officers (86%) said in 2016 that high-profile fatal encounters between black people and police officers had made their jobs harder. Sizable majorities also said such incidents had made their colleagues more worried about safety (93%), heightened tensions between police and blacks (75%), and left many officers reluctant to use force when appropriate (76%) or to question people who seemed suspicious (72%).

Officers say fatal encounters between police and blacks have made policing harder

% of officers saying high-profile incidents between police and blacks have made ...

12% No difference

No answer

86%
Their job harder

Note: Less than 0.5% said these incidents have made their job easier.

% of officers saying each has happened in their department as a result of high-profile incidents involving blacks and the police

Officers have become more concerned about their safety	**93%**
Officers have been more reluctant to use force when it is appropriate	**76**
Interactions between police and blacks have become more tense	**75**
Officers have become less willing to stop and question people who seem suspicious	**72**

Source: Survey of law enforcement officers conducted May 19-Aug. 14, 2016.
"Behind the Badge"

PEW RESEARCH CENTER

Print Citations

CMS: DeSilver, Drew, Michael Lipka, and Dalia Fahmy. "10 Things We Know about Race and Policing in the U.S." In *The Reference Shelf: Policing in 2020,* edited by Micah L. Issitt, 26-36. Amenia, NY: Grey House Publishing, 2021.

MLA: DeSilver, Drew, Michael Lipka, and Dalia Fahmy. "10 Things We Know about Race and Policing in the U.S." *The Reference Shelf: Policing in 2020,* edited by Micah L. Issitt, Grey Housing Publishing, 2021, pp. 26-36.

APA: DeSilver, D., Lipka, M., & Fahmy, D. (2021). 10 things we know about race and policing in the U.S. In Micah L. Issitt (Ed.), *The reference shelf: Policing in 2020* (pp. 26-36). Amenia, NY: Grey Housing Publishing.

Why Statistics Don't Capture the Full Extent of the Systemic Bias in Policing

By Laura Bronner
FiveThirtyEight, June 25, 2020

Across the U.S., demonstrators have spent the past few weeks protesting against racial disparities in the country's criminal justice system. There's plenty of data to back them up: Black and Hispanic people are stopped more frequently, including traffic stops, and are more likely to be arrested. Once stopped, police are more likely to use force against, shoot and kill Black citizens. And then once in jail, Black defendants are more likely to be denied bail, which in turn makes conviction more likely. And when convicted, sentencing is also biased against Black defendants, with Black defendants more likely to be incarcerated.

The data seems to overwhelmingly point to a criminal justice system riven by racial bias. But, remarkably, it could be even more overwhelming than some studies make it seem. That's because of a statistical quirk called "collider bias," a kind of selection bias that means that the crime data that shows racial bias is, itself, biased by racist practices. If you thought crime data showed clear evidence of racism before, understanding how collider bias affects these analyses might make it even clearer.

To understand how all this works, we're going to get mathy. In particular, we're going to be talking a lot about denominators, which, if you'll remember your fourth grade math lessons, are the numbers on the bottom of a fraction. For our purposes, though, you can think of them as the universe of people who are being studied.

Police engage with only a small subset of the population they see, so if we look at statistics about those interactions, the stats we get are informed by that smaller sample. And if there's bias in who the police choose to interact with—if it's not a random sample—that can change the relationships you see in the data.

There are two main ways that researchers approach this problem—by using a "population denominator" and an "encounter denominator."

The former, for example, compares the fraction of Black people in the general population who are arrested or harmed to that same statistic for white people. That's how you get studies that show 96 out of 100,000 Black men and boys will be killed by police over the course of their lifetimes, compared to 39 out of 100,000 white men and boys—a risk that is 2.5 times higher. Seems straightforward enough. But because Black and white people encounter the police at different rates to begin with, using population denominators might not lend itself to an apples-to-apples comparison; being more likely to encounter police means that you're more likely to encounter police force, too.[1]

For this reason, many researchers choose to look at the set of people who have encountered the police. This is the "encounter denominator." The setup is simple: You look at all the people who had recorded encounters with police—data which is not always easy to obtain—and calculate the proportion that involved the use of force. But this approach has a different issue, as a recent paper pointed out—if there's bias in who gets stopped in the first place, then looking at discrepancies in the resulting interactions won't give you the full picture. This is because of something called "collider bias."[2]

"The vast majority—99.9 percent of the data—we never get to see," said Dean Knox, a professor of politics at Princeton and one of the authors of the study. "We just don't see all the times when police officers are encountering civilians on the street. And that's a huge problem, because among the data that you *do* get to see— the stops, and the arrests, and the use of force that officers record—those are already contaminated, because officers have discretion in who they choose to engage."

The fact that researchers' data comes from a biased sample—who the police choose to stop—rather than the full sample of *possible* stops might skew the conclusions we draw from it. "If we're using administrative data, we always need to be aware of what world those data capture, and what they don't capture," said Allison P. Harris, a political science professor at Yale who studies racial disparities in the criminal justice system. "With policing, we just can never know what there's no record of."

One example of an encounter denominator approach is a 2019 study by Roland Fryer, an economist at Harvard. He found that police shoot white, Black and Hispanic Americans whom they've stopped at equal rates.[3] At first blush, that would seem like evidence that the police are not racially biased—every demographic is being treated equally, after all.

But we know that police officers are more likely to stop Black and Hispanic people than white ones—and that more of those stops are unfounded. Researchers measure this with something called the "hit rate," or the rate at which contraband is actually found on the people who were stopped. A lower hit rate implies bias because it means that the decision to search someone was made with less evidence. White people stopped in New York City, for example, were more likely to be carrying a weapon than Black and Hispanic people who were stopped. White drivers stopped by the police were more likely to have contraband than Black and Hispanic drivers nationally.

As political scientists Knox, Will Lowe and Jonathan Mummolo, among others, have pointed out, that complicates Fryer's findings. All of a sudden, what at first appeared to be *equal* treatment actually suggests *unequal* treatment. Because of the initial discrimination in who gets stopped, the sample of stopped people isn't the same across races. The different hit rate indicates that stopped white people are actually more likely to have contraband, on average, than stopped Black people. In other words, in a world without discrimination in who was stopped—if the Black and white people who were stopped were equally likely to be engaged in criminal activity—you'd see an even bigger disparity in outcomes. . . .

A statistical quirk called "collider bias" . . . means that the crime data that shows racial bias is, itself, biased by racist practices.

"The data we have pick up halfway through the encounter, after officer bias very likely has already exerted an effect," said Mummolo, a professor at Princeton. And without knowing the racial composition of the people who are sighted by police but *aren't* stopped, it's impossible to fully correct for the bias. The paper provides a suggestion for how to estimate bias in one part of the chain—use of force in encounters—but it doesn't capture any of the potential disparities that occur beforehand that make the encounter likelier.

So if racial bias in police *stops* makes it hard to estimate racial disparities in how people are treated while stopped, you might be wondering: well, doesn't this affect all of the other components of the chain, too?

"We need to think about this as this complex system," said Knox. There are biases layered on biases—social decisions like how society allocates resources in education versus policing, and individual decisions like who police choose to stop or arrest and who is ultimately charged or convicted. "It just compounds all the way down the line," Knox said.

The thing about systemic racism is it's just that: systemic.

Ultimately, the fact that these biased events build on each other should be a reminder that we're not capturing the entire process surrounding the stats we're looking at. Essentially, all the discrimination we *can* actually measure at each specific stage is an underestimate of how much is actually happening.

1. Other studies, aware of the difficulties with the population denominator, disregard the idea of a denominator entirely and find, for example, that people who are shot are no more likely to be Black or Hispanic than white. However, estimating differences among people who are shot is not the question of interest — what we're really interested in is whether some people are more likely to be shot than others. Failing to include a denominator at all doesn't solve the problem, it just means that the original study doesn't address the relevant question.

2. The term got its name because if you're drawing a sloppy diagram of the directions in which you think causal effects go, the arrow heads pointing to one of the boxes in the diagram will collide. I wish I was kidding.

3. He did find some differences in non-shooting uses of force.

Print Citations

CMS: Bronner, Laura. "Why Statistics Don't Capture the Full Extent of the Systematic Bias in Policing." In *The Reference Shelf: Policing in 2020,* edited by Micah L. Issitt, 37-40. Amenia, NY: Grey House Publishing, 2021.

MLA: Bronner, Laura. "Why Statistics Don't Capture the Full Extent of the Systematic Bias in Policing." *The Reference Shelf: Policing in 2020,* edited by Micah L. Issitt, Grey Housing Publishing, 2021, pp. 37-40.

APA: Bronner, L. (2021). Why statistics don't capture the full extent of the systematic bias in policing. In Micah L. Issitt (Ed.), *The reference shelf: Policing in 2020* (pp. 37-40). Amenia, NY: Grey Housing Publishing.

2
Policing in Place

By Carl Wycoff, via Wikimedia.

Iowa police officers taking part in community outreach during a Police Week.

Community Policing and the Role of Police

At a time when trust in police is at its lowest historical level, those seeking to initiate reform or to rehabilitate the public image of policing in America must deal with a host of issues beyond allegations of racial prejudice and violence. Police have also frequently been critiqued for failing to effectively represent the public that they are assigned to protect and of relying on ineffective or inappropriate militant and adversarial tactics. One of the reasons that policing has become so controversial is because of differing political and public pressures on police officers, and this has frequently placed officers in difficult positions as symbols of unpopular or controversial political directives.

What Is the Role of Police?

While controversy is sometimes the result of police misconduct, it is often related to politics. For instance, since 2017 the Trump administration has embraced some of the most extreme and controversial immigration policies in American history. Separating immigrant children from their parents and confining them without judicial oversight was so controversial that U.S. citizens protested these policies continuously for several years, and the United States drew the kind of criticism from international governments typically levied only at autocratic regimes. The administration's aggressive anti-immigration policies affected every level of the government. States were pressured to do more to locate and imprison or deport undocumented migrants. In many states, local police were asked to make immigration enforcement part of their job. A police officer performing a traffic stop might, therefore, be ordered to check the immigration status of the driver or passengers, a task that would typically be left to federal authorities.[1] Some cities refused to obey the Trump administration's policies on immigration, and these "sanctuary cities" became one of the great controversies of the first two years of Trump's time in office.

Whether working in a sanctuary city or in a community more aligned with controversial immigration goals, police were placed in a difficult position during Trump's time in office. Those who participated in immigration enforcement risked public condemnation, as a majority of Americans opposed the Trump administration's stance on aggressive enforcement. But police were also under pressure from local and national political leaders. Critics have raised a number of concerns about asking or requiring local police to play a role in immigration enforcement. Some argue that police resources are limited and that police should not be expending resources to address issues that are federal priorities. When police officers in a city or county spend time checking the immigration status of individuals who are apprehended in a traffic stop or other minor violation, or if local police apprehend and detain individuals with questionable immigration status, this uses time and resources that might be better spent addressing local crime.

There is a deeper issue involved when police begin addressing immigration enforcement as well. In addressing local crime, police are dependent on the cooperation of local citizens and noncitizens within their communities. Very few successful investigations conducted by police are the result of police effort alone. Police depend on members of the public to report crimes and to supply the essential information that ultimately leads to successful investigations. Police also frequently rely on informants whose lives intersect with criminals or criminal organizations. It has been argued that local police enforcement of immigration issues, especially given the wide variety of Americans who disapprove with the anti-immigrant positions of the Trump administration, could potentially hinder the ability of police to secure cooperation from citizens. Undocumented migrants, or citizens whose families or social groups contain undocumented migrants, may be less likely to report information to police out of the fear of increased police scrutiny.[2]

Another arena in which local police have been positioned in the political crossfire is in the use of police during civil rights protests. The Trump administration's polarizing policies brought about some of the largest protest movements in the history of America, and the most controversial of these were those that followed allegations of police violence against African Americans. Protest movements united behind the "Defund the Police" and the "Black Lives Matter" movements spread to cities around the United States, and police were called upon to confront these protests. Over two months of sporadic protests, an investigation by *The Guardian* found that U.S. police engaged in 950 instances of violence against protestors and journalists across the United States.[3] In some cases, such as in New York City, civil rights organizations sued local government and police departments, alleging brutality against protestors.[4]

The right to gather and to conduct peaceful protests is enshrined in the Constitution of the United States. By extension, all those who represent any branch of American government, either at the federal, state, or municipal level, are sworn to uphold this right. On the other hand, riots in some cities and towns resulted in the destruction of property. The riots were not directly connected to the protests, and many independent reports from journalists provided data suggesting that protestors were largely peaceful. Nonetheless, some politicians, most notably Donald Trump, claimed that the protests were part of a larger surge in violent lawlessness and called on police and, in some cases, federal authorities to violently end the protest movement. This political messaging placed police officers in a difficult position, associating them with a controversial political administration and exacerbating claims of authoritarianism among police officers. The fact that the protests were labeled and widely perceived as "antipolice" protests was also likely a factor, inciting some officers involved to feel personally or professionally targeted. In any case, police response to the protests has been widely criticized by activists, civil liberties experts, and international observers and journalists. The public perception of police abuse and the unnecessary use of force became a serious problem that threatened to further erode public trust.

Representation and Responsiveness

Police around the country are also dealing with the perception that police departments don't effectively represent the communities in which police serve. For instance, in some cases police departments in predominantly minority communities might consist primarily of white officers. Critics argue that police will be more effective if they reflect the economic and racial diversity of the communities in which they operate. Some critics argue further that officers serving a specific community should come *only* from that community or the immediate surrounding area. This runs contrary to how some police departments operate, with officers pulled from sometimes distant regions. Again, critics argue that police will be more effective at dealing with citizens if the police themselves are familiar with, or better yet residents of, the communities in which they serve.[5]

Critics of this theory argue that police departments might often be unable to effectively staff their departments if limited to officers living in the municipal area in which a police department is located. Further, officers who once lived within a community might seek to leave that community for a suburban area, and this raises a question as to how to define the extended community in which officers might live to qualify for work at a specific police station. In some regions officer shortages are not uncommon, and this problem has increased as police budgets have been reduced. In the 2010s, police departments in many parts of the country reported increased difficulty in finding and hiring personnel, especially for highly trained positions within police departments.

One of the reasons that police departments face personnel shortages is because the profession has an increasing level of attrition, with officers retiring or changing careers more often than professionals in other professions. The rate at which officers leave the profession has increased as public perception of police has declined and as police have faced increasing conflict with citizens. Increasingly negative public perception is also a factor in an overall reduction in the number of individuals joining police training programs.[6] Essentially, then, the loss of the public trust is a problem that will intensify over time as fewer people decide to become police officers, leaving police departments lacking in personnel as well as new ideas and fresh perspectives.

One of the ways that police departments might increase interest in the profession is to take steps to diversify police departments to appeal to a wider swath of candidates. Addressing public image problems is also an important factor as higher levels of public support would likely translate to higher levels of interest from potential applicants.

One of the most frequent suggestions from reformers has been that police need to return to the principles of "community policing," the idea that officers and departments must actively try to build, maintain, and improve relationships with members of a community. Community policing has been around since the 1960s. But the basic strategy of making police officers work with other kinds of community leaders does not blend well with the military-style tactics promoted by "get tough on crime" politicians and police administrators. Further, the decline in public trust has made it more difficult for police to secure the cooperation of community members needed to make community policing work. Even as some communities have invested in training police to engage in community policing, research on the effectiveness of this effort has been conflicting, and it is unclear whether or not the adoption of community policing has been successful. Supporters of this approach argue, however, that for community policing to be effective, police administrators and officers must fully embrace the principles behind this style of policing, which might mean de-emphasizing reliance on more aggressive or militaristic policing methods.

The Community Is the Key

There are some Americans who feel that policing in America is desperately broken, and others who feel that no serious reforms are needed, and there are many whose views fall somewhere in between these extremes. As with many other challenges facing police in the 2020s, the loss of public trust provides evidence that the current model is at least in some situations insufficient. A healthy and trusting relationship between police and members of a community is an essential factor in effective policing, and when this relationship deteriorates, it creates stress and conflict for both citizens and police. Whether the answer to this conundrum lies in returning to some form of community policing, or increasing racial diversity and representation in police departments, or limiting the role of police to avoid political controversy, it is essential for the future of American policing as a career and culture a way is found to strengthen the relationship between police and the citizens they are supposed to serve.

Works Used

Gross, Elana Lyn. "New York City Civil Rights Organizations Sue NYPD and City Officials for Alleged 'Police Brutality' at Protests." *Forbes*. Oct 26, 2020. https://www.forbes.com/sites/elanagross/2020/10/26/new-york-city-civil-rights-organizations-sue-nypd-and-city-officials-for-alleged-police-brutality-at-protests/?sh=4aebb6ba6810.

Ingraham, Christopher. "Two Charts Demolish the Notion That Immigrants Here Illegally Commit More Crime." *Washington Post*. Jun 19, 2018. https://www.washingtonpost.com/news/wonk/wp/2018/06/19/two-charts-demolish-the-notion-that-immigrants-here-illegally-commit-more-crime/.

Maciag, Mike. "Where Police Don't Mirror Communities and Why It Matters." *Governing*. Aug 28, 2015. https://www.governing.com/topics/public-justice-safety/gov-police-department-diversity.html.

Ortiz, Aimee. "Confidence in Police Is at Record Low, Gallup Survey Finds." *New York Times*. Aug 12, 2020. https://www.nytimes.com/2020/08/12/us/gallup-poll-police.html.

"Judiciary Committee Releases Report on Trump Administration Family Separation Policy." *House Committee on the Judiciary*. Oct 29, 2020. https://judiciary.house.gov/news/documentsingle.aspx?DocumentID=3442.

Solomon, Danyelle, Tom Jawetz, and Sanam Malik. "The Negative Consequences of Entangling Local Policing and Immigration Enforcement." *Center for American Progress*. Mar 21, 2017. https://www.americanprogress.org/issues/immigration/reports/2017/03/21/428776/negative-consequences-entangling-local-policing-immigration-enforcement/.

Thomas, Tobi, Adam Gabbatt, and Caelainn Barr. "Nearly 1,000 Instances of Police Brutality Recorded in US Anti-Racism Protests." *The Guardian*. Oct 29, 2020. https://www.theguardian.com/us-news/2020/oct/29/us-police-brutality-protest.

Tuccille, J.D. "U.S. Cops Are Facing a Recruitment Crisis: Will It Force Them to Change Their Ways?" *Reason*. Jun 25, 2019. https://reason.com/2019/06/25/us-cops-are-facing-a-recruitment-crisis-will-it-force-them-to-change-their-ways/.

Notes

1. "Judiciary Committee Releases Report on Trump Administration Family Separation Policy," House Committee on the Judiciary.
2. Solomon, Jawetz, and Malik, "The Negative Consequences of Entangling Local Policing and Immigration Enforcement."
3. Thomas, Gabbatt, and Barr, "Nearly 1,000 Instances of Police Brutality Recorded in US Anti-Racism Protests."
4. Gross, "New York City Civil Rights Organizations Sue NYPD and City Officials for Alleged `Police Brutality' at Protests."
5. Maciag, "Where Police Don't Mirror Communities and Why It Matters."
6. Tuccille, "U.S. Cops Are Facing a Recruitment Crisis: Will It Force Them to Change Their Ways?"

Polling Finds a Divide in How Americans View Police and Protestors

By Timothy Rich, et al.
The Hill, August 11, 2020

Recent polls show that 97 percent of Americans are aware of George Floyd's death, with other data showing an increased awareness of police brutality and racial injustice. Public perceptions of protests against police brutality remain politically divisive. Progressives argue that the violent actions of a few protesters distracts from the protests' overall peaceful nature, while President Trump and other conservatives downplay or deny police brutality claims, asserting that a few "bad apples" do not reflect police departments as a whole. Furthermore, once championed by a progressive minority, broader public discourse now considers calls to reform, defund, or abolish police departments in response to recurring police violence.

We address three interrelated issues about these protests and policing. First, how does the public view these protests in comparison to civil rights era protests? Second, does the public judge protesters or the police by the actions of so-called "bad apples"? Third, how does the public view terms like "defund the police"?

Many have drawn parallels to 1960s civil rights protests, due to the emphasis on racial injustice, their size and geographic spread across the country, and the force used by police in response. Yet, this comparison may paint a glorified picture of the past, ignoring that protests were highly controversial at the time.

Historically, regardless of partisanship, most Americans viewed police favorably and especially their local police. However, Americans also increasingly view police brutality as problematic, and majorities believe recent peaceful protests were justified yet oppose violent protests. Meanwhile, evaluating police actions and protests remains contentious, as some view violence as isolated, non-representative actions of the group whereas others view these violent acts as core components.

Various local police reforms have also resulted from protests, though implementation remains to be seen. Cities such as Minneapolis voted to dissolve the police force, while New York City plans to reallocate an undetermined amount of funds from law enforcement to youth services. Yet, calls to "defund" or "abolish" the police remain controversial and perhaps misunderstood.

To address these issues of protests and police and with assistance from the International Public Opinion Lab (IPOL) at Western Kentucky University, we conducted a web survey via mTurk of 1,027 American respondents on July 7, 2020.

Acknowledging that web surveys commonly underrepresent Black people and other ethnic minorities, we focused our attention on partisan differences.

Respondents first were randomly assigned to one of four prompts to evaluate using a five-point Likert scale (strongly disagree to strongly agree).

Version 1:

I support protests against racial injustice like those seen regarding George Floyd.

Version 2:

I support protests against racial injustice like those organized by Martin Luther King, Jr.

Version 3:

Police departments should not be judged as a whole by the violent actions of a minority of its members.

Version 4:

Protests should not be judged as a whole by the violent actions of a minority of its members.

For clarity, we recoded the five-point scale into three categories by combining "strongly disagree" with "disagree" and "strongly agree" with "agree." We find that more than 80 percent of Democrats expressed support for protests, regardless of the framing, with only a minor increase when Martin Luther King, Jr. was referenced. In contrast, a majority (57.14 percent) of Republicans agreed with the King prompt, but support dropped nearly 18 percent when Floyd was referenced.

So why the difference? Democrats perhaps see a clearer continuity between issues from the civil rights era to the present, supporting anti-police brutality and anti-racism platforms. If Republicans focus more on protest violence, then views of King-era protests may be sanitized views that disregard the looting, riots, and chaos that frequent major protests. The age distribution between the parties may also contribute if young people are more likely to see police brutality and protest coverage via social media.

Moving to the third and fourth versions, again, we see a stark difference. Among Democrats, more than 80 percent agree that protests should not be judged by the violent actions from a minority of its members. However, when the prompt focuses on police departments, only a plurality (47.46 percent) disagree with the statement. Among Republicans, we see nearly a mirror image, with more than 80 percent agreeing with the police department prompt while a slim majority (55.39 percent) agree with the protest version.

It should be noted that institutional protection for individuals differs greatly between police departments and protest groups. The "Blue wall of silence" describes the informal system amongst police officers who agree not to report another officer's misconduct. In doing so, many police departments fail to report excessive force, as required by the Violent Crime Control and Law Enforcement Act. Broader institutional protections, from qualified immunity to the role of police unions, further protect police so much so that from 2005 to 2011 only 13 on-duty police officers were charged with armed aggravated assault in the United States despite over 1,000 police shootings each year. In contrast, protesters lack such institutional structures while their actions are more likely to be in public and documented.

Next, all 1,027 respondents were asked to rate their first impressions of the following three phrases on 1 to 5 scale:

"Reform the police"

"Defund the police"

"Abolish the police"

Half of respondents, through random assignment, were given additional information about the three terms to clearly evaluate whether the public understood the differences between the terms. The additional information included: "Reform the police" means a long-term process that has usually involved putting more funding toward police and limiting officers' use of force and holding police accountable.

"Defund the police" means divesting some money from police budgets to invest in education, mental health care, housing, workforce development and other social services.

"Abolish the police" means reducing, with the vision of eventually eliminating, our reliance on policing to secure our public safety.

We see the public most supportive of "reform" and least of "abolish," with a much larger difference in support between "reform" and "defund" among Republicans. However, we see limited evidence that additional definitions influence views, with at best Democrats supporting "defund" and Republicans supporting "reform." This suggests that the media discourse about the terms have already generated clear beliefs on what these terms mean. To Democrats, defunding the police implies a reallocation of funds to public services whereas Republicans think fewer officers means increased crime. This suggests a fundamental disagreement on the nature of policing.

What does this all mean? Disagreements on how to judge "bad apples" contributes to partisan disagreements on police reform as Democrats and Republicans, in general, view one side as undeserving of judgement based on the actions of a few violent offenders, but do not extend more broadly. The multifaceted nature of the issues surrounding police brutality also make finding consensus extremely difficult. Although city budgets for

> **"Defund the police" means divesting some money from police budgets to invest in education, mental health care, housing, workforce development and other social services.**

public services rarely take a front seat in national political discourse, we're likely to see issue-based, local government functions continue to compound into a national partisan political debate.

The survey results also have clear implications for the 2020 presidential election. Studies suggest that protests have fused with the anti-Trump movement aiming to elect Democratic candidate Joe Biden. The protests have pushed prominent Republicans to reserve their vote for Biden and encouraged tens of thousands of Americans to register to vote.

Meanwhile, President Trump, focusing on protest violence, has embraced campaign strategies reminiscent of Nixon and Reagan's presidencies by claiming to be the "law and order" candidate, precisely at a time when the Democratic Party attempts to distance itself from "law and order" policies from the Johnson and Clinton administrations. Even if the size and scope of protests decline ahead of the election, the electoral rhetoric of injustice versus law and order is likely to endure precisely because of the chasm in perceptions between those party identifiers.

Print Citations

CMS: Rich, Timothy, et al. "Polling Finds a Divide in How Americans View Police and Protestors." In *The Reference Shelf: Policing in 2020,* edited by Micah L. Issitt, 49-52. Amenia, NY: Grey House Publishing, 2021.

MLA: Rich, Timothy, et al. "Polling Finds a Divide in How Americans View Police and Protestors." *The Reference Shelf: Policing in 2020,* edited by Micah L. Issitt, Grey Housing Publishing, 2021, pp. 49-52.

APA: Rich, T., et al. (2021). Polling finds a divide in how Americans view police and protestors. In Micah L. Issitt (Ed.), *The reference shelf: Policing in 2020* (pp. 49-52). Amenia, NY: Grey Housing Publishing.

The Negative Consequences of Entangling Local Policing and Immigration Enforcement

By Danyelle Solomon, Tom Jawetz, and Sanam Malik
Center for American Progress, March 21, 2017

"Trust between law enforcement agencies and the people they protect and serve is essential in a democracy. It is key to the stability of our communities, the integrity of our criminal justice system, and the safe and effective delivery of policing services."[1]

– The President's Task Force on 21st Century Policing, 2015

Law enforcement personnel across the nation today are facing complex challenges. Whether it is through interacting with individuals who have mental health or substance abuse issues, dealing with gun crimes, or responding to domestic violence, officers must address difficult realities on a daily basis. In the midst of heightened racial and ethnic tensions, they must tackle these challenges with constrained resources, including limited training, inadequate and outdated police equipment, enormous technological and data gaps, uneven recruitment, and reduced support services for officers.[2]

But on top of law enforcement officers' primary mission of keeping their communities safe, President Donald Trump has consistently called for the creation of a "deportation force" to maximize the number of immigrants removed from the country and has proposed a range of efforts that would supercharge the role of state and local law enforcement agencies, or LEAs, in federal immigration enforcement.[3] From signaling plans to aggressively promote the 287(g) program around the country to withholding federal grants from so-called sanctuary jurisdictions, the Trump administration has made clear that it aims to enlist state and local law enforcement in its civil immigration enforcement efforts through both inducement and coercion.[4]

State and local elected officials and LEAs are now, or soon will be, faced with a choice: whether and how to assume a greater role in enforcing federal immigration laws. As this issue brief illustrates, exercising that role could lead to significant financial burdens, increased litigation, and diminished public trust—all at the expense of public safety and the general welfare of all members of U.S. communities.

A Brief History of the 287(g) Program and Sanctuary Policies

The 287(g) program

Section 287(g) was added to the Immigration and Nationality Act in 1996. It authorizes state, county, and local LEAs to perform federal immigration enforcement duties pursuant to written memorandums of agreement, or MOAs, with U.S. Immigration and Customs Enforcement, or ICE.[5]

Historically, 287(g) agreements have taken three forms: 1) task force agreements that allow local law enforcement officers to perform immigration enforcement functions in their communities; 2) jail enforcement agreements that allow officers to question and screen individuals already being held in jail; and 3) hybrid agreements that combine the features of task force and jail enforcement agreements.[6]

The first 287(g) agreement was signed in 2002, shortly after the September 11 terrorist attacks, and the program grew from there. In 2007, ICE signed 26 new MOAs and added another 28 in 2008; by May 2009, there were 66 active MOAs.[7]

In 2010, the Office of Inspector General at the U.S. Department of Homeland Security, or DHS, identified serious concerns about the program and noted that the lack of training and oversight provided to task force jurisdictions by ICE increased the risk of civil rights violations.[8] Partly in response to this and other developments, the Obama administration phased out the use of task force and hybrid agreements at the end of 2012.[9] The Trump administration, however, hopes to increase the number of 287(g) agreements signed nationwide, as well as reintroduce the task force and hybrid models.[10]

Sanctuary policies

While there is no one definition, sanctuary jurisdictions generally are those that have adopted resolutions, ordinances, laws, or policies that limit local law enforcement's involvement in federal immigration enforcement efforts. These policies are intended to facilitate trust and increase public safety by ensuring that one's immigration status will not affect the ability to, for example, come forward as a witness or victim of a crime. Overall, more than 600 cities and counties and a few states have adopted sanctuary policies.[11]

The number of sanctuary jurisdictions—particularly those that limit when people may be held in custody based solely upon an ICE detainer or a request to hold someone past the point at which they would ordinarily be released—increased in response to the Secure Communities program. This program was launched under the George W. Bush ad-

> **Because racial profiling worsens already strained relationships with communities of color, it also makes it harder for law enforcement to build lasting trust.**

ministration and expanded nationwide under the Obama administration. Through Secure Communities, federal immigration officials received fingerprint information collected during booking by state and local LEAs and shared it with the Federal

Bureau of Investigation for use in criminal background checks. With this information, ICE significantly increased its issuance of detainer requests.[12]

Other jurisdictions adopted sanctuary policies to reduce their liability exposure after a series of federal court rulings on ICE detainer requests. These rulings call into question whether depriving people of liberty based on an ICE detainer request violates their constitutional rights to due process and to be free of unlawful seizure.[13]

How Local Entanglement in Federal Immigration Enforcement Harms Communities

In the coming months, the Trump administration is expected to conduct significant outreach to states and localities to enter into new 287(g) agreements or to add task forces onto existing jail enforcement agreements. The administration is also expected to make some effort to deny federal grants to jurisdictions that the Secretary of DHS—in his discretion—deems to be sanctuary jurisdictions.[14]

Such efforts fly in the face of law enforcement best practices, particularly those of community policing. While there is no universal definition of community policing, one common tenet is that "[r]educing crime and disorder requires that the police work cooperatively with people in neighborhoods to (1) identify their concerns, (2) solicit their help, and (3) solve their problems." Failure to maintain trust and open lines of communication with the public results in an unwillingness to cooperate or share information.[15]

Research shows that the general principles of community policing apply with equal force when looking at effective policing in immigrant communities. A study by the University of Illinois at Chicago found that Latinos, whether citizens or noncitizens, are "less likely to volunteer information about crimes because they fear getting caught in the web of immigration enforcement themselves or bringing unwanted attention to their family or friends." The study further found that 70 percent of unauthorized immigrants and 44 percent of Latinos are less likely to communicate with law enforcement if they believe officers will question their immigration status or that of people they know.[16] Reviewing several recent instances in which unauthorized immigrants assisted law enforcement as victims or witnesses to crime, Chuck Wexler, executive director of the Police Executive Research Forum, observed: "Had these undocumented people, and countless others in cities across America, not stepped forward to report crime and cooperate with the police, we would have more dangerous offenders committing more crime—and more serious crime—against innocent victims."[17]

287(g) agreements are expensive and litigation-prone and undermine public safety and community trust

In deciding how to respond to the Trump administration's 287(g) efforts, jurisdictions need to consider how limited resources and potential increases in racial profiling and litigation will affect their primary mission of ensuring public safety.

Strains on already limited resources

Under the 287(g) program, participating jurisdictions perform federal immigration enforcement functions largely at their own expense.[18] While ICE may provide some reimbursement for detention costs in some cases, it provides minimal funding for training and information technology equipment and services. Local agencies are entirely responsible for the salaries and benefits of their personnel as well as travel costs, housing, and per diem for required training.[19]

Many jurisdictions that have participated in 287(g) programs have found them to be a raw deal. A 2009 study conducted by the Brookings Institution found that Prince William County, Virginia, had to increase property taxes and pull money from its rainy day fund to implement its 287(g) program. Overall, the program cost the county $6.4 million in its first year and was estimated to cost $26 million over five years.[20] An analysis of North Carolina, the state with the highest nationwide number of 287(g) jurisdictions, found that the program cost Mecklenburg and Alamance counties together more than $10 million in the first year alone.[21] Sheriff Ed Gonzalez in Harris County, Texas, recently terminated his 287(g) agreement to make better use of the $675,000 in associated salary expenses; according to the sheriff, incorporating ICE-trained deputies elsewhere in the jail complex could reduce the $1 million in overtime costs the county incurs every two weeks managing the overcrowded facility.[22]

Increased racial profiling and litigation

A frequent complaint against jurisdictions operating 287(g) task force agreements was the broad discretion provided to law enforcement to detain and arrest people believed to be in the country unlawfully created opportunities for abuse, especially when not closely monitored. Racial profiling—the practice of targeting a set of individuals based on their race, ethnicity, religion, or national origin—has long been a troubling policing tactic.[23] Even with proper training, law enforcement officers, as all humans, are susceptible to relying on racial or ethnic stereotypes. Because racial profiling worsens already strained relationships with communities of color, it also makes it harder for law enforcement to build lasting trust. Mayors and other elected officials, police chiefs, and residents understand that without that trust, public safety is diminished.

Perhaps the most prominent case of discriminatory policing by a 287(g) jurisdiction involved the Maricopa County Sheriff's Office, or MCSO, under Sheriff Joe Arpaio. In 2006, the MCSO entered into an MOA to operate a 287(g) task force, which was scaled back to a jail enforcement agreement in 2009. In 2011, the U.S. Department of Justice found that the MCSO engaged in discriminatory policing practices, leading the DHS to terminate the agreement.[24] A federal court later ruled that Maricopa County engaged in unconstitutional racial profiling and pretextual stops.[25] In addition, a 2008 Goldwater Institute study found that the MCSO's significant investment in immigration enforcement efforts detracted from the office's public safety mission and blew an enormous hole in its budget.[26]

The MCSO's unlawful and discriminatory conduct was determined to have been intentional.[27] But even without meaning to, any LEA performing immigration enforcement functions with insufficient oversight, training, and guidance is at a heightened risk of making unlawful stops of individuals who look or sound foreign. Such conduct also creates a heightened risk of litigation. Furthermore, it increases the likelihood that people of color will stop communicating and working with their local LEAs to solve crimes.

Sanctuary Policies Reduce Litigation Risks and Are Associated with Lower Crime Rates

Faced with the threat of losing important federal funds, some sanctuary jurisdictions may be considering changes to their policies, and other jurisdictions may be reconsidering whether to adopt such policies. In making those choices, jurisdictions should consider the fiscal and public safety costs associated with increased cooperation, as well as the likelihood that the administration will overcome significant legal obstacles to withholding federal funds.

Reduced litigation risks due to unlawful detention

The proliferation of sanctuary policies limiting when local LEAs can hold people pursuant to ICE detainer requests can be traced, in part, to a growing body of lawsuits that have resulted in court judgments and hefty settlements. Many of these cases have concluded that warrantless ICE detainer requests fail to provide the probable cause required under Fourth Amendment jurisprudence to allow a state or locality to deprive a person of liberty.[28] The city of Allentown, Pennsylvania, and Lehigh County, Pennsylvania, for example, settled with a U.S. citizen who was detained for three days pursuant to a detainer request that ICE mistakenly issued. The lawsuit cost the city $25,000 and the county $95,000.[29] Salt Lake County, Utah, paid $75,000 to settle a case brought by an individual held on an ICE detainer for 46 days after he had posted bail.[30] Clackamas County, Oregon, settled a case for $30,100 brought by a woman detained for two weeks based solely on an ICE detainer request.[31]

In light of the Trump administration's threat to punish sanctuary jurisdictions by withholding federal funds—discussed in the next section—the constitutional deficiencies with ICE's current detainer practices place law enforcement agencies in a difficult place. Jurisdictions that respond to the threat by deciding to hold people regularly pursuant to ICE detainers will be more likely to encounter legal challenges.[32] These litigation risks should be taken seriously when jurisdictions determine what detainer policy is in the best interest of public safety and overall resource management.

Lower crime rates

The Trump administration has attempted to justify a crackdown on sanctuary policies by claiming that such jurisdictions "have caused immeasurable harm to the American people and to the very fabric of our Republic."[33] Yet research finds that, on average, there are 35.5 fewer crimes per 10,000 people in sanctuary counties than in non-sanctuary counties.[34] According to the Major Cities Chiefs Association, or MCCA, entangling local law enforcement with federal immigration enforcement "would result in increased crime against immigrants and in the broader community, create a class of silent victims and eliminate the potential for assistance from immigrants in solving crimes or preventing future terroristic acts."[35] The MCCA has consistently cited five major areas of concern with linking local law enforcement with federal immigration enforcement, including undermined community trust, lack of resources, and overly complex and time-consuming training that detracts from the public safety mission.[36]

Threats to Withhold Federal Funding from Sanctuary Cities May Be Legally Impermissible

President Trump's January 25 executive order purports to allow the government to withhold federal grant money from sanctuary jurisdictions. It also broadly directs the attorney general to "take appropriate enforcement action" against any entity with a policy that "prevents or hinders the enforcement of [f]ederal law."[37] However, the administration's threats to withhold funding from or otherwise punish sanctuary jurisdictions will be constrained by longstanding 10th Amendment jurisprudence that prevents the federal government from commandeering state and local resources.[38] Additionally, Supreme Court precedent under the spending clause limits when, under what circumstances, and to what extent the federal government can impose conditions on the granting of federal funds.[39]

Although the administration has not yet described the specific funds it would seek to withhold, in recent years, congressional Republicans have attempted to pass legislation that would jeopardize several law enforcement, economic development, and community development grant programs.[40] This sledgehammer approach would have broad and dangerous consequences for jurisdictions that are already feeling the pinch of smaller budgets—which in turn would make communities less safe and less prosperous.[41]

Conclusion

Today, law enforcement is faced with many challenges that are beyond the scope of their primary duties and functions. Efforts to increase police involvement in federal immigration enforcement illustrate the Trump administration's disconnect with the real challenges facing local law enforcement. Instead of working to meet these growing challenges, the administration is choosing to add to them by pursuing an agenda guided by anti-immigrant ideologues such as Kris Kobach and Stephen Bannon—not by community priorities, public safety data, or research.[42]

As a candidate and as president, Trump has labeled immigrants as criminals who pose a threat to public safety.[43] These statements fly in the face of a range of evidence that immigrants are actually less likely to commit serious crimes than the U.S.-born and that increases in immigration are associated with decreases in crime.[44] Although the country badly needs a responsible solution to our outdated immigration system, as former Los Angeles Police Chief William Bratton wrote in 2009, "[T]he solution isn't turning every local police department into an arm of Immigration and Customs Enforcement."[45] Given the evidence presented in this brief, local law enforcement should think twice about engaging in federal immigration enforcement.

Endnotes

1. Office of Community Oriented Policing Services, *Final Report of the President's Task Force on 21st Century Policing* (U.S. Department of Justice, 2015), available at https://cops.usdoj.gov/pdf/taskforce/taskforce_finalreport.pdf.

2. Office of Community Oriented Policing Services, *2016: The State of Policing in the United States,* Volume 1 (U.S. Department of Justice, 2016), available at https://ric-zai-inc.com/Publications/cops-w0815-pub.pdf.

3. Michelle Mark, "Trump's immigration crackdown is paving the way for a 'deportation force'," Business Insider, February 23, 2017, available at http://www.businessinsider.com/trump-dhs-memos-pave-way-for-deportation-force-2017-2; Tom LoBianco, "Donald Trump promises 'deportation force' to remove 11 million," CNN Politics, November 12, 2015, available at http://www.cnn.com/2015/11/11/politics/donald-trump-deportation-force-debate-immigration/.

4. U.S. Immigration and Customs Enforcement, "Delegation of Immigration Authority Section 287(g) Immigration and Nationality Act," available at https://www.ice.gov/factsheets/287g (last accessed March 2017); The White House, "Executive Order: Enhancing Public Safety in the Interior of the United States," Press release, January 25, 2017, available at https://www.whitehouse.gov/the-press-office/2017/01/25/presidential-executive-order-enhancing-public-safety-interior-united.

5. U.S. Immigration and Customs Enforcement, "Delegation of Immigration Authority Section 287(g) Immigration and Nationality Act."

6. Cristina Rodriguez and others, "A Program in Flux: New Priorities and Implementation Challenge for 287(g)" (Washington: Migration Policy Institute, 2010), available at http://www.migrationpolicy.org/research/program-flux-new-priorities-and-implementation-challenges-287g.

7. Ibid.

8. Office of Inspector General, *The Performance of 287(g) Agreements* (U.S. Department of Homeland Security, 2010), available at https://www.oig.dhs.gov/assets/Mgmt/OIG_10-63_Mar10.pdf.

9. William A. Kandel, "Interior Immigration Enforcement: Criminal Alien Programs" (Washington: Congressional Research Service, 2016), available at https://fas.org/sgp/crs/homesec/R44627.pdf.

10. Secretary John Kelly, *Implementing the President's Border Security and Immigration Enforcement Improvement Policies* (U.S. Department of Homeland Security, 2017), available at https://www.dhs.gov/sites/default/files/

publications/17_0220_S1_Implementing-the-Presidents-Border-Security-Immigration-Enforcement-Improvement-Policies.pdf.

11. Lena Garber and Nikki Marquez, "Searching for Sanctuary: An Analysis of America's Counties & Their Voluntary Assistance With Deportations" (San Francisco: Immigrant Legal Resource Center, 2017), available at https://www.ilrc.org/sites/default/files/resources/sanctuary_report_final_1-min.pdf.

12. U.S. Immigration and Customs Enforcement, "Secure Communities," available at https://www.ice.gov/secure-communities (last accessed February 2017).

13. Law Enforcement Immigration Task Force, "A Path to Public Safety: The Legal Questions around Immigration Detainers," February 27, 2017, available at http://immigrationforum.org/blog/the-legal-questions-around-immigration-detainers/.

14. See, for example, Eric T. Schneiderman, "Guidance Concerning Local Authority Participation In Immigration Enforcement And Model Sanctuary Provisions" (Albany, NY: New York State Attorney General, 2017), available at https://ag.ny.gov/sites/default/files/guidance.concerning.local_.authority.particpation.in_.immigration.enforcement.1.19.17.pdf.

15. Police Foundation, "Community Policing," available at https://www.police-foundation.org/projects/community-policing/ (last accessed March 2017).

16. Nik Theodore, "Insecure Communities: Latino Perceptions of Police Involvement in Immigration Enforcement" (Chicago: University of Illinois at Chicago, 2013), available at http://www.policylink.org/sites/default/files/INSECURE_COMMUNITIES_REPORT_FINAL.PDF.

17. Chuck Wexler, "Police chiefs across the country support sanctuary cities because they keep crime down," *Los Angeles Times*, March 6, 2017, available at http://www.latimes.com/opinion/op-ed/la-oe-wexler-sanctuary-cities-immigration-crime-20170306-story.html.

18. *Immigration and Nationality Act, 287(g)(1)* (1996), available at https://www.uscis.gov/ilink/docView/SLB/HTML/SLB/0-0-0-1/0-0-0-29/0-0-0-9505.html.

19. Office of Inspector General, *The Performance of 287(g) Agreements.*

20. Audrey Singer, Jill H. Wilson, and Brooke DeRenzis, "Immigrants, Politics, and Local Response in Suburban Washington" (Washington: Brookings Institution, 2009), available at https://www.brookings.edu/wp-content/uploads/2016/06/0225_immigration_singer.pdf.

21. Mai Thi Nguyen and Hannah Gill, "The 287(g) Program: The Costs and Consequences of Local Immigration Enforcement in North Carolina Communities" (Chapel Hill, NC: The University of North Carolina, 2010), available at http://isa.unc.edu/files/2012/06/287g_report_final.pdf.

22. James Pinkerton and St. John Barned-Smith, "Sheriff cuts ties with ICE program over immigration detentions," *Houston Chronicle*, February 23, 2017, available at http://www.chron.com/news/houston-texas/article/Sheriff-cuts-ties-with-ICE-program-over-10949264.php.

23. National Institute of Justice, "Racial Profiling," January 10, 2013, available

at https://www.nij.gov/topics/law-enforcement/legitimacy/pages/racial-profiling.aspx.

24. U.S. Department of Homeland Security, "Statement by Secretary Napolitano on DOJ's Findings of Discriminatory Policing in Maricopa County," Press release, December 15, 2011, available at https://www.dhs.gov/news/2011/12/15/secretary-napolitano-dojs-findings-discriminatory-policing-maricopa-county.

25. *Manuel de Jesus Ortega Melendres et al. v. Joseph M. Arpaio*, U.S. District Court for the District of Arizona (May 24, 2013) (No. PHX-CV-07-02513), available at https://www.aclu.org/sites/default/files/field_document/arpaio_decision.pdf.

26. Clint Bolick, "Mission Unaccomplished: The Misplaced Priorities of the Maricopa County Sheriff's Office" (Phoenix: Goldwater Institute, 2008), available at https://goldwater-media.s3.amazonaws.com/cms_page_media/2016/8/31/12.02.2008%252c%20Mission%20Unaccomplished.pdf.

27. *Ortega Melendres et al. v. Arpaio*, p. 125. ("The Court finds direct evidence of discriminatory intent based on the MCSO's policies, operations plans and procedures.")

28. Laurence Benenson, "The Trouble with Immigration Detainers," National Immigration Forum, May 24, 2016, available at http://immigrationforum.org/blog/the-trouble-with-immigration-detainers/.

29. American Civil Liberties Union of Pennsylvania, "Galarza v. Szalczyk, et al.," available at https://www.aclupa.org/our-work/legal/legaldocket/galarzavszalczyketal/ (last accessed March 2017).

30. Ashton Edwards, "Man settles immigration lawsuit against Salt Lake County, awarded $75,000," Fox 13 News, August 25, 2014, available at http://fox13now.com/2014/08/25/man-settles-immigration-lawsuit-against-salt-lake-county-awarded-75000/.

31. Steve Mayes, "Woman at center of landmark immigration case settles suit that changed jail holds in state, nation," *The Oregonian*, May 18, 2015, available at http://www.oregonlive.com/clackamascounty/index.ssf/2015/05/woman_at_center_of_landmark_im.html.

32. Major County Sheriffs' Association, "Sheriffs Respond to Sanctuary City Executive Order," January 2017, available at http://www.mcsheriffs.com/pdf/news/sanctuary_city_eo_jan_2017.pdf.

33. The White House, "Executive Order: Enhancing Public Safety in the Interior of the United States."

34. Tom K. Wong, "The Effects of Sanctuary Policies on Crime and the Economy" (Washington: Center for American Progress and National Immigration Law Center, 2017), available at https://www.americanprogress.org/issues/immigration/reports/2017/01/26/297366/the-effects-of-sanctuary-policies-on-crime-and-the-economy/.

35. Craig E. Ferrell Jr. and others, "M.C.C. Immigration Committee Recommendations For Enforcement of Immigration Laws by Local Policy Agencies"

(Charlotte, NC: Major Cities Chiefs Association, 2006), available at https://www.majorcitieschiefs.com/pdf/news/MCC_Position_Statement.pdf.

36. Major Cities Chiefs, "Immigration Policy" (2013), available at https://www.majorcitieschiefs.com/pdf/news/2013_immigration_policy.pdf.

37. The White House, "Executive Order: Enhancing Public Safety in the Interior of the United States."

38. Ilya Somin, "Federalism, the Constitution, and sanctuary cities," *The Washington Post*, November 26, 2016, available at https://www.washingtonpost.com/news/volokh-conspiracy/wp/2016/11/26/federalism-the-constitution-and-sanctuary-cities/?utm_term=.54d3b65a57f7; Ilya Somin, "More on Federalism, the Constitution, and Sanctuary Cities," *The Washington Post*, December 12, 2016, available at https://www.washingtonpost.com/news/volokh-conspiracy/wp/2016/12/12/more-on-federalism-the-constitution-and-sanctuary-cities/?utm_term=.51f4b95eefc6; Noah Feldman, "Sanctuary Cities Are Safe, Thanks to Conservatives," *Bloomberg View*, November 29, 2016, available at https://www.bloomberg.com/view/articles/2016-11-29/sanctuary-cities-are-safe-thanks-to-conservatives.

39. *South Dakota v. Dole*, U.S. Supreme Court (April 28, 1987) (No. 86-260), available at https://supreme.justia.com/cases/federal/us/483/203/case.html; *National Federation of Independent Business v. Sebelius* (June 28, 2012) (No. 11–393, 11–398, 11–400), available at https://supreme.justia.com/cases/federal/us/567/11-393/opinion3.html.

40. *Stop Sanctuary Policies and Protect Americans Act*, S. 2146, 114th Cong. (2014), available at https://www.congress.gov/bill/114th-congress/senate-bill/2146?q=%7B%22search%22%3A%5B%22Stop+Sanctuary+Policies+and+Protect+Americans+Act%22%5D%7D&r=1.

41. Angelo Mathay and others, "How Much Funding for Sanctuary Jurisdictions Could Be at Risk?", Center for American Progress, March 7, 2017, available at https://www.americanprogress.org/issues/immigration/news/2017/03/07/427438/how-much-funding-for-sanctuary-jurisdictions-could-be-at-risk/.

42. Tara Goshan, "Steve Bannon in 2016: legal immigration is the real 'problem'," Vox, February 2, 2017, available at http://www.vox.com/policy-and-politics/2017/2/2/14472404/steve-bannon-legal-immigration-problem; Jonathan Blitzer, "Trump's Ideas Man for Hard-Line Immigration Policy," *The New Yorker*, November 22, 2016, available at http://www.newyorker.com/news/news-desk/trumps-ideas-man-for-hard-line-immigration-policy; Emily Ekins, "Policing in America: Understanding Public Attitudes Toward the Police. Results from a National Survey." Working Paper (CATO Institute, 2017), available at https://www.cato.org/publications/working-paper/policing-america-understanding-public-attitudes-toward-police-results.

43. Peter Beinart, "Trump Scapegoats Unauthorized Immigrants for Crime," *The Atlantic*, March 1, 2017, available at https://www.theatlantic.com/

politics/archive/2017/03/trump-scapegoats-unauthorized-immigrants-for-crime/518238/.

44. Walter Ewing, Daniel E. Martínez, and Rubén G. Rumbaut, "The Criminal-ization of Immigration in the United States" (Washington: American Immi-gration Council, 2015), available at https://www.americanimmigrationcoun-cil.org/research/criminalization-immigration-united-states; Drake Baer, "The Two Big Ways Immigrants Drive Down Crime," *New York Magazine*, March 1, 2017, available at http://nymag.com/scienceofus/2017/03/does-immigration-increase-crime-no.html.

45. William J. Bratton, "The LAPD fights crime, not illegal immigration," *Los Angeles Times*, October 27, 2009, available at http://articles.latimes.com/2009/oct/27/opinion/oe-bratton27.

Print Citations

CMS: Solomon, Danyelle, Tom Jawetz, and Sanam Malik. "The Negative Consequences of Entangling Local Policing and Immigration Enforcement." In *The Reference Shelf: Policing in 2020,* edited by Micah L. Issitt, 53-63. Amenia, NY: Grey House Publishing, 2021.

MLA: Solomon, Danyelle, Tom Jawetz, and Sanam Malik. "The Negative Consequences of Entangling Local Policing and Immigration Enforcement." *The Reference Shelf: Policing in 2020,* edited by Micah L. Issitt, Grey Housing Publishing, 2021, pp. 53-63.

APA: Solomon, D., Jawetz, T., & Sanam, M. (2021). The negative consequences of entan-gling local policing and immigration enforcement. In Micah L. Issitt (Ed.), *The reference shelf: Policing in 2020* (pp. 53-63). Amenia, NY: Grey Housing Publishing.

Has ICE Found a Way to Get around Sanctuary Policies?

By Jack Herrera
PacificStandard, May 7, 2019

When Immigration and Customs Enforcement announced its new training program for local law enforcement on Monday, the agency billed the program as a way for police in so-called "sanctuary" cities and states to cooperate with ICE.

Does ICE's new program really allow police to skirt around their state and city's sanctuary policies? According to legal experts, probably not.

Though sanctuary policies vary greatly, most people agree that, for such a policy to have teeth, it must limit ICE's ability to issue "detainer requests." An ICE detainer request works like this: When local law enforcement officers arrest somebody, they take that person's fingerprints and send the information to the federal government. If ICE determines that the person is in the country illegally, the agency might issue a detainer request asking local police to keep the person in jail. Even if a judge has ordered someone's release, or if police realize they arrested the wrong person, an ICE detainer request asks the police to hold that person in jail for up to 48 hours longer, in order to give ICE agents time to come re-arrest them.

Multiple courts around the country have ruled that ICE detainers are *requests*, not orders: That's where sanctuary policies come in. Local jurisdictions have the option to refuse detainer requests, and many cities (and a few states) have passed laws compelling state law enforcement to refuse the requests.

Now, ICE claims it's found a way to get around those sanctuary policies. In a press release on Monday, ICE claimed that its new "Warrant Service Officer" training program is "intended for local law enforcement that wish to honor immigration detainers but are prohibited due to state and local policies that limit cooperation with the agency." By training local law enforcement officers to act as pseudo-immigration officers, the agency claims that those officers will be able to act on detainer requests.

But nothing about the training program would make detainer requests into orders. "They would continue to be optional, and they have to optional under the Tenth Amendment," says Spencer Amdur, a staff attorney with the American Civil Liberties Union. "The federal government can't force anybody to do one of these agreements."

Amdur says federal statute limits the kind of cooperation agreements ICE

enters into with local law enforcement. Specifically, the
agreements have to be consistent with state and local law—
meaning ICE can't empower
police in sanctuary jurisdictions to break local laws.

> ### ICE can't empower police in sanctuary jurisdictions to break local laws.

Why, then, is ICE billing the program as a way to cooperate with local police in sanctuary jurisdictions?

According to Amdur, the new training program is likely intended for law enforcement agencies that have already decided to cooperate with detainer requests. In other words, the new policy could give local police a sort of legal cover: If a sheriff is challenged in court for honoring a detainer request, the sheriff could argue: *ICE said it was OK.*

However, Amdur says that local law enforcement should be cautious: ICE cooperation agreements might not shield sheriffs from lawsuits. ICE has made similar guarantees to sheriffs in the past, and that hasn't stopped those sheriffs from ending up in court.

In January of 2018, a collection of Florida counties entered into what are known as Basic Ordering Agreements with ICE. Under the agreements, ICE would pay sheriffs $50 for every immigrant they held. In a press release, ICE said the Basic Ordering Agreements would mean that local law enforcement would be "afforded liability protection" for lawsuits regarding detainers. But then the agency made a mistake: In a jail in Key West, ICE sent a detainer request for a man named Peter Brown, who turned out to be an American citizen. Brown and the ACLU then sued Monroe Country Sheriff Rick Ramsay for illegal detention in violation of the Fourth Amendment.

Ramsay claims that the detention was out of his hands. "It is important to also note that when an inmate is held under an ICE matter, I, as Sheriff, do not have the legal authority to release that person," he wrote in a statement that Pacific Standard obtained from the police department in December. Ramsay's argument is legally suspect—the detainer document for Brown clearly states that his detention is "requested," not ordered. Ramsay's statements indicated that he believed the Basic Ordering Agreement he signed with ICE put the responsibility for the mistaken detainer request in ICE's hands. But the ACLU lawsuit against Ramsay is moving forward.

Amdur sees the new Warrant Service Officer training programs as similar to the Basic Order Agreement policy: another attempt by ICE to convince local law enforcement to sign on to cooperation agreements and honor detainer agreements.

"ICE [has always] tried to convince localities that detainers are mandatory," Amdur says. "I don't think that they're fooling anybody: Everybody knows at this point that detainers are not mandatory."

Print Citations

CMS: Herrera, Jack. "Has ICE Found a Way to Get around Sanctuary Policies?" In *The Reference Shelf: Policing in 2020,* edited by Micah L. Issitt, 64-66. Amenia, NY: Grey House Publishing, 2021.

MLA: Herrera, Jack. "Has ICE Found a Way to Get around Sanctuary Policies?" *The Reference Shelf: Policing in 2020,* edited by Micah L. Issitt, Grey Housing Publishing, 2021, pp. 64-66.

APA: Herrera, J. (2021). Has ICE found a way to get around sanctuary policies? In Micah L. Issitt (Ed.), *The reference shelf: Policing in 2020* (pp. 64-66). Amenia, NY: Grey Housing Publishing.

Calls for Reform Bring Renewed Focus to Community Policing, but Does It Work?

By Candice Norwood
PBS NewsHour, September 18, 2020

Amid protests over racial injustice spurred by the killing of George Floyd by police in May, the concept of community policing is getting a new look as lawmakers, reform advocates and some law enforcement consider whether it could help promote systemic changes in policing.

In a June column for USA Today, former Vice President and Democratic nominee Joe Biden discussed his proposal for a $300 million investment in community policing initiatives aimed at "getting cops out of their cruisers and building relationships with the people and the communities they are there to serve and protect."

That same month, President Donald Trump signed an executive order calling for legislation that would enhance existing federal grant programs to help police agencies grow community engagement.

For about 60 years, law enforcement agencies have turned to the community policing philosophy to serve a variety of purposes, including crime reduction and changes to how police interact with the residents they serve. Despite funding from the federal government and support among many police departments, community policing has become a broad, amorphous concept that encompasses a myriad of tactics that departments use to engage civilians. The outcomes of these strategies will differ depending on a particular department's implementation, as well as the specific needs of the residents, researchers told the *PBS NewsHour*.

These differences mean some community policing efforts may build community trust, change officer behavior or reduce use of force against civilians, while others may not.

The Origins of Community Policing

Interest in community policing in the U.S. dates back to the 1960s and 1970s, a period of high tension and clashes between law enforcement and protesters against the backdrop of the Civil Rights and Anti-War movements. By the 1980s, the more formalized concept sought to train officers to police and interact with communities in new ways, said Tracey Meares, a professor and founding director of the Justice Collaboratory at Yale Law School.

In its early iteration this included officer foot patrols, knocking on doors, counseling crime victims and setting up neighborhood police stations, according to a 1988 paper by criminologists George Kelling and Mark Moore.

Kelling and Moore wrote that the key elements of community policing are organizational decentralization, such as neighborhood police stations; developing an intimate relationship between police and residents; and fostering communication that encourages people to bring issues within the neighborhood directly to officers.

But community policing that advanced alongside other crime fighting approaches, critics say, disproportionately targeted poor people and communities of color. One of these was the broken windows theory, popularized by Kelling, which asserted that smaller signs of crime or disorder, like a broken window in a neighborhood building, will lead to further deterioration, or more frequent crimes. Therefore, Kelling argued, swiftly addressing small instances of disorder like panhandling or loitering, will in theory, promote lawfulness and order in a city.

During this period, the country's "tough on crime" approach included the War on Drugs that led to laws establishing minimum sentences for possession of controlled substances like cocaine, heroine and marijuana.

> **The goal is for the officers to develop relationships with residents to address any neighborhood problems based on their particular needs.**

The Violent Crime Control and Law Enforcement Act of 1994, which Biden played a lead role in writing, is frequently criticized for mandating the three-strike sentencing rule and contributing to increased incarceration. It also allocated $8.8 billion over six years and established the federal Community Oriented Policing Services office to manage and distribute these funds.

Between 1980 and 2000, the total U.S. prison population increased from 329,000 people to more than 1.3 million, with 46.2 percent of those serving sentences longer than one year being Black, 35.7 percent being white and 16.4 percent being Hispanic.

Despite the push for community-based approaches to law enforcement in the 1980s and 1990s, policing in practice showed "extreme inequality," said Daniel Lawrence, a principal research associate in the Urban Institute's Justice Policy Center. "Individuals from communities of color—specifically Black communities—instead experience dehumanizing behaviors repeatedly in their interactions with police officers."

As crime rates decreased and public support for criminal justice and policing reform evolved, so did approaches to community policing. In 2011, President Barack Obama's administration established the Collaborative Reform Initiative (CRI), under which departments could request a Justice Department assessment of its policing practices that included recommendations. Departments could also receive federal funding and training to help implement the changes.

In 2014, the Justice Department under Obama also provided $4.75 million in funding for a three-year pilot program called the National Initiative for Building

Community Trust and Justice. Through the initiative, six police departments received guidance and training from experts on addressing implicit biases, improving public interactions and building trust.

During his time in office, Trump has repeatedly called for "law and order" and shown public support for law enforcement, particularly amid a series of sustained protests across the United States that have called for racial equality and an end to police brutality. Trump's administration has provided military equipment, tactical training and some financial support for police.

But, the administration discontinued funding for the National Initiative, restructured the Collaborative Reform Initiative to scale back federal oversight of local departments and has repeatedly proposed large budget cuts to a COPS office program meant to provide funding to hire more local officers.

The 2021 White House budget proposal released in February included a 58 percent cut to the hiring program from $235 million to $99 million to reallocate funds to federal law enforcement. The administration stated that resources for the program "are spread thin and are not well targeted to achieve public safety outcomes."

Community Policing Approaches Vary

Lawmakers frequently discuss community policing as if it is a cohesive set of recommendations that can bring about police reforms. In reality, community policing can mean whatever individual police departments decide.

In the 1980s, Houston police set up "storefront" police stations at malls to give people more accessibility to officers, said Jihong Zhao, a professor of criminal justice and criminology at Sam Houston State University in Texas. In Spokane, Washington, in the 1990s, Zhao said he shadowed police officers who were assigned to monitor apartment complexes in a lower income neighborhood with higher volumes of 9-1-1 calls.

In 1991, the Elgin Police Department in Illinois established the Resident Officer Program of Elgin (ROPE), which placed nine officers in residence in different areas of the city where the department had determined crime rates were higher, in order to build partnerships between police and residents, said Commander Adam Schuessler, who became an early ROPE officer.

"We put officers in those neighborhoods to work with the community, not run the community," Schuessler said. "We are going to let them know we live in this neighborhood with you. We're here with you. We're here for you. We're here to listen to you. We're here to help solve the problems that you see."

A 2014 *FiveThirtyEight* analysis determined that of the 75 U.S. cities with the largest police forces, 60 percent of officers lived outside city limits. ROPE now has just four participating officers, but has become a model for similar efforts in other cities. Elgin police also run other community programs and events, including assigning neighborhood officers, holding camps for children and a civilian police academy to recruit community members.

A different community policing approach in Grand Rapids, Michigan, designates community policing "specialists" who work to make nonenforcement "informal" contacts with the residents of a specific region or neighborhood. This can involve anything from playing basketball with kids, to attending community events. The goal is for the officers to develop relationships with residents to address any neighborhood problems based on their particular needs, Sgt. John Wittkowski of the Grand Rapid Police Department said.

Beyond these specialists, Wittkowski said his department makes the principles of community policing part of the entire department's culture. An acceptance of that culture is something they look for when hiring new personnel, he added.

"Over the last few years we have made a push to ensure that officers realize that those informal contacts—those community contacts getting out of your car, shooting hoops with a kid, speaking to parents at an event—are hugely important to developing relationships and most importantly, developing a level of trust in the community," Wittkowski said.

Neither Elgin nor Grand Rapids could provide metrics showing the effects of their community policing efforts on crime levels, arrests or community satisfaction. Policing researchers said the inconsistency in how departments use certain community-based policing approaches creates challenges for isolating the outcomes of a particular strategy.

"There certainly have been studies that try to figure out if policing under the guise of community policing leads to particular outcomes you might expect like lower levels of crime, increased citizen satisfaction with police, lower fear of crime. … but the research is mixed," said Christopher Harris, associate professor of criminology and justice studies with the University of Massachusetts, Lowell.

One 2019 study examined how positive nonenforcement interactions affect public perceptions of law enforcement. The study worked with police in New Haven, Connecticut, who knocked on doors and briefly engaged with residents in a nonenforcement capacity. The study found significant improvements in the civilians' feelings toward the officers, with the biggest positive effect among Black residents.

In a 2014 report, researchers conducted a systematic review of 25 reports containing 65 independent tests of community-oriented policing. It determined that these efforts had positive effects on citizen satisfaction, perceptions of disorder and police legitimacy. But the impact on crime and fear of crime was limited, the study concluded.

Among the body of research, it's unclear what effect community-focused strategies have on officer behavior and use of force—a primary concern for reform advocates. "Certain kinds of community policing can improve the community's perception of police legitimacy and trust … that is not the same thing as enhancing public safety," said Michael Sierra-Arévalo, an assistant professor with the University of Texas at Austin who co-authored the 2019 New Haven study. "You can have people trust the police, and the police can still violate their rights. They can still uphold unjust laws."

Use of force data can be a challenge to collect from police agencies generally, and there is no mandatory nationwide database for such information. A number of researchers and news organizations have collected figures looking at police killings, shootings or use of force against civilians, which indicate racial disparities. One analysis from *The Guardian* found that in 2016, police killed Native Americans at the highest rates (10.13 per million people), followed by Black people (6.66 per million). The rate for Latino people was 3.23 per million, and 2.9 per million for white people.

To assess the potential effects of community-oriented policing programs, an Urban Institute report from last year, co-authored by Lawrence, looked at the Obama administration's National Initiative and its outcomes on five of the six participating cities: Birmingham, Alabama; Fort Worth, Texas; Minneapolis, Minnesota; Pittsburgh, Pennsylvania; and Stockton, California.

Only three of the cities provided data on use of force by police officers. While two of the cities did experience decreases in the number of instances in which police used force, none saw a change in racial disparities in the use of force that existed prior to the program. Beyond police use of force, the researchers found a reduction in violent crime during the program period in just one of the five cities: Pittsburgh. Meanwhile, there was an increase in violent crime in Fort Worth and no changes for Birmingham, Minneapolis and Stockton.

Researchers, Lawmakers and Activists Consider What Will Bring About Reform

The makeup and needs of communities vary, which means the goals and results of community policing tactics will look different. One important step is for residents to determine what purpose policing should serve in their communities, Meares of Yale University said. "Citizens of the United States need to come to a consensus about the meaning of public safety that includes the perspective of those most affected by both the problems that the state deploys police to solve, and the way that the state responds to those problems," Meares and Tom Tyler, a professor and founding director of the Justice Collaboratory at Yale Law School, wrote in *The Atlantic*.

Daniel Lawrence of the Urban Institute said empirical evidence indicates that the principles of procedural justice can have positive outcomes for civilians. Procedural justice focuses on how police interact with people through dignity and respect, transparency, impartiality and giving individuals a voice. That concept is "grounded in the idea that people's perceptions of police legitimacy will be influenced more by their experience of interacting with officers, than by the end result of those interactions," Yale's Justice Collaboratory wrote.

The Obama administration's Taskforce on 21st Century Policing released a report in 2015 outlining key recommendations for reforms that have been embraced by numerous policing scholars. One of the pillars calls for procedural justice and another emphasizes the importance of community policing.

But many activists demanding structural changes to law enforcement argue that community policing strategies will not help historically marginalized populations. "Community policing is based on this false notion that knowledge keeps people safe, that if the police just knew the people who they were surveilling and harassing, that they could somehow police safer," said Derecka Purnell, a human rights lawyer, activist and writer. Purnell argued that enhanced proximity to law enforcement would instead be detrimental for vulnerable groups and would lead to more frequent interactions that could turn aggressive.

Purnell and other supporters of the Defund the Police movement are calling for money to be reinvested in services that will address the roots of crime and inequality in the country, such as financial instability or the lack of adequate mental health services.

Ultimately community policing will not fix systemic racism within law enforcement, Sierra-Arévalo with UT Austin said, noting the importance of residents' lived experiences with discrimination and excessive force.

"That's a conversation that I think academics are interested in having," Sierra-Arévalo said about the defund movement. "What policing we do keep, what facets of the policing system do remain as we move towards something smaller should keep in mind what we know about these positive nonenforcement interactions."

Print Citations

CMS: Norwood, Candice. "Calls for Reform Bring Renewed Focus to Community Policing, but Does It Work?" In *The Reference Shelf: Policing in 2020,* edited by Micah L. Issitt, 67-72. Amenia, NY: Grey House Publishing, 2021.

MLA: Norwood, Candice. "Calls for Reform Bring Renewed Focus to Community Policing, but Does It Work?" *The Reference Shelf: Policing in 2020,* edited by Micah L. Issitt, Grey Housing Publishing, 2021, pp. 67-72.

APA: Norwood, C. (2021). Calls for reform bring renewed focus to community policing, but does it work? In Micah L. Issitt (Ed.), *The reference shelf: Policing in 2020* (pp. 67-72). Amenia, NY: Grey Housing Publishing.

3
Plague Policing

By Becker1999, via Wikimedia.

Enforcing lockdowns and other measures became the responsibility of police departments during the COVID-19 pandemic, with varying degrees of success.

Policing in the Age of COVID-19

For many, the COVID-19 pandemic dramatically changed life in America. Activities once considered safe suddenly became potentially deadly, and Americans in every sector of society were forced to weigh their personal liberty against the collective welfare of society. While some Americans were fortunate enough to transition to remote work or were working in businesses able to mitigate COVID-19 risk with new policies, workers in jobs designated as "front line" or "essential workers" were faced with a more difficult challenge. For these workers, whose jobs necessarily involve frequent contact with unfamiliar members of the public, COVID-19 represented a more potent and continuous threat. But the continued service of essential workers was also absolutely necessary for American society to endure the changes brought about by the disease.

The Dangers of Policing

Police officers are called upon to intervene in conflict and must sometimes willingly place themselves at risk of injury or even death. Each year, approximately thirteen out of every 100,000 officers are injured on the job, which means that around 100 American police officers are injured on the job each year.[1] While this is a high level of risk, on-the-job injury and death is relatively rare for police officers. Workers in America's most dangerous jobs, such as logging, commercial fishing, and waste collection, endure up to 900 times the risk of injury or death as police. However, for police officers working during the COVID-19 pandemic, the risk of on-the-job injury or death increased dramatically.

Police, like many other essential workers, work in a profession where contact with the public is an important part of the job. Police minimize the risk of dangerous encounters by working in groups, utilizing protective equipment, and establishing sometimes controversial policies for engaging with the public. During COVID-19, however, simply being in close proximity to members of the public and managing routine tasks carried the risk of infection. This risk was even more elevated for officers whose families or social circles contained elderly individuals or those at high risk of serious complications from COVID-19 infection.

As COVID-19 spread in early 2020, police departments around the country issued new policies for officers in an effort to minimize the risk of contracting the disease and, secondarily, to minimize the risk of infected officers spreading COVID-19 among the public. Typically, COVID policies included wearing masks, maintaining social distancing when able to do so, and being aware of symptoms that might indicate infection. Despite these measures, COVID-19 became the leading cause of officer injury and death in 2020, greatly outpacing all other dangers. To highlight the seriousness of the situation, the number of officers and other emergency responders injured or killed by COVID-19 surpassed the number of first responder deaths after the 9/11 terrorist attacks. The number of deaths and injuries surpassed the average injury and on-the-job fatality rates in the years before the pandemic.[2]

Public safety advocates argued that the threat of transmitting COVID-19 meant that the basic strategies utilized by police needed to be temporarily altered. Speaking to *American Progress*, former Police Chief Ron Davis argued that police should treat arrest and confrontation as a tool of last resort, both to prevent officers from contracting COVID-19 and to prevent officers from becoming vectors for the disease. Davis and other public safety strategists recommended that police should limit traffic stops and other types of routine arrests, and that police departments should reduce the number of public interactions for each officer during a routine shift.[3]

A number of public safety advocates also argued that the recent increase in local police assistance in tracking and/or identifying potential undocumented migrants was a waste of resources and an unnecessary risk during the pandemic, forcing police into potentially dangerous encounters during a time when processing, imprisoning, or deporting unauthorized migrants was especially difficult and dangerous. The controversy surrounding local law enforcement involvement in immigration enforcement overlapped with the broader controversy of immigration enforcement at the federal level, with a number of advocates arguing that the risk involved in imprisoning and deporting undocumented migrants was too great and that federal authorities should reduce emphasis on combating illegal migration until the end of the COVID-19 crisis.

While police departments around the country responded in very different ways to the pandemic, many police divisions did reduce emphasis on traffic stops and low-level crimes and took other steps to reduce officer contact with the public. However, the response differed from region to region, and some police departments made few changes to standard procedures. As a result, some areas experienced far higher levels of infection and COVID-19 deaths among police officers and staff. Texas was one of the states that made fewer changes to address the threat of COVID-19, resulting in the highest level of COVID-19 infection among officers. Though the final analysis of police-department-oriented COVID-19 management has not yet been completed, it appears that states in which COVID-19 policies were more relaxed experienced higher rates of officer infection and death.[4]

Exacerbating Challenges

Studies of crime during the COVID-19 crisis showed that some types of crimes decreased as more members of the public avoided social situations. Other types of crimes increased, most notably burglaries targeting businesses that were temporarily or permanently closed. The COVID-19 crisis also saw unemployment and poverty rates rise sharply, which typically results in a surge in economic crime. Changes in patterns of crime posed a major challenge for the nation's police, especially in the arena of funding and the allocation of resources. Adjusting quickly to changes in crime rates is a difficult task for any police department, but it was especially difficult during COVID-19, as police in many communities were already dealing with significant policy changes and reduced staff due to officer quarantines and illnesses.

While police departments in many parts of the country have been struggling with insufficient funding for many years, the COVID-19 crisis intensified budgetary problems. Studies from the summer of 2020 indicated that police departments across the nation had experienced the most significant budget cuts in more than a decade. The Police Executive Research Firm announced in June that 258 police departments had reduced budgets or were facing the likelihood of future budget reductions. Funding fluctuations increased further as the "Defund the Police" movement, which asked for sharp reductions in police budgets, spread across the nation.

Some police reform advocates argued that the reduction in funding might actually delay police reforms, as many proposals involve instituting new training for newly hired officers and for those enrolled in training.[5] Several reports also suggested that funding cuts were reducing emphasis on community policing, a strategy of increasing cohesion between officers and citizens living in the communities where officers work.

Police as a COVID-19 Response

One of the effects of COVID-19 was that communities established new laws and policies dictating public behavior. In some communities, bars, restaurants and other recreational activities were suspended or limited. In some cities or counties, residents were legally prohibited from engaging in large-scale gatherings. Many businesses were ordered to reduce capacity and/or to establish new protocols to protect visitors and employees from infection. In some places, citizens were required to wear masks when in public. These laws meant that police and other representatives of the state were expected to enforce new guidelines and protocols. In many cases, police were held responsible for helping to enforce new COVID-19 guidelines, with varying degrees of success.

Following the spring spike in COVID-19 cases across the United States, public policy analysts began looking at whether or not police were effective in enforcing COVID-19 regulations at the state and municipal level. Evidence suggests that the effectiveness of police intervention varied by region. For instance, in Los Angeles, California, where COVID-19 restrictions were among the strongest in the nation, studies indicated that police often declined to intervene directly even though they were empowered to enforce the state's curfew, mask mandate, and other regulations. In November of 2020, a number of Southern California police departments reported that they would not issue fines or arrest citizens for violating COVID-19 regulations.[6] As of December 2020, it is unclear whether police enforcement of COVID-19 regulations had a positive or negative impact on community adoption, but achieving police enforcement was controversial, in part because of the political controversy surrounding COVID-19.

A number of public health experts argued that police should not be expected or required to strictly enforce COVID-19 regulations, and some argued that forcing officers to do so could exacerbate police abuse and inequality by intensifying prejudice in the application of the law.[7] However, widespread failure to follow COVID-19 regulations was a problem in many regions, especially in areas where COVID-19 regulations took on a more overtly political and controversial character. In some states, activists protested mask mandates and stay-at-home orders, and there were widespread instances of citizens who opposed COVID-19 regulations engaging in confrontations with business owners attempting to enforce local or institutional regulations. It is unclear whether the threat of police enforcement might have limited anti-regulation demonstrations. Some argued further that because of the intense scrutiny on law enforcement across the country, police enforcement of COVID-19 restrictions was more likely to bring about conflict between police and citizens. However, in some regions police did begin actively enforcing regulations like mask mandates and issuing citations or fines for violators. In Florida, for instance, the state reported that more than $300,000 had been earned from fines issued to individuals violating mask mandates and other regulations.[8]

It is unclear how police enforcement impacted rates of infection, the spread of the virus, and broader perceptions of police. During a time of intense controversy and changing norms, the COVID-19 crisis proved to be another serious challenge to many states and police departments and brought additional political controversy. As 2021 progresses, statistics from local and municipal agencies may shed more light on how police responses impacted communities facing the COVID-19 threat, and this may provide helpful data for those considering how best to utilize police resources when the next pandemic arrives in the United States.

Works Used

Bates, Josiah. "'We Cannot Police Our Way Out of a Pandemic.' Experts, Police Union Say NYPD Should Not Be Enforcing Social Distance Rules Amid COVID-19." *Time*. May 7, 2020. https://time.com/5832403/nypd-pandemic-police-social-distancing-arrests/.

Greenberg, Jon. "PolitiFact: Has Coronavirus Killed More Cops Than All Other Causes?" *Tampa Bay Times*. Sep 6, 2020. https://www.tampabay.com/news/health/2020/09/06/politifact-has-coronavirus-killed-more-cops-than-all-other-causes/.

Jennings, Wesley G., and Nicholas M. Perez. "The Immediate Impact of COVID-19 on Law Enforcement in the United States." *American Journal of Criminal Justice*. Jun 6, 2020. https://www.ncbi.nlm.nih.gov/pmc/articles/PMC7275851/.

Johnson, Kevin, and Kristine Phillips. "'Perfect Storm': Defund the Police, COVID-19 Lead to Biggest Police Budget Cuts in Decade." *USA Today*. Jul 31, 2020. https://www.usatoday.com/story/news/politics/2020/07/31/defund-police-covid-19-force-deepest-cop-budget-cuts-decade/5538397002/.

Phillips, Kristine. "Many Face Mask Mandates Go Unenforced as Police Feel Political, Economic Pressure." *USA Today*. Sep 16, 2020. https://www.usatoday.com/story/news/politics/2020/09/16/covid-19-face-mask-mandates-go-unenforced-police-under-pressure/5714736002/.

"Police Responses to COVID-19." *Brennan Center*. Jul 8, 2020. https://www.bren-nancenter.org/our-work/research-reports/police-responses-covid-19.

Sauter, Michael B., and Charles Stockdale. "The Most Dangerous Jobs in the US Include Electricians, Firefighters and Police Officers." *USA Today*. Jan 8, 2019. https://www.usatoday.com/story/money/2019/01/08/most-dangerous-jobs-us-where-fatal-injuries-happen-most-often/38832907/.

Valdez, Jonah. "Some Police Agencies Won't Enforce New Stay-at-Home Coronavirus Orders, Others Will as a 'Last Resort.'" *OC Register*. Nov 19, 2020. https://www.ocregister.com/2020/11/19/some-police-agencies-will-not-enforce-new-stay-at-home-orders-is-a-last-resort-for-others/.

Notes

1. Sauter and Stockdale, "The Most Dangerous Jobs in the US Include Electricians, Firefighters, and Police Officers."
2. Greenberg, "PolitiFact: Has Coronavirus Killed More Cops Than All Other Causes?"
3. "Police Responses to COVID-19," *Brennan Center*.
4. Jennings and Perez, "The Immediate Impact of COVID-19 on Law Enforcement in the United States."
5. Johnson and Phillips, "'Perfect Storm': Defund the Police, COVID-19 Lead to Biggest Police Budget Cuts in Decade."
6. Valdez, "Some Police Agencies Won't Enforce New Stay-at-Home Coronavirus Orders, Others Will as a 'Last Resort.'"
7. Bates, "'We Cannot Police Our Way Out of a Pandemic.' Experts, Police Union Say NYPD Should Not Be Enforcing Social Distance Rules Amid COVID-19."
8. Phillips, "Many Face Mask Mandates Go Unenforced as Police Feel Political, Economic Pressure."

Policing during the Coronavirus Pandemic

By Ed Chung, Betsy Pearl, and Lea Hunter
Center for American Progress, April 14, 2020

With the criminal justice system vulnerable to the rapid spread of COVID-19, maintaining the status quo means jeopardizing the lives of those connected to the system. Many officials and advocates have rightfully focused on the need to immediately reduce jail and prison populations, especially since the lack of sufficient medical attention, unsanitary conditions, and overcrowding, among other obstacles, combine to create environments where the coronavirus can spread precipitously. The Cook County jail in Chicago, for example, currently has the largest cluster of COVID-19 cases in the country. Guidance from policy experts and advocates has provided a roadmap of how to safely and expeditiously lower the jail and prison population, and governors in Illinois and Kentucky have been taking initial steps. There may also be federal funding available to achieve this, as Congress included $850 million in the CARES Act for law enforcement to prevent and respond to the coronavirus.

At the same time, jurisdictions must do all they can to ensure that more people are not sent to jails and prisons during the pandemic. This begins with changing or modifying policing practices to make them consistent with public health guidelines to maintain physical distancing, which is essential for the health and safety of the public and of police officers themselves. Staffing levels at a number of law enforcement agencies have already been affected due to the spread of COVID-19. More than 2,000 New York City Police Department officers, for example, have tested positive for the coronavirus, and 20 percent of the 45,000-person police force is out sick. Meanwhile, in Detroit, 369 officers have been placed in quarantine, even after more than 400 recently returned from quarantine.

This column provides several recommendations for how police agencies can safely modify their practices in a fair and just manner to prevent the further spread of COVID-19. In an interview with the Center for American Progress, Ron Davis, the former East Palo Alto, California, police chief and former head of the Office of Community Oriented Policing Services at the U.S. Department of Justice, argues that these changes are consistent with principles of policing in the 21st century:

> Police must now apply the public health model of "do no harm first" in making decisions, from arrests to uses of force. Making arrests must transition from being a common tool used by law enforcement to becoming literally a tool of last resort. This

counters the notion that the only way to hold someone accountable in our society is to put handcuffs on him, because putting handcuffs now has a different meaning—not only for the person whose freedom is taken, but for the law enforcement officer who has to come within 6 feet to make that arrest. We, as a society, must find viable alternatives to incarceration.

Davis also dispels the notion that incorporating physical distancing or making other changes to policing practices will jeopardize public safety:

Police agencies must make a lot of adjustment to protect their officers and staff from this virus while assuring the public safety needs of the community. In making these changes, we must remember that less is not necessarily bad. The police alone cannot make a community safe. And we have learned over the years that simply adding more police does not equate to more public safety. It takes an entire community working with the police to sustain long-term public safety. So, as we decrease the physical footprint of law enforcement in the community, it doesn't automatically mean that public safety is compromised or that crime is going to go up. It does mean, however, that the community must fill in the gaps that may exist with the reduction of police intervention—for example, increasing mental health services, drug rehabilitation, youth mentoring programs, etc., as alternatives to arrests, or using technology to reduce the need for police physical interactions. In short, we must reimagine policing so that it relies less on physical interventions and more on community partnerships.

Furthermore, it is essential that these policy recommendations are not only enacted by a department or jurisdiction but also implemented in a consistent manner. CAP tracked recently announced policies for ensuring that the general public adhered to state and local directives for social distancing. While many of those policies were appropriately restrained and focused on educating the public, news reports have shown some significant problems with their implementation. Thus, while announcing key steps is crucial, it is equally important that the entire agency understands the policy and consistently adheres to it.

Recommendations for Policing during the COVID-19 Pandemic

Below are several key recommendations that police departments from across the country have begun to implement to help mitigate the effects of the pandemic and ensure communities' safety.

Drastically reduce the number of police stops and custodial arrests

Departments should instruct officers to focus on the most serious cases and minimize enforcement actions for lower-level offenses. Individuals should be taken into custody only if they pose a clear risk to public safety. Philadelphia Police Department Commissioner Danielle Outlaw, for example, issued guidance instructing officers to delay arrests for many categories of nonviolent crimes, including all narcotics offenses, burglary, prostitution, vandalism, and others. Meanwhile, in Washington, D.C., Metropolitan Police Department Chief Peter Newsham issued an order to expand the types of offenses that are eligible for citation and release, in an effort to reduce the volume of custodial arrests.

Limit the amount of calls for service that officers respond to in person

To reduce the spread of COVID-19 among police officers, agencies should issue guidance to reduce in-person responses to nonemergency issues. They should instead reserve in-person responses for issues that present an imminent threat to public safety or instances where investigation or evidence collection cannot be delayed. Agencies should also encourage the public to report nonurgent complaints via an online portal or nonemergency phone line.

Police agencies nationwide—including in Arlington, Virginia; Burbank, California; and Dallas—have encouraged the community to utilize their online reporting system for nonemergency incidents.

And in Syracuse, New York, the police department implemented a temporary shift in the way it handles calls for service, emphasizing the use of online and over-the-phone incident reporting.

Prioritize responding to and preventing domestic violence

While the majority of people under stay-at-home orders are safer in their homes, many, including survivors and those at risk of domestic violence, are not. Police responding to domestic-violence-related calls for services should be trained on the increased risks and warning signs of intimate partner violence in the context of the COVID-19 pandemic. They should also work with local service providers to readily advertise hotline numbers and other resources alongside all public guidance related to COVID-19.

The Minnesota Department of Public Safety, for instance, issued guidance to members of local law enforcement on its stay-at-home order, which listed "Relocation to ensure safety" as the No. 1 allowable activity. This means that those who are not safe in their homes may relocate to a safer place, such as the home of a family member, friend, or designated shelter, without violating the governor's executive order. As another example, the French

> **Departments should instruct officers to focus on the most serious cases and minimize enforcement actions for lower-level offenses.**

government has contracted with hotels to dramatically expand the country's capacity for emergency shelter for survivors of domestic violence. And Mayor Lori Lightfoot (D) of Chicago announced a partnership with ride-sharing services to provide free rides for individuals who contact the Illinois Domestic Violence Hotline and need to relocate.

Obtain and distribute personal protective equipment (PPE) to every officer to use while on duty

Agencies and departments should educate officers on personal safety precautions, such as procedures for hand-washing, sanitizing surfaces and work equipment, and identifying symptoms of COVID-19. Agencies must also provide COVID-19 testing for officers and require them to remain at least 6 feet away from members of the public whenever possible.

Several police departments, including in Austin, Texas, and Philadelphia, are now requiring officers to wear masks while on duty, based on Centers for Disease Control and Prevention (CDC) guidance that recommends Americans wear face coverings in public settings. In Los Angeles, patrol officers have received a PPE kit that contains a mask, goggles, and multiple pairs of gloves. The Los Angeles Police Department has also issued guidelines for officers on using PPE, interacting with the public, and protecting their health while on duty.

Consider contracting with local hotels to allow officers to isolate

As first responders, police are at high risk of contracting and spreading COVID-19. Officers may need options to safely distance themselves from their own household and colleagues. Cities and districts should take steps to ensure police have access to alternative places to stay if necessary.

The city of Seattle, for example, contracted an entire hotel to provide accommodations for first responders and other essential city employees, including police, firefighters, emergency medical services (EMS), and transportation workers.

Conclusion

This COVID-19 pandemic serves as a reminder that the safety of the community and officers are interrelated. Cities across the country must take immediate steps to ensure that everyone responsible for public safety—law enforcement and the community—is protected from this virus and future pandemics.

Print Citations

CMS: Chung, Ed, Betsy Pearl, and Lea Hunter. "Policing during the Coronavirus Pandemic." In *The Reference Shelf: Policing in 2020*, edited by Micah L. Issitt, 81-84. Amenia, NY: Grey House Publishing, 2021.

MLA: Chung, Ed, Betsy Pearl, and Lea Hunter. "Policing during the Coronavirus Pandemic." *The Reference Shelf: Policing in 2020*, edited by Micah L. Issitt, Grey Housing Publishing, 2021, pp. 81-84.

APA: Chung, E., Pearl, B., & Hunter, L. (2021). Policing during the coronavirus pandemic. In Micah L. Issitt (Ed.), *The reference shelf: Policing in 2020* (pp. 81-84). Amenia, NY: Grey Housing Publishing.

Explainer: Why Police Will Be Crucial Players in the Battle against Coronavirus

By Terry Goldsworthy and Robyn Lincoln
The Conversation, March 26, 2020

As coronavirus continues to affect all aspects of life, law enforcement agencies are playing a more pivotal role in enforcing new health and social regulations while ensuring society continues to function in a civil manner.

So why is law enforcement important in our battle against COVID-19, and what role will it play?

Police Help Contain the Virus

Several Australian police services have set up dedicated resources to assist in containing the virus. These include major incident rooms and operations and specific new taskforces.

Victoria has established a 500-strong contingent to compel the closure of all but essential services. As well as the shutdown measures, police and authorised officers will be enforcing mandatory self-isolation periods for anyone entering Victoria from overseas. Under Victoria's state of emergency, breaking quarantine conditions carries fines of up to A$20,000 for individuals and nearly A$100,000 for businesses.

In New South Wales, police have been required to limit large gatherings in public and restrict access to beaches, removing swimmers and surfers where necessary.

The state government this week granted police enhanced powers to enforce public health orders relating to COVID-19. This includes the power to arrest people breaching their quarantine. Police will be able to compel suspected COVID-19 cases to remain in isolation. The bill will:

> allow a police officer to arrest a person who the officer reasonably suspects of contravening a public health order in relation to COVID-19 and returning the person to their usual place of residence or their place of detention.

In conducting similar checks, Victoria Police discovered seven people were not self-isolating as required during spot checks this week.

Such enforcement activity brings with it a unique set of problems. Reports this week indicated up to 200 Victorian police staff are already in quarantine. Concerns were raised about a lack of protective equipment for officers. The powerful Police

---

Association wants a state of disaster declared to free up police to act with greater efficiency and additional powers.

In Queensland, police recruits have been fast-tracked through the academy to provide extra personnel. In addition, Operation Sierra Linnet was launched, a multi-agency taskforce that will ensure compliance with restrictions for all pubs, registered and licensed clubs, gyms, indoor sporting venues, casinos and night clubs.

From midnight Wednesday this week Queensland police have been harnessing their random roadside breath-testing skills to curtail non-approved border crossings.

> **There will be surges in some crime categories and reductions in others due to conditions created by the crisis.**

What Impact Might Coronavirus Have on Crime?

While police are being asked to extend their range of duties into our everyday activities, in other areas they are pulling back from traditional roles. For example, Queensland police have stopped static random breath test sites because of coronavirus fears.

It is probable police will respond to essential call-outs only, as has happened in some other countries. Even then response times might be longer than before.

We should not be concerned that fewer uniformed police will have an impact on public safety—it is common for police to exercise largely peacekeeping functions. This was highlighted in the Kansas City Patrol Experiment in the 1970s, which found formal police patrols did not impact on crime rates or community fear of crime.

As a consequence of the virus, we have seen criminal elements attempt to take advantage of emerging markets. In the UK, police arrested men who had allegedly stolen toilet paper and hand wash. In Sydney, two men threatened staff with a knife while trying to steal toilet paper.

The strain on our social cohesion is showing, with fights erupting between shoppers as they try to obtain items now in short supply.

In response, the prime minister this week announced his government was creating a new offence to target people hoarding essential goods in an effort to prevent price gouging and exports of products needed to reduce the spread of coronavirus. He said:

> These measures will help prevent individuals purchasing goods including face masks, hand sanitiser and vital medicines and either reselling them at significant mark-ups or exporting them overseas in bulk, which prevents these goods from reaching people who need them in Australia.

It isn't only New York that has two-hour wait queues for firearms and ammunition—consumers are stocking up on ammunition here as well.

What Does the Future Hold?

Trying to predict crime transformations due to coronavirus is difficult. It is likely there will be surges in some crime categories and reductions in others due to conditions created by the crisis.

"Break and enter" offences in private dwellings will probably decline under a widespread lockdown that keeps people in their homes. Alcohol-fuelled violence in public spaces is certain to drop significantly with the closures of pubs, clubs, casinos and restaurants. However, domestic violence incidents are predicted to rise over time, with interpersonal tensions in restricted living arrangements.

Given the uncertainty and the ever-changing situation facing us all, policing needs to be agile and flexible in its response to the needs of society and the demands of governments.

Our law enforcement agencies will perform a critical role in combating the virus and ensuring public safety.

Print Citations

CMS: Goldsworthy, Terry, and Robyn Lincoln. "Explainer: Why Police Will Be Crucial Players in the Battle against Coronavirus." In *The Reference Shelf: Policing in 2020,* edited by Micah L. Issitt, 85-87. Amenia, NY: Grey House Publishing, 2021.

MLA: Goldsworthy, Terry, and Robyn Lincoln. "Explainer: Why Police Will Be Crucial Players in the Battle against Coronavirus." *The Reference Shelf: Policing in 2020,* edited by Micah L. Issitt, Grey Housing Publishing, 2021, pp. 85-87.

APA: Goldsworthy, T., & Lincoln, R. (2021). Explainer: Why police will be crucial players in the battle against coronavirus. In Micah L. Issitt (Ed.), *The reference shelf: Policing in 2020* (pp. xxx-xxx). Amenia, NY: Grey Housing Publishing.

Do We Really Need the COVID-19 Police?

By Marc Siegel
The Hill, December 1, 2020

Over Thanksgiving holiday week, I was glad to see more people wearing masks in public than ever before. This compliance was consistent with a growing body of population research from the Centers for Disease Control and Prevention (CDC) and elsewhere revealing that masks and mask mandates (in Kansas, Nebraska, Thailand and throughout over 200 countries) are associated with decreased spread of COVID-19. The public messaging on behalf of masks has grown stronger and more persuasive and pervasive than ever before.

But there are limits to the science. Here's what a population study can't possibly show you: Is it the masking or the distancing that is preventing spread? And how appropriately are people doing either one?

Unfortunately, I have observed that most people I encounter are not wearing their masks firmly or securely over their mouths and noses—too many use them as "chin-wear." Too many are touching their masks frequently, and too many wear their masks over their mouths only, exposing their droplet-laden noses to the air. Worse than that, too many seem to think that as long as they have some kind of mask on, they can't possibly be spreading COVID-19. Unfortunately, this is not true.

I took a plane flight over the holiday, wearing a KN95 mask and a shield in a solo cabin. Recent studies have shown that the large HEPA filters and the rapidly filtered air quite likely protected me, but when I reached the airport, I was herded into a shuttle bus with dozens of others who were not distanced from each other. The same was true at the airport itself.

I took a PCR test before I left, and another when I returned, self-quarantining until I knew the results, but I feared that not enough travelers were following this test-in, test-out strategy for a virus that is so easily transmissible and

> **By this point in the pandemic, I believe you should be able to know what to do based on common sense.**

leads to a high percentage of asymptomatic, contagious cases. And how many have truly quarantined themselves after they have been exposed to a close contact with COVID-19?

A vaccine is coming soon, and while we wait for it we need to make science-based decisions consistently. Instead, our leaders remain inconsistent. In Los Angeles County, for example, restaurants—including fast food—are now closed except for takeout, despite the fact that they account for less than 3 percent of 204 recent outbreaks, whereas government offices, where close to 7 percent of the cases have occurred during these outbreaks, remain open.

Here in New York, it took a SCOTUS ruling to block church and synagogue restrictions. By contrast, liquor stores, bicycle shops, lawyers, accountants and even insurance brokers are considered essential, whereas churches are not. This despite the fact that large churches and synagogues throughout New York have gone to great lengths to follow guidelines of social distancing, whereas liquor stores and bike shops clearly cannot. I am an avid cyclist, but would definitely survive if my local bike shop was closed for a while and I have to fix my own tire.

It makes sense to close the bars but keep the schools open, as Rhode Island is now doing, because the former can fuel super spreader events and the later has been studied and not been found to be a source of sustained spread.

The inconsistencies extend right to the hospitals, where essential surgeries and procedures and screening tests are deemed non-essential and are put on hold as COVID-19 cases increase. On the one hand this is understandable because of how contagious and difficult it is to contain COVID-19, on the other hand, it is important that all the public health damage caused by COVID-19, even if it is indirect, be considered at the same time if proper public health decisions are to be made. Perhaps designated COVID-19 hospitals need to once again be considered in hot zones as the total number of hospitalized patients in the U.S. rises over 90,000.

Vermont has the fewest COVID-19 cases per 100,000 population in the country, at 595. To get there and to stay there, they have focused consistently on basic public health measures including masking, distancing and reducing the size of gatherings. They shut down quickly and reopened slowly. But now in their continuing zeal to ensure public health compliance, I believe they have taken things a step way too far. Vermont Gov. Phil Scott has authorized schools to interrogate their students about whether—during Thanksgiving—they or their parents violated the state's non-essential travel restrictions requiring quarantine, or their gathering rules. An admission of guilt leads to mandatory participation in online school. If this were the honor system I wouldn't object, but the notion of a child turning in his or her parents to the state is quite disturbing and could create a deep rift in a family. Score one for the COVID-19 police.

Instead of waiting for a vaccine to save you while you continue to gather and risk your health and those of others; instead of relying on political dogma (which too easily ignores your depression and anxiety) to guide you, by this point in the pandemic I believe you should be able to know what to do based on common sense.

Wearing a mask in public and not crowding into an elevator or a store and washing or disinfecting your hands frequently are basic public health measures all Americans are aware of by now, and shouldn't need a mandate or fear to follow.

Print Citations

CMS: Siegel, Marc. "Do We Really Need the COVID-19 Police?" In *The Reference Shelf: Policing in 2020,* edited by Micah L. Issitt, 88-90. Amenia, NY: Grey House Publishing, 2021.

MLA: Siegel, Marc. "Do We Really Need the COVID-19 Police?" *The Reference Shelf: Policing in 2020,* edited by Micah L. Issitt, Grey Housing Publishing, 2021, pp. 88-90.

APA: Siegel, M. (2021). Do we really need the COVID-19 police? In Micah L. Issitt (Ed.), *The reference shelf: Policing in 2020* (pp. 88-90). Amenia, NY: Grey Housing Publishing.

U.S. Policing after Wave One of COVID-19

By Vanda Felbab-Brown
Lawfare, May 20, 2020

Police and law enforcement officers are on the frontline of the coronavirus response. Both policing and crime have been deeply affected by the virus and will be shaped by the pandemic for a long time to come, though some effects will be more profound and lasting than others. In a forthcoming May 28 piece—part of a Brookings series on how on the United States should reopen various parts of the economy, public life and external engagement after the initial lockdown—I reflect on immediate, coronavirus-specific challenges and priorities for domestic law enforcement—including how to reinforce and prepare police forces, what kind of unrest to expect when new lockdowns become necessary, how to deal with prisons and how to respond to domestic violence. In this piece, I will analyze other short-term and medium-term policing priorities as well as law enforcement distractions.

Reinforce Reductions in Gang Violence and Emphasize Police Responsiveness

Around the world as well as in various parts of the U.S., the coronavirus lockdown disrupted local patterns of street crime; predatory crime, such as mugging and robberies, decreased dramatically as potential victims did not mingle on the streets. After this initial drop, however, burglaries of closed storefronts and car theft increased. As the country reopens, these two patterns may change again; with more potential victims on the street, muggings and pickpocketing may rise again and burglaries of better guarded stores, along with car theft, could decrease.

The question is what will happen to homicides in the U.S., and here the coronavirus disruption provides a unique opportunity. Homicides have been declining in the United States over the past two decades—except for difficult pockets of persisting high violence, such as in Chicago and Baltimore.

But the coronavirus disrupted—at least temporarily—this entrenched violence that has been resistant to numerous policy interventions. During the coronavirus lockdowns, gang violence driven by tit-for-tat honor killings and fights over local retail drug markets declined dramatically at first, including in places where numerous policing strategies failed to reduce gang violence—such as Chicago or El Salvador. In contrast, premeditated strategic warfare among organized crime groups did not, for the most part, decrease during the worldwide lockdowns; in Mexico, in March and April, homicides continued to break monthly records and significantly surpass official, if suspect, counts of Mexico's COVID-19 deaths. Unfortunately, the immediate reduction in violence early on in the lockdown is already being lost: By the end of April, Chicago saw 15 percent more gun violence than in the same period last year.

Reinforcing the reduction in gang violence in U.S. cities should be a priority for law enforcement forces as well as civil society, even during the pandemic. One strategy to deploy is a focused deterrence approach. Backed by influential actors in civil society—such as religious authorities, community leaders and mothers—law enforcement representatives should engage with gang leaders, indicating to them that the current violence disruption presents an opportunity to avoid lengthy imprisonment for gang members while being clear that homicides and violent assault will be prosecuted with determination. The drop in homicides allows investigators and prosecutors the opportunity to resolve a greater number of new homicides and obtain guilty verdicts, thus boosting not just the effective prosecution rate but also deterrence effects. Powerful and consistent evidence shows that it is the prevalence of effective prosecution far more so than the severity of penalty that deters crime. A former U.S. deputy attorney general once assessed in a conversation with me that in his experience in the United States, South Africa, Colombia and Guatemala, creating deterrence effects for homicides requires an effective prosecution rate of some 40 percent. Intervention strategies to keep gang violence down also include maintaining and expanding behavioral therapy and counseling—including via virtual platforms—to gang members to dissuade them from rash, violent retaliations for perceived dishonor. As the coronavirus wiped out many of the jobs that can be presented to gang members as reasons and opportunities to disengage from violence, reinforcing online behavioral therapy approaches and teaching skill sets in problem solving and conflict resolution can be all the more important.

Such a focus is all the more urgent as gang violence is likely to increase, in part because finances of gang members—like those of most Americans—will be depleted and street crime, such as drug dealing, may be driven by food insecurity. Already, some U.S. localities have experienced a rise in shooting, including fatal attacks, over local drug retail markets. In addition to an important focus on well-tested and effective problem-oriented policing, responses for avoiding a renewed rise in violence may include engagement with local community leaders to organize food banks and to discourage street violence and retaliation.

> **Social media platforms of groups that call for violence need to be shut down diligently.**

Do Not Waste Police Resources on Targeting Undocumented Migrants

The Trump administration has spent its entire tenure hunting for undocumented migrants and threatening to penalize police departments that refused to aggressively participate in such a misguided policing focus, setting off ongoing complex litigation as to when the federal government can withhold money from police departments in sanctuary cities. The administration has ignored warnings from police chiefs of many major U.S. cities that such a policing approach is counterproductive.

Pressuring local police forces to check immigration papers of residents and obligating them to prioritize hunting undocumented individuals will ultimately hurt law enforcement. The George W. Bush administration tried that policy; it did not help reduce crime, and local police departments resented it and found it counterproductive, diverting them from other anti-crime priorities and alienating local communities. Communities in fear, including those with legal immigration status but whose relatives are undocumented, shut down and refuse to interact with police forces; the sense of alienation grows; and protests against police can escalate—in the process, vital information on serious crime can be lost.

It is not just a matter of undocumented workers being afraid to cooperate with the police in addressing violent crime. Entire communities, including U.S. citizens and legal residents, might turn away from the police. In order to identify and stop criminals, the police need to know and be accepted by the community.

All of these imperatives are amplified by the coronavirus. The illness can persist among populations—such as undocumented migrants fearing arrest—who do not have access to health care but who must work because they have no livelihood reserves. Although the Trump administration is poised to pressure police departments to track down undocumented migrants, this is not an effective use of police resources. Among all the complex issues that exhausted police departments will need to deal with during reopening, hunting down undocumented migrants is not only the least important—it is directly counterproductive to the facilitation of healthy recovery by U.S. communities and the minimization of coronavirus outbreaks. No community should fear seeking health care if the progress of the disease makes isolation at home inadequate. Pushing any community into the shadows by bad policies risks reinfecting much larger communities. Not only is targeting undocumented populations unnecessary right now, but the Trump administration should worry that it will cause an extended lockdown period and increased spread of the pandemic.

Meanwhile, detention of undocumented residents by Immigration and Customs Enforcement (ICE) has already set off the extensive spread of the virus in detention centers. Even after a federal judge ruled that 22 people at high risk for COVID-19 should be released from immigration detention in Pennsylvania jails, ICE transferred some undocumented detainees from those same jails to other jurisdictions. Such a policy places detainees in danger—even after judges have affirmed the health risks posed by immigration detention centers in the midst of the pandemic—and could spread the infection around the country, including to workers at those centers. As of May 9, 27,908 immigrants were being held, and 965 cases of COVID-19 were confirmed in these centers, even though testing of detainees was vastly inadequate. The data is poor, but even with those likely significant undercounts, the 1.2 percent infection rate among detainees is almost three times as high as among the U.S. population overall. Many have become infected in detention, where health facilities are disastrously insufficient, particularly for those who have COVID-19.

Worse yet, the Trump administration has been deporting infected migrants abroad, failing in the basic humanitarian obligation to garner medical help for the infirm— and leaving struggling, vulnerable and unprepared governments and communities in Mexico, Central America and the Caribbean scrambling to respond. Previously, U.S. deportation policies spread dangerous gang violence to Central America; now the Trump administration is spreading infection.

Overall, the Trump administration has exploited the coronavirus to discharge several salvos of anti-immigrant policies so as to minimize even legal immigration. Indifferent to how the policies also hurt U.S. citizens, such as the spouses and children of the undocumented, the administration is preparing further policies to prevent migration to the United States and remove immigrants. Nor does the administration recognize that many of the undocumented are employed to nurse the elderly, or work in U.S. agriculture and slaughterhouses. In the U.S. health care industry, 16 percent of workers are foreign born. The U.S. food processing industry employs 3.8 million immigrants—though not all are undocumented. And nearly 28 percent of the country's agricultural workers are foreign born. They provide essential help in avoiding food shortages and reducing the crisis in the U.S. health care sector, even as they risk their lives to infection by having to work in close proximity with others without taking the proper precautions. Few of the U.S. citizens who have lost their jobs due to the coronavirus will seek out these back-breaking and dangerous jobs. As U.S. agribusinesses protested the anti-immigrant fervor of the Trump administration—even against those who hold temporary visas—the Trump administration eased regulations for H-2A agricultural visas. But as the U.S. presidential election approaches, the Trump administration continues to beat a vicious and counterproductive anti-immigration drum, at the worst possible moment during a crisis that requires the help of undocumented frontline workers.

Target Right-Wing, Neo-Nazi Groups and U.S. Militia Groups That Incite Violence

Far-right groups in the U.S. and some anti-immigrant, anti-federal-government and survivalist U.S. militias who envision a coming civil war in the U.S. have seized on the economic desperation and dislocation of the pandemic to advance their dangerous and sometimes outright violent agendas. To a large extent mimicking the coronavirus rhetoric of violent jihadists, far-right extremists in the U.S. have moved beyond calling the coronavirus a hoax to falsely claiming that the pandemic was purposefully arranged by China or Jews. They have scapegoated immigrants, African Americans, law enforcement officials and Democratic Party politicians. Online, they have called for spreading the virus to Jewish people, by getting themselves infected and hanging around synagogues. They have urged sabotaging infrastructure to provoke race riots. They have even gone so far as to urge their followers to spray bullets on city streets and into car windows to promote panic, chaos and social strife. Seeking a total collapse of governance, they have posted formulas for citizens to make their own bombs and toxic gases.

Distressingly, their potent propaganda during the lockdown has generated a significant uptick in online traffic on their social media platforms and in response to their recruitment appeals, though it is not yet clear how large an increase in membership this has produced.

Much of this far-right and militia subculture lives in an expectation of a second civil war, as I mentioned earlier, often coded as "the boogaloo" or race war in the United States—and much of their activity seeks to accelerate its envisioned arrival. At least 125 boogaloo-promoting groups were identified on Facebook by mid-April, with 60 percent of them created in just the past three months and a combined online membership of 73,000—though it is not clear how many members belong to multiple groups. A YouTube video with 340,000 views—called "Top 5 Boogaloo Guns"—preaches the need to "take to the streets and take care of business" against a "tyrannical government" in the United States.

The right to carry weapons is a common theme among such extremist and U.S. militia groups, and some gun shop owners and pro-gun activists have been catering to these groups, cultivating them and supplying them with propaganda. Alarmingly, gun sales in the U.S. experienced their greatest spike in the first month of the lockdown, rising by 85 percent compared to March 2019.

Far-right groups and militias, such as the Michigan Liberty Militia, have sought to intimidate government officials into prematurely calling off lockdowns—including the recent case in Michigan when they stormed the state house to threaten Democratic Governor Gretchen Whitmer. Although they claim to have a right to carry weapons to demonstrate their Second Amendment rights, clearly their purpose is to intimidate those who disagree with them.

Increasingly, individual militias as well as entire militia groups have moved to forcefully assist in the reopening of stores and businesses in defiance of local ordinances. In doing so, they are intimidating not just local authorities and elected government officials, but also law enforcement officials who are needed to counter their activities. More than through other mechanisms, the militias have been able to use their declared support for protecting law-violating businesses to build up political capital with a wide set of conservative actors—not just gun stores and right-wing politicians, but also ordinary conservative citizens. Being able to deliver services to a broader segment of the population—that is, enabling disgruntled business owners no longer willing to comply with lockdowns to open their businesses—allows the militia groups to transform themselves from limited fringe entities catering mostly to their members into groups with political capital among a much wider segment of the public. A buildup of broader popular support may shield them from law enforcement actions as local politicians or government officials refuse to authorize law enforcement actions against them or act against their intimidation. This political capital derived from protecting and encouraging law violations through intimidation is a threat to the rule of law in the United States.

Some individuals affiliated with these far-right groups have moved beyond intimidation and the incitement of violence to the attempt to carry out violence. In Missouri, Navy veteran Timothy Wilson—who frequented far-right webpages and had been the subject of a months-long FBI investigation—attempted to blow up a hospital treating COVID-19 patients by using a vehicle laden with explosives, but he was intercepted and killed by FBI agents. Online, he claimed that the federal government sought to use the pandemic as "an excuse to destroy our people," in what he called "a Jewish power grab." In Arkansas, Aaron Swenson—who frequented boogaloo Facebook pages—announced on April 12 that he was hunting for a law enforcement officer to kill and was ultimately arrested by the Texarkana police.

Law enforcement officials so far have been successful in disrupting these violent planned crimes. They must place the highest priority on prosecuting any efforts to intimidate or target law enforcement officials. They need to remain vigilant against the possibility of more violent attacks by far-right groups and militias and must anticipate that more violent recruitment and incitement, as well as actual attempts, will follow—particularly if a second lockdown locally or nationally becomes necessary.

The big increase in recruitment by far-right groups and militias provides an opportunity for local and state police forces as well as federal law enforcement agencies to infiltrate the groups and build up networks of informants. Social media platforms of groups that call for violence need to be shut down diligently. At the same time, U.S. law enforcement officials should mount sting operations and conspiracy-charge-based prosecutions that have been highly effective in preventing and disrupting jihadi terrorist attacks in the United States and leading to the apprehension and effective prosecution of criminals with global notoriety, such as Viktor Bout. Adopting focused deterrence strategies, law enforcement officers should also build up portfolios of prosecutable crimes against far-right and militia leaders—particularly violent members—both to indict them and to deter other members from crossing into illegality and violent action.

The rise of such violent political militancy in the United States poses an even greater danger to public safety and the quality of democracy than most criminal groups could ever mount.

Conclusion

U.S. law enforcement forces are key responders against the coronavirus pandemic, often toiling under difficult circumstances to preserve public safety. Many improvements in U.S. policing that long preceded the pandemic—including regarding racial fairness—remain urgent and imperative. While the pandemic creates new challenges for policing and exacerbates others, the hardships related to the coronavirus also present new opportunities for strengthening citizens' safety and improving relations between communities and law enforcement. Reducing gang violence and strengthening the safety of minority and marginalized communities is one important facet; resolutely acting against far-right groups and militias that promote violence and work to undermine the rule of law and law enforcement forces is another.

Print Citations

CMS: Felbab-Brown, Vanda. "U.S. Policing after Wave One of COVID-19." In *The Reference Shelf: Policing in 2020,* edited by Micah L. Issitt, 91-97. Amenia, NY: Grey House Publishing, 2021.

MLA: Felbab-Brown, Vanda. "U.S. Policing after Wave One of COVID-19." *The Reference Shelf: Policing in 2020,* edited by Micah L. Issitt, Grey Housing Publishing, 2021, pp. 91-97.

APA: Felbab-Brown, V. (2021). U.S. policing after wave one of COVID-19. In Micah L. Issitt (Ed.), *The reference shelf: Policing in 2020* (pp. 91-97). Amenia, NY: Grey Housing Publishing.

COVID-19 Curbs Community Policing at a Time of Diminishing Trust

By David Montgomery
The Pew Charitable Trusts, October 1, 2020

AUSTIN—The funeral last month for Jorge Cabrera featured familiar tributes to a fallen officer. Cabrera's flag-draped coffin sat at the front of the church, near a large replica of a police badge with black ribbon. The strains of a bagpipe accompanied the entry of a uniformed honor guard.

Cabrera was a ubiquitous figure in his hometown of Mission, Texas, serving a dozen years as a police patrol officer and traffic investigator in the border town of 85,000. Hundreds paid their respects in person or watched his funeral online as eulogists praised his service to the community.

The 42-year-old Cabrera didn't die in a crash or a shootout; he succumbed to COVID-19 on Aug. 24, after a 21-day struggle against the virus. Mission Police Chief Robert Dominguez said Cabrera may have been infected while escorting a prisoner.

In the seven months since the start of the pandemic, COVID-19 has emerged as the nation's deadliest police killer, felling far more officers than violence or accidents. It also has changed the way police do their jobs, and hampered trust-building measures at a time when many people have taken to the streets to condemn police brutality and racism.

"Given the current climate, community policing is even more important because it allows law enforcement to not have all their hours on the job devoted just to 'crime-fighting,'" said Wesley G. Jennings, a professor of criminal justice and legal studies at the University of Mississippi. "It allows them to get in the community, engage with the community."

But because of restrictions imposed by the pandemic, Jennings said, "regularly scheduled activities where the police and the community would interact … are not occurring."

In Washington, D.C., for example, community leaders and police officers concede that COVID-19 safeguards have slowed or impeded bridge-building activities in the Sixth District, an area that includes parts of the Northeast and Southeast quadrants of the city. The area, comprised of single-family detached and row houses, along with a significant number of public housing projects, is predominantly Black.

"Community policing is definitely affected by COVID-19 because of the inability to have face-to-face contact," said the Rev. Dr. Lewis Tait Jr., minister of The Village, a church 5 miles east of the U.S. Capitol that was founded by Tait's father 60 years ago. "Whether you're the police, or the public that you're dealing with, everybody is just a little bit anxious in terms of how you deal with them."

Before the pandemic, police officers convened at least monthly with clergy and neighborhood community leaders, typically over breakfast. Since April, the meetings have been conducted via Zoom, which allows participants to talk but prevents the personal contact that helped them build real relationships.

"Sometimes you want to have that candid conversation with them," said Officer Jason Medina, the police department's community outreach coordinator for the Sixth District. "You want to be able to look them in the eye and tell them that everything's going to be okay. And by not being able to do that, it's kind of harder."

Remote Policing

The pandemic also has changed policing in other ways. Some departments are declining to make arrests for minor crimes, restricting public access to police stations, allowing some officers and civilian employees to work from home and collecting crime reports via phone or email instead of sending officers to the field.

"You can't have a global pandemic like this and things not change," said Assistant Chief Joseph Chacon of the Austin Police Department, describing the litany of safeguards Austin officers routinely incorporate into their daily routine, from face masks and social distancing to applying "a ton of hand sanitizer" to their work stations and squad cars.

"It's our new normal and it sounds like it will be for some time to come."

Dallas Police Sgt. Mike Mata, president of the Dallas Police Association, said the changes have added barriers between officers and residents, at a time when street encounters are more likely to be fraught.

"You don't want to be just a report writer and grab the facts," Mata said. "You want to be attentive to the citizen, and that's a great part of community policing."

"But dealing with COVID right now, we're not able to sit around that kitchen table or living room and have those discussions with family members."

In Houston, officers posted at the department doors take temperatures of arriving employees. Those with fevers are denied entry and required to get tested immediately. Officers and employees don full PPE—masks, goggles and gloves—when they meet somebody on a call and are required to keep their masks on inside headquarters, unless they're in their own space.

Residents in many cities have reported bare-faced officers in their neighborhoods—despite policies requiring masks—and participants in racial justice protests have lodged similar complaints, according to the *New York Times* and other news outlets.

But Medina of the Washington, D.C., police and several other officers said in interviews that they always wear masks to protect themselves, the public and their families.

In Yonkers, New York, a northern suburb of New York City, Police Commissioner John Mueller said his officers don masks when they interact with residents but may not when in the field riding in a squad car.

> **COVID-19 has changed the way police do their jobs, and hampered trust-building measures at a time when many people have taken to the streets to condemn police brutality and racism.**

"We try to our best to encourage this, to make sure that everybody wears them," he said in a recent telephone interview, "but we can't be everywhere they are at all times."

In Texas, the blazing heat dissuades some officers from following mask protocols. "Asking them to put something over their face—it's restrictive; it makes it harder to breathe," Chacon of the Austin Police Department said. "But they've got to do it. They've got to set the example and they've got to keep themselves and the public safe."

Hundreds of Cases

Despite the precautions, police departments have reported hundreds of positive cases, and many officers have died.

Estimates of the total death toll vary, but the Fraternal Order of Police attributes at least 235 law enforcement deaths to COVID-19 based on media reports, with the numbers reaching into the double digits in at least eight states. The states with the highest numbers of coronavirus-related law enforcement deaths as of Sept. 30 were Texas (51), New York (35) and Louisiana (20), according to the organization.

The Officer Down Memorial Page Inc., a nonprofit organization that honors fallen officers, reports that 114 of the 208 line-of-duty deaths it has confirmed this year were caused by the virus, more than all other categories combined. The next largest category was gunfire, with 35 cases.

Jessica Rushing, the group's communications director, said line-of-duty deaths increased by 90% this year compared with last year, and the spike was caused almost entirely by COVID-19. She said the final count is likely to exceed 200, once the group has reviewed 150 additional COVID-19 deaths to determine whether officers contracted the virus while working.

To be sure, COVID-19 has taken a much heavier toll on health care workers. A database compiled by *The Guardian* and Kaiser Health News suggests that more than 1,200 health care workers have died from the virus.

The pandemic has had a less deadly impact on firefighters and emergency medical service personnel, even though they are often the first to have contact with COVID-19 patients. According to the International Association of Fire Fighters, at least 26,000 of their members have been exposed to the virus, and 17 have died.

Officer Rosie Perez, a 41-year-old community liaison with the Austin Police Department, tested positive for the virus in early June after 12 days of virtually nonstop work including during protests in downtown Austin. She said she tried to abide by anti-coronavirus protocols but "it didn't slow down the fact that we still had a job to do."

After recovering and returning to work, she talked openly about the ordeal with fellow officers and urged them to get tested.

In mid-April, Marvin Wayne Trejo, police chief of the Texas Panhandle town of Dumas, came home from work and told his wife of 22 years he was feeling "a little under the weather." Twenty-four days later, Lisa Trejo was at her husband's side in the hospital, holding his hand during the last hour of his life. It was May 10—Mother's Day.

Trejo said she is unsure how her husband contracted the disease but noted that, at the time he became ill, the Dumas area was experiencing a fierce outbreak partly linked to a nearby meatpacking plant.

The surge of infections throughout prisons and jails has made corrections officers particularly vulnerable. Nearly 21,700 inmates and 4,800 staff have tested positive in the Texas prison system. The virus has claimed the lives of 161 inmates and 20 employees, including Akbar Nurid-Din Shabazz, the first Muslim chaplain in the Texas Department of Criminal Justice, who died in April.

As of Sept. 18, the Houston Police Department had a total of 450 positive cases among officers. No officers have died, but the department lost two long-time civilian employees: Nicole Rodriguez, 38, and Latonya Lewis, 36.

Given the heightened challenges facing law enforcement and the lurking threat of a fatal disease, Houston police's Assistant Chief Sheryl Victorian said maintaining morale has been a pressing concern. Houston officers are frequently reminded about the availability of counseling, peer support and other support services, Victorian said, because "2020 has really been a tough year."

Print Citations

CMS: Montgomery, David. "COVID-19 Curbs Community Policing at a Time of Diminishing Trust." In *The Reference Shelf: Policing in 2020,* edited by Micah L. Issitt, 98-101. Amenia, NY: Grey House Publishing, 2021.

MLA: Montgomery, David. "COVID-19 Curbs Community Policing at a Time of Diminishing Trust." *The Reference Shelf: Policing in 2020,* edited by Micah L. Issitt, Grey Housing Publishing, 2021, pp. 98-101.

APA: Montgomery, D. (2021). COVID-19 curbs community policing at a time of diminishing trust. In Micah L. Issitt (Ed.), *The reference shelf: Policing in 2020* (pp. 98-101). Amenia, NY: Grey Housing Publishing.

4
Training Days

US CBP—US Customs and Border Protection, via Wikimedia.

Supporters of reform criticize the militarization of the police force. Above, a U.S. Customs and Border Protection agent in a cloud of tear gas during violent protests in Portland, Oregon, in July 2020.

Police Education and Policy

The history of policing in America is rich and varied. In some states, organized policing grew out of the systems that colonial British governments established for enforcing colonial laws. In other states, policing was entangled with the slave trade, with groups of local men recruited into teams whose primary purpose was to capture slaves that tried to escape. At each stage of development, the establishment of policing systems reflected Americans' greatest hopes for what their communities could become, but also incorporated prejudice and ignorance. What this means is that the philosophy of policing has evolved in different ways in different communities. In some communities, police emphasize "keeping the peace," intervening only when necessary to protect citizens, to arbitrate disputes, and to address any disturbance to the peace. In other communities, police are used as "law enforcers," and are encouraged to actively seek out violations of law and to aggressively punish infractions.

The basic philosophy of policing is important because it determines how new and veteran police officers are trained and encouraged to perform their jobs. Police departments that emphasize aggressive enforcement tend also to subscribe to the idea that the fear of police or of aggressively punitive policies will deter crime. It is a fear-based approach to preventing disturbances within a community. Those who subscribe to the peace-officer approach tend to emphasize rehabilitation and problem solving. Police under this model are expected to try to avoid disturbing the peace through their own actions as well as addressing the actions of others. The underlying idea is that members of a community should view their police as protectors and problem solvers and that deterring crime is best achieved by utilizing community resources.

Over the past century, the peace officer model has been eclipsed by the law enforcement model, and this has made policing increasingly confrontational and aggressive. The reason for this is primarily political. The fear of crime is a powerful motivator, and politicians have frequently tried to increase their appeal with voters by offering more aggressive and punitive approaches to crime. Such politicians market themselves as "law and order" leaders and promote the idea that the way to "solve" a crime problem is to get tough. In practice, decades of research show that this approach is ineffective, but it remains an expedient political strategy that has proven perennially popular with voters.

Domestic War Zones

The shift from rural agricultural life to industrial life pushed American policing away from peace keeping toward law enforcement, and this is one of the factors that has seen an increasing level of conflict and distance between police and citizens.

The Industrial Revolution saw a dramatic increase in poverty in America's cities, resulting in the rise of organized crime. Aided by America's lax laws on weapons ownership, criminal gangs proliferated in the early twentieth century and, when the Prohibition movement succeeded in banning the sale of alcohol, these gangs filled the void with bootleg liquor. Competition for access to this lucrative industry fueled rising violence, and crime became one of the most controversial issues of the era. A 24 percent increase in crime over the early years of Prohibition made crime control one of the top political priorities. The solution arrived at was to provide more weapons and tactical training to police officers, and this was the beginning of a trend that has been called the "militarization of police." Another major factor was the reorganization of the national police model, through a series of reforms introduced in the early twentieth century that sought to reorganize the structure of police ranks using the U.S. military as a model. Concurrent with the addition of tactical weapons and equipment, the training given to police officers began to more closely resemble the kinds of training used in the military. The idea behind this was to increase officer safety while also preventing corruption and misconduct by creating a more rigid chain of command and to introduce more rigorous officer training.[1]

One of the problems with the military model is that it encourages members of police departments to view citizens as potential enemies rather than as charges to be afforded protection and assistance. Militaristic and aggressive methods have also been unevenly utilized against minority and poor communities, exacerbating racial discrimination and reducing the trust of the poor and minority Americans in both the government and policing. During the 1960s civil rights movement, police around the nation were criticized for their aggressive and confrontational approach to protests and marches, and film of police abusing protestors in the South was one of the factors that helped motivate public support for new civil rights legislation at the federal level. But what grew out of this was the perception among many African Americans who had witnessed police hostility firsthand that police were enforcers of political will, not protectors of the peace. In the 1980s, the "War on Drugs" saw American police organizations going further and further down the militarization path. SWAT teams and military-grade equipment became a standard feature in policing in the effort to get tough on crime or to win the alleged war against drugs. The primary problem with this is that police are not at war, and citizens in America's cities and towns are not enemy combatants, whether or not they break the law. Drugs and violent crime are complex problems arising from sociological factors and, over the decades, sociologists have produced numerous studies indicating that the militarization approach has been ineffective at reducing crime and has decreased police safety by making violent confrontations more common.[2]

The Community Reforms

In the 1960s and 1970s, reformers urged police departments to change the way that police were being trained to increase cohesion between police and the public. This was not a new idea at the time, but drew from some of the early philosophies of modern policing. Sir Robert Peel, the man credited with establishing London's

Metropolitan Police, left a lasting mark on policing philosophy and was a major proponent of what is today called "community policing." Peel famously said, "The police are the public and the public are the police," and he saw this as a central principle in policing, that police should see themselves as members of the societies they were policing and should always seek to work with members of the community when addressing disturbances.[3]

Opinion polls show that the relationship between police and citizens has dramatically deteriorated, to the point where a majority of Americans no longer trust police or other individuals occupying positions of power within their society.[4] There has been, overall, a net loss in terms of support and trust in the quality of policing and in the intentions and capabilities of police officers. This is part of the reason that a majority of crimes in America go unreported. Though the community policing reforms of the 1960s are not considered to have been widely effective, there are many who believe that instituting community policing reforms could still help to heal the rift between policing and the public.

There are newer versions of the basic community policing model that have also begun to gain some attention among some facets of the reform movement. For example, a method known as "Insight Policing" seeks to train officers in the psychological principles of "Insight Conflict Analysis and Resolution," which is based on the idea that the behaviors that humans engage in when in conflict, boiled down to "fight or flight" reactions, are universal and are the basis for most criminal behavior. Insight Policing is meant to help officers control their own instinctual reactions during conflict, enabling them to maintain emotional control to prevent escalation.

George Mason University researcher Megan C. Price, one of the primary proponents of Insight Policing, argues that the training methods used in this program are meant to boil down the intricacies of "de-escalation," methods used to avoid and control conflict. The program also incorporates ideas from community policing, including the concept of utilizing civilians to help de-escalate conflicts before conflicts escalate to the use of force. Continued integration of officers within community outreach and organizational institutions is intended to further provide officers with intelligence on the community, and this provides insight that can be used when officers are called upon to resolve a conflict. Because Insight Policing is a relatively new police training system, the full impact of this or similar types of training remains unclear, but the idea of Insight Policing provides another example of how traditional reform methods might be utilized to reduce the potential for problematic encounters between police and members of the public.[5]

Defusing Conflict

One of the arenas in which police handling of sensitive situations has come into focus is how police handle mental illness. While there are officers in police departments around the country with the training, experience, or temperament to effectively manage interactions with individuals who have mental health issues, there are also numerous documented instances of police perceptively mishandling encounters with individuals with mental health issues, sometimes resulting in violence or serious injury. Some advocates believe that police are simply inappropriate for addressing mental health disturbances and have argued that social workers or other mental health professionals should be charged with addressing problems involving individuals with mental health issues. Alternatively, some have argued that police need to receive special training in how to manage interactions with individuals suffering from mental health issues and that departments need to conduct monitoring and oversight to avoid unnecessary confrontations and to de-escalate sensitive situations.[6]

Mental illness is also closely linked to another major issue in America, drug abuse and addiction. The aggressively punitive approach to drug enforcement pursued by American policing in the twentieth century has led to a situation in which individuals with drug problems often feel they cannot call on police for help or assistance, even when facing problems unrelated to drug use. As with addressing mental illness, many officers lack the training needed to effectively address situations involving drug abuse or addiction, and this limits the effectiveness of police as a first-line response to some drug-related issues.

In situations where police officers are asked to deal with citizens who have mental health issues, drug abuse issues, or both, aggressive tactics can escalate the situation into conflict. These individuals may lack the ability to control their reactions and emotions, exacerbating the problem. These are extreme examples of what many reformers consider a broader overarching problem, which is that police too often lack the psychological and social skills that might help to de-escalate situations. This applies not only to dealing with citizens who suffer from mental health issues, but also to many situations in which emotions are heightened, leading to confrontational interactions.

Over the years, reformers have encouraged police departments to train officers specifically in how to manage and de-escalate conflicts, and many police departments have invested in de-escalation training, though the effectiveness of these initiatives remains in question. Pilot programs training officers in de-escalation have shown limited success in applying the training to real-life situations, but the problem may be that some officers are resistant to the idea of learning and applying new techniques.[7]

The difficulty in getting police departments to embrace reforms is one of the major challenges faced by those promoting reform. As with any profession facing pressure to change procedures or to adjust to new policies, there are always some individuals who are more resistant to embracing those changes. The fact that the relationship between the police and the public has become more contentious and less productive exacerbates this problem, leaving some officers feeling defensive and aggrieved as they perceive that their entire profession is being maligned for behaviors that not all officers engage in. There are and have always been some officers and administrators who already embrace and try to implement the kinds of strategies that reformers are calling for, such as getting to know and working with members of a community or engaging in interactions with an eye toward reducing, rather than intensifying, confrontation. Reviews of programs introducing new training methods indicate that police in this category, those who already on some level embrace the basic philosophy behind such reforms, are more likely to improve when provided with new training. Other officers, however, feel justified in their existing approach to their job and view new reform methods or training as unnecessary or even intrusive.

The success of any institutional change is based on the degree to which members of the institution are able to embrace and accept the changes. As calls for reform intensify, therefore, it is important that politicians and administrators cooperate to unify their messaging to police and local governments. Highlighting the ways that reforms could benefit police, by reducing stress levels, keeping them safer on the job, and increasing cohesion with the public, could potentially help resistant officers and administrators to see the potential benefits and might therefore increase adoption of new methods and strategies.

Works Used

Miller, Brian. "The Militarization of America's Police: A Brief History." *FEE*. May 24, 2019. Retrieved from https://fee.org/articles/the-militarization-of-americas-police-a-brief-history/.

Price, Megan, and Jamie Price. "Insight Policing and the Role of the Civilian in Police Accountability." *Clearinghouse Review*. Aug. 2015. https://www.insightconflictresolution.org/uploads/1/5/5/0/15508726/insight_policing_police_accountability_price_2.pdf.

Rice, Johnny II. "Why We Must Improve Police Responses to Mental Illness." *NAMI*. National Alliance on Mental Health. Mar 2, 2020. https://www.nami.org/Blogs/NAMI-Blog/March-2020/Why-We-Must-Improve-Police-Responses-to-Mental-Illness.

Schultz, David. "A Long, Powerful History: How We Militarized the Police." *Minnpost*. https://www.minnpost.com/community-voices/2014/08/long-powerful-history-how-we-militarized-police/.

Schumaker, Erin. "Police Reformers Push for De-Escalation Training, but the Jury Is Out on Its Effectiveness." *ABC News*. Jul 5, 2020. https://abcnews.go.com/Health/police-reformers-push-de-escalation-training-jury-effectiveness/story?id=71262003.

"Understanding Community Policing." *NCJRS*. Office of Justice Programs. 1994. https://www.ncjrs.gov/pdffiles/commp.pdf.

"Why Americans Don't Fully Trust Many Who Hold Positions of Power and Responsibility." *Pew Research Center*. Sep 19, 2019. Retrieved from https://www.pewresearch.org/politics/2019/09/19/why-americans-dont-fully-trust-many-who-hold-positions-of-power-and-responsibility/.

Notes

1. Schultz, "A Long, Powerful History: How We Militarized the Police."
2. Miller, "The Militarization of America's Police: A Brief History."
3. "Understanding Community Policing," BJA. U.S. Department of Justice.
4. "Why Americans Don't Fully Trust Many Who Hold Positions of Power and Responsibility," *Pew Research Center*.
5. Price, "Insights Policing and the Role of the Civilian in Police Accountability."
6. Rice, "Why We Must Improve Police Responses to Mental Illness."
7. Schumaker, "Police Reformers Push for De-Escalation Training, but the Jury Is Out on Its Effectiveness."

Police Reformers Push for De-escalation Training, but the Jury Is Out on Its Effectiveness

By Erin Schumaker
ABC News, July 5, 2020

De-escalation training.

It's on the tip of the tongue of both police departments and reformers—the idea that officers can be trained effectively to throttle their use of force to avoid deadly escalations.

In the wake of George Floyd's death at the hands of police in Minneapolis, it was embraced by Senate Republicans, led by the party's lone Black senator, Tim Scott, of South Carolina—an effort that was blocked by the body's Democrats.

"One of the challenges in these split-second decisions is the need for more training, that's why the de-escalation aspect is so important," Scott said after Rayshard Brooks, who is Black, was shot and killed by police in a Wendy's parking lot in Atlanta earlier this month, one in a series of recent events that has galvanized the police reform movement.

The Republican initiative sought "alternatives to use of force and de-escalation tactics," according to the bill. That "includes techniques and strategies that are designed to protect the safety of the person experiencing the behavioral health crisis, law enforcement officers and the public," teaching officers, in other words to be "guardians," who only use force as a last resort instead of "warriors."

But a crucial question is whether teaching police officers to rely on communication and negotiation tactics rather than physical force can effectively teach a guardian-style mentality and whether training can actually drive down use of force in police departments across the country. De-escalation training has been adopted by a number of departments around the country in various forms, with 15 to 17% of departments practicing a form of crisis intervention training that includes de-escalation techniques.

Experts who study de-escalation, as well as law enforcement officials who mandate it for their forces, say it's a mixed bag. On the one hand, there's no conclusive evidence that de-escalation training works. There's also no evidence that it doesn't work. And the training has never been rigorously studied at all.

Law enforcement leaders who require de-escalation training in their departments are enthusiastic about its potential on an anecdotal level. But some say they aren't sure every officer can be trained.

"I think we would find that there's people who can't be reached by training," said Sylvia Moir, chief of police in Tempe, Arizona, whose department is currently involved in a de-escalation training study conducted by Arizona State University and partially funded by the Bureau of Justice Assistance.

> **Teaching the national law enforcement body to de-escalate conflict and embrace a guardian mindset would require buy-in from the agency leadership on a department-by-department basis.**

That's where appropriate screening comes in, Moir added. A mechanism to screen out "hyper-masculine traits" in recruits and individuals who aren't open to training could keep so-called bad actors out of the force, she said.

Moir rejected the "warrior" vs. "guardian" binary.

"So little of what I do is binary," Moir said. "We are guardians always and warriors when the situation needs us to be."

The Limits of De-escalation Training for Police Officers

De-escalation is a broad term, explained Chuck Wexler, executive director of the nonprofit Police Executive Research Forum, an organization focused on improving policing.

Wexler, who has worked extensively with American and British police forces over the course of his career, often makes comparisons to Scotland, where police officers rarely carry lethal weapons and which is considered a model for de-escalation training in the U.S.

But comparisons to Scotland fail to account for a key difference between the two nations. Americans own more guns per capita than any other nation in the world. Scotland doesn't even break the Top 10.

"That's why American police tend to be more cautious and protective," Wexler said. "If somebody appears to have a bulge in their jacket, police get very nervous. You can't do anything with any of this unless the officer feels safe," he added.

Traditional policing often escalates tense situations involving civilians, according to Wexler. "A person has a rock, they take out a baton," Wexler said.

"That's part of the culture. When I say 'back away,' some police officers recoil. Police are taught you never give up," Wexler said. In some situations it's okay to back off, he added, or even physically leave the scene.

"How do we teach the police, so that everybody can go home safely?" he asked.

That's where it gets complicated. Unlike in the United Kingdom and in many European countries, which have national police agencies, policing in the United States is highly fractured. Teaching police officers de-escalation techniques and philosophy here has to happen one department at a time.

In the U.S., there are roughly 18,000 separate police agencies and no national standards for use-of-force training. Half of local police departments have fewer than 10 full-time officers, according to the Bureau of Justice Statistics. Teaching the national law enforcement body to de-escalate conflict and embrace a guardian mindset would require buy-in from agency leadership on a department-by-department basis.

In small departments, with tighter budgets and staffing constraints, sparing one of 10 officers for hours or days of classroom learning may be a difficult proposition.

"It's a slow turn to change an entire field," said Robin Engel, a criminology professor at the University of Cincinnati, who studies policing policy.

"15 Different Answers"

Without standardization, there's also confusion about what counts as de-escalation training in the first place.

"If you asked 15 different departments about de-escalation training, they would give you 15 different answers," Wexler said.

To help cut to the chase, Wexler puts officers in a classroom and has someone pull out a knife and threaten them. Their training, or lack thereof, shines through.

De-escalation training varies dramatically from department to department, in delivery, dosage and content, Engel said.

Indeed, a 2015 survey of police academies conducted by PERF found that recruits spent eight hours each on de-escalation, crisis intervention and use of force training. They spend 58 hours on firearm training and 49 hours on defensive tactics.

"None of it has been systematically tested," she added.

Until the coronavirus pandemic hit, the New York Police Department, the largest law enforcement agency in the country, held de-escalation training involving classroom lectures, panels with community members with mental illness and live-action role play between officers and actors hired by the department, sometimes played out on sets designed to look like a bodega, a subway car or a New York City apartment.

The eight-hour, multi-day training, known as crisis intervention training, or CIT, includes teaching de-escalation techniques, with a focus on de-escalating interactions with civilians who are mentally ill. A quarter of the 1,000 people shot and killed by police officers in 2018 had mental illness.

Since the program began in 2015, 16,800 members of the NYPD or a little less than half of overall personnel, have been CIT certified, according to Lt. Angela Ho, one of the coordinators of the of NYPD's CIT training unit.

Fifty-eight percent of the patrol force have been certified, she added.

While the NYPD says its goal is to train its entire force, the department has no hard timeline for when the full force is expected to complete CIT training, according to Ho. The department has also previously been criticized for being so slow to roll out the training to everyone. Until a critical mass of the patrol force is trained, an officer responding to an assault in progress or a mental illness call could potentially be untrained in de-escalation.

"We shouldn't wash it down by rushing everybody in," Ho said, explaining that quickly training more officers might compromise the program's effectiveness.

But even when officers are trained, there's no guarantee it will translate to better behavior in the field.

Garrett Rolfe, the officer who was charged with fatally shooting Brooks in Atlanta, was trained in de-escalation and cultural awareness just to months before the shooting, the Atlanta Police Department said. Rolfe's lawyer said the charges were rushed and that his client's actions "were appropriate."

And prior to George Floyd's killing, the Minneapolis police department had attempted to institute reforms, including trainings sessions as an alternative to disciplining cops.

It apparently wasn't enough. According to the Marshall Project, which reviewed court documents, state legislation and a 2015 report by the U.S. Justice Department, even after those changes were instituted, law enforcement in Minneapolis had a clear pattern being reluctant to remove bad officers from patrol.

"They have also failed to set clear criteria on the use of force and de-escalation," Marshall Project reporters found. Neither the police department nor the police chief responded to requests from the Marshall Project to comment on their findings.

Inside the NYPD's De-escalation Training

During the NYPD de-escalation training the actors didn't hold back, performers involved with the project told *ABC News*.

They would scream in officers' faces and curse at them, trying to get them to snap in the classroom the way they might be inclined to do during tense interactions on the street.

There were heartening interactions where officers seemed either naturally inclined towards guardian-style policing or to have learned from their de-escalation training. Renan Kanbay, age 31, an actor who spent three years working on crisis intervention training with the NYPD, said she often played the part of a woman with depression, who wouldn't leave a park the officer had been ordered to clear after dark.

One female officer treated her softly. The scene ended with the officer giving her a hug, she said. On another occasion, the same scene wrapped when a frustrated officer handcuffed Kanbay, who is slight, with a 5-foot-5 frame, to the floor.

There were also troubling indications of racial biases that were evidenced during the training, a white actor, who didn't want to share their name, told *ABC News*. Officers seemed to disproportionately handcuff the black actor among them, the white actor said, but there was never a critical analysis of that disparity in the classroom.

For her part, Kanbay said that the one character she felt like the officers couldn't connect with was a recurring scene in which she played a Muslim woman with a headscarf. Kanbay, who is Turkish, would scream at the officers in Turkish while portraying a character with severe mental illness, she said.

"You shouldn't only depend on your language to subdue the other person," she added, noting that body language and tone of voice are important de-escalation tools.

Focus on Crime Reduction Left Police Policy Research Underfunded

Engel, the researcher, doesn't want to give the impression that she's against investing in de-escalation training.

On the contrary, she wants the federal government to spend the money to rigorously study de-escalation.

Last week, when Engel testified before President Donald Trump's commission on law enforcement, she outlined what we don't know about de-escalation training's effectiveness.

Although "de-escalation use of force policies and training are widely viewed as a common-sense approach," she testified, "there is no uniformly accepted definition of de-escalation within the policing field, and little is known about the development, delivery, and impact of police de-escalation training."

In addition to concerns about whether or not the training works, little is known about how de-escalation training affects officer safety.

Earlier this year, Engel and her colleagues conducted a systematic review of the studies on de-escalation training for the police. There was just one problem. There were no such studies. Of the 64 rigorous studies conducted over the past 40 years, they were primarily done in nursing or psychiatric settings.

"We found zero studies in policing," Engel told *ABC News*. "Not one."

The result is that recommendations for and conversations about de-escalation training "rely heavily on anecdotal evidence and untested propositions about best practice," Engel concluded.

Decades of neglect and prioritizing research on reducing crime over research on policing policy has left us with little idea of what works and what doesn't, she said.

"The particular crisis we find ourselves in has exposed how big the gap is between research and practice right now," Engel said.

While the United States' fractured policing system makes it difficult to put a national price tag on de-escalation training, it's safe to say that it's a multi-million dollar expenditure. When CBS polled 155 police agencies on their racial bias training last year, including the three largest in each state, every department that completed the survey said they offered some form of de-escalation training.

Despite scant evidence, Wexler believes that de-escalation training works. "If we want police to be more humane, we should be investing in them, not walking away from them," he said. "If you have one bad car stop it will pay for years of de-escalation training," he added.

Change in the Works?

In June, Rep. Eddie Bernice Johnson, D-Tx.,introduced legislation to use federal funding from the National Science Foundation for social and behavior research on policing policy.

"We must explore the legacy of policing and the root cause of the racial disparities we observe," Johnson said in a statement. "In our search for solutions, we must be guided by evidence grounded in data and scientific research."

Still, Engel is sympathetic to the bind that police leadership finds itself in.

"The solution can't be to wait for evidence," she said. "They need to make decisions now."

She hopes that police executives will allow researchers like herself to tag along to collect data and evaluate use of force reforms to find out if they work. She also stressed that de-escalation training needs to happen in conjunction with strong policies to hold leadership and rank-and-file officers accountable.

In Oklahoma City, she said, officers are required to fill out a form every time they use force, detailing which de-escalation techniques they attempted first, if any.

"If you just do the training, you might change attitudes but you are less likely to change behavior," she said. "

As for the theory that de-escalation training makes good cops better and doesn't help bad cops, "that's exactly why the training can not stand alone," Engel said.

Print Citations

CMS: Schumaker, Erin. "Police Reformers Push for De-escalation Training, but the Jury Is Out on Its Effectiveness." In *The Reference Shelf: Policing in 2020,* edited by Micah L. Issitt, 111-116. Amenia, NY: Grey House Publishing, 2021.

MLA: Schumaker, Erin. "Police Reformers Push for De-escalation Training, but the Jury Is Out on Its Effectiveness." *The Reference Shelf: Policing in 2020,* edited by Micah L. Issitt, Grey Housing Publishing, 2021, pp. 111-116.

APA: Schumaker, E. (2021). Police reformers push for de-escalation training, but the jury is out on its effectiveness. In Micah L. Issitt (Ed.), *The reference shelf: Policing in 2020* (pp. 111-116). Amenia, NY: Grey Housing Publishing.

Private Company Moves to Profit from New York's Police Reforms

By Alice Speri

The Intercept, August 9, 2020

The protests in response to the police killing of George Floyd in Minneapolis have accelerated changes in New York state that police reform advocates had fought to enact for years. Within days of the protests spreading to New York City and across the state, legislators moved to ban chokeholds and repeal a controversial law that has long protected records of police abuse from public scrutiny.

On June 12, Gov. Andrew Cuomo signed a sweeping executive order requiring the state's more than 500 police agencies to "to develop a plan that reinvents and modernizes police strategies and programs in their community based on community input." Departments across the state have until April 2021 to do so, or they risk losing state funding.

"The protests taking place throughout the nation and in communities across New York in response to the murder of George Floyd illustrate the loss of community confidence in our local police agencies," Cuomo said in a statement. "This emergency regulation will help rebuild that confidence and restore trust between police and the communities they serve."

The mandate to comprehensively review existing police strategies, policies, procedures, and practices was in part an effort by state officials to return the conversation to police reform at a time when most protesters on the street had started demanding that police be defunded instead. But the order also left local officials across the state, and particularly those in small communities, scrambling and overwhelmed at the prospect of having to rewrite their police rulebooks from scratch.

"Our village police chief literally did not know exactly what to do," said Clyde Rabideau, the mayor of Saranac Lake, a village of 5,400 people in the Adirondack region.

Following Cuomo's order, Saranac Lake's police chief reached out to colleagues across the state and found a solution: Lexipol, a California-based consulting company that has quietly drafted the policies of thousands of police departments across the country, would rewrite Saranac Lake's for $11,000, plus additional yearly fees. "We're a small village, we have 12 sworn officers including the chief," said Rabideau.

In the past, local police policy "was basically on the fly as different situations presented themselves," he added. "They did the best job they could given their

limited time and resources. But now, given all the executive orders and new directives, we have got to step back, get some professional help, engage the public, and
reformulate our policies and procedures."

Saranac Lake officials had never heard about Lexipol until the recent executive
order sent them looking for it, but the story of how the village came to contract
with the company has
been repeated dozens of
times across the country.
Lexipol, founded in 2003
by two former cops, rap-
idly took over California's

> **"Lexipol's rise is an indication of the
> failure of our government to regulate law
> enforcement."**

law enforcement agencies, contracting with more than 95 percent of them. But its
influence has quickly grown nationwide as well, as the company has seized on police protests—and the reforms they prompted—to pitch its services to departments
looking to keep up with a changing landscape.

Critics of Lexipol warn that the company is committed to its bottom line rather
than transformed policing: The policies it sells tend to be conservative interpreta-
tions of the law that prescribe the bare minimum to keep police departments from
getting sued—a promise that is central to Lexipol's aggressive marketing campaigns.
And critics fear that by outsourcing the drafting of their policies to a private company, departments can maintain an appearance of professionalism while de facto
hindering transparency and cutting local communities out of the process.

In New York, community organizers whose work and activism prompted changes
like Cuomo's recent executive order, now fear their efforts will be co-opted by a
company looking for profit. "Obviously wide-spread privatization of police policy
would have a pretty spectacular impact on New York state," said Zohar Gitlis, a
member of the High Peaks DSA chapter, which organizes the northeastern Adirondack region, including Saranac Lake. "And [it] would be a really grim outcome of an
executive order that was celebrated for its intent to address racist policing after the
murder of George Floyd."

Shannon Pieper, a spokesperson for Lexipol, wrote in an email to *The Intercept*
that the company does not collect information on the reasons behind agency decisions to subscribe to Lexipol's services. But on July 30, she wrote, Lexipol held
an informational webinar, in partnership with the New York State Association of
Chiefs of Police, reviewing much of the recent New York police reform legislation,
including Cuomo's executive order. "Our appeal to potential customers today is
consistent with our message since we first started providing policies to New York
law enforcement agencies in 2015: Lexipol's policy management system is a cost-
effective solution that provides comprehensive policies and policy updates, Daily
Training Bulletins to help officers apply policies, and reporting features to track
policy acknowledgment."

"Lexipol encourages agencies that subscribe to our policies to review and customize the policies to address community and agency needs," she added. "Our

customers can—and have—involved community members in review of the policies before they are implemented and integrate changes as a result of that process."

Jason Conwall, a spokesman for Cuomo, wrote in an email to *The Intercept* that officials are finalizing guidance, including resources, that municipalities may consider as they work to comply with the executive order, but did not specifically comment on Lexipol.

"Governor Cuomo's executive order is clear—it calls on community members, stakeholders, local elected officials and police to come to the table and be part of a collective effort to create transparent and fair law enforcement policies that reflect the community's desires," Conwall wrote. "Once a municipality has finalized a plan and its legislative body has approved it, the municipality is required to file a certification with the state Division of Budget and certify that all stakeholders contributed to the process."

Rabideau, Saranac Lake's mayor, believes a number of other towns are considering contracting with Lexipol as a result of recent legislation. That should be cause of alarm, said Joanna Schwartz, a professor at the UCLA School of Law who has closely studied the company.

"I am very concerned about the prospect of Lexipol crafting these policies in New York and across the country without transparency and engagement," Schwartz told *The Intercept*. "I appreciate that the governor wants to make sure that police policies are being written in a good way, but if that ends up being Lexipol's way I fear that the underlying goals of the initial reforms aren't going to be met."

Police Consultants

Lexipol's approach, in the 3,500 public safety agencies in 35 states in which the company operates, has been mostly sticking to the minimum legal standard of what police are and are not allowed to do. The company promises departments regularly updated policies that keep up with changing laws, and its marketing materials pitch "legally defensive content" and call on officials to "protect" their agencies from lawsuits.

In fact, those promises have not always panned out, and a number of departments relying on Lexipol policies have been sued when those policies were found to violate constitutional standards or other laws. Civil rights advocates have particularly taken issue with Lexipol's policies regulating the cooperation between local law enforcement and U.S. Immigration and Customs Enforcement, but Lexipol has also been challenged in Illinois for promoting policies that illegally discriminate against pregnant officers. Lexipol lobbied against a recent California law restricting the use of police force and drafted the policies of the Pomona police department, which was sued last month by the American Civil Liberties Union of Southern California over its defiance of the law.

"The entire policy philosophy of Lexipol is based on the idea that if the policies just describe the legal standard and don't give operational guidance to officers, don't direct them how to behave in particular situations, they believe that that will minimize individual officer liability," said Carl Takei, a senior staff attorney at the ACLU.

"All of their policy really tries very hard to avoid having bright-line rules or directing officers to do or not do any particular thing in a particular circumstance."

In workshops, promotional material, and the policies it sells to police departments, Lexipol has regularly opposed de-escalation policies, the regulation of use of force, and growing calls to forbid police from shooting into moving vehicles. In 2019, after the police killing of Eric Logan in South Bend, Indiana, threatened to derail the presidential ambitions of Mayor Pete Buttigieg, it emerged that the officer who killed Logan had been wearing a body camera, but that the camera was off. South Bend's police manual, which Lexipol wrote for nearly $95,000, mandated officers wear body cameras—but it didn't specify that the cameras had to be turned on.

Pieper, Lexipol's spokesperson, pushed back against criticism of the company. "In many cases our policies go beyond what is required by law," she wrote. She added that Lexipol "requires officers to consider and use de-escalation tactics when time and circumstances permit" and that "a complete ban on shooting at moving vehicles would prevent officers from intervening to save lives in situations such as a vehicular-based terror attack." She declined to comment on lawsuits against police departments using Lexipol's services, and she argued that California's AB 392 law "does not create a new legal standard for the use of deadly force"—an interpretation that the ACLU contests.

Lexipol's copyrighted policies have largely replaced free draft policies that were previously circulated by law enforcement associations. And the company has specifically pitched police departments, law enforcement associations, and insurance companies, speaking to "the current challenges" police are facing at a time of widespread protests, the company wrote, for instance, to the chief of the San Francisco police department. "With recent racial tensions rising, now would be the perfect opportunity to re-examine ways Lexipol can help ensure the safety of your officers to avoid any potential risks," a Lexipol representative also wrote to the chief of the Beverly Hills police department.

"Lexipol has been involved in the past when there have been high-profile incidents or when cities have thought systematically about reforms," said Schwartz, whose research documents Lexipol's pitches to various departments. "I would not be surprised if they are taking the opportunity of New York's executive order to expand."

Lexipol's success is largely a result of the severe decentralization of policing in the U.S.: there are 18,000 different law enforcement agencies across the country, and each sets its own policies.

The fact that Lexipol is relatively unknown, even as it has become the single most influential provider of police policy nationwide, doesn't bode well for police transparency, critics say. Instead, they suggest, Lexipol's role should be played by government agencies, with the involvement of a range of community stakeholders beyond police themselves, and in a public and transparent way.

"If I had a magic wand, I would create a government agency and state accreditation agencies that were involved in drafting model policies that were regularly updated and that departments could adapt," said Schwartz. "I do think that Lexipol's rise is an indication of the failure of our government to regulate law enforcement."

"It's just a classic neoliberal privatization thing, it's like, 'Well, we've got a few experts who can work on this full time, and you're a dinky police department with very little experience, so just buy our policy products,'" echoed Alex Vitale, who runs the Policing and Social Justice Project at Brooklyn College. "It's a bad idea. Police consultants should not be making policy, it should be a public process."

A Seat at the Table

In Saranac Lake, residents first heard about the village's plans to contract with Lexipol at a village board of trustees meeting. A group of local advocates had attended to ask the village to hire community health workers and devote more resources to dealing with mental health and substance abuse issues, which they said was a much greater concern to the community than crime. Policing takes up about 45 percent of Saranac Lake's general funds.

The village, a popular tourist destination, had recently installed lamppost banners that said "Racism is a public health crisis." Gitlis, one of the advocates at the meeting, hoped to make the case for the village to invest in Saranac Lake's own public health crisis. "Police is the number one spending priority in the village and it seems like our problem, which is true in many small rural towns, is much more around mental health," she said. "Perhaps we should shift the conversation and funding patterns."

But at the meeting, after the time allocated to public comment had ended, the police chief updated participants about Cuomo's recent executive order, and said that the village was looking to partner with Lexipol. He said the contract would cost around $6,000 and would be put up for a vote by the village's board soon. Shortly afterwards, officials issued the agenda for the next meeting: It included a vote on the contract with Lexipol, for $11,000; notably the vote was scheduled before the time allocated to public comment. Alarmed, local advocates flooded village leaders with emails, and successfully moved up the public comment time slot to happen before the vote. At the meeting, one person after the other raised opposition to the plan, and the vote was ultimately postponed.

Still, Rabideau told *The Intercept* he believes the board will approve the contract with Lexipol at the next meeting, scheduled for this week. Rabideau said local advocates opposing Lexipol were "well-meaning but very inexperienced with police work" and dismissed Schwartz's research on Lexipol as a "scholarly opinion piece." Rabideau added that he saw no problem contracting with a for-profit company, and that once Lexipol's policy for the village was drafted, there would be hearings to present it to the public and solicit their input. He added criticism that Lexipol's focus was to limit police liability "doesn't make sense at all."

"Yeah we want to limit our liability exposure," he said. "We want to conform to all the existing laws and procedures, and we don't want to be sued. We don't want to cause harm to people and we want to do our best job possible. Our insurance companies always ask us to limit our exposure and that is our duty to our taxpayers. For someone to complain about that is totally ridiculous."

In fact, insurance companies frequently function as a broker between Lexipol and local municipalities, offering discounted rates to departments that subscribe to the company's services. Lexipol did not answer questions about how many clients it has in New York state and whether it works with local insurers. But William Worden, the chief of police in Port Jervis, a small city in New York's Orange County that is also in the process of subscribing to Lexipol, noted that several agencies in the county have contracted with the company in recent years, also thanks to a deal with the local chiefs association.

"By purchasing as a consortium, group services discounts are offered to Orange County Police Agencies and New York State Police Agencies," Worden wrote to *The Intercept*. "Once the Lexipol program is fully incorporated, we will research the potential of negotiating a discount through the City's insurance carrier based upon the services Lexipol provides to the City."

In an email repeating much of the company's marketing language, Worden wrote that "Lexipol provides an effective format that links police agencies across the state to customized policy managements, daily updates and training that incorporates industry best practices." He said that Port Jervis police plans to implement Lexipol's policies by March 2021, just in time for the April deadline set by Cuomo's executive order. But Worden said nothing of a key component of the order: that the new plans be developed "based on community input."

In Saranac Lake, Rabideau repeatedly said that input was important but that ultimately people who were not police had limited understanding of the issues at stake. "If somebody walks in off the street, never been a cop in their life, never rode in a cop car in their life, only googled stuff, and comes in and says, 'Oh, I want the police department to do x, y, and z.' Well, does it make sense?" he said. "You have to start with a basis of fact, in conformance with laws and executive orders, and not just lay people coming off the street giving us their wish list. We listen to the wish list, some of it may make a lot of sense, but we have to have a reference point."

To those who had hoped Cuomo's executive order would be a first step toward a radically different approach to policing in New York, the outsourcing of that process to Lexipol has felt like a betrayal. "It's been pretty disappointing to see how this is playing out on a local level, and how it actually doesn't have much potential to change anyone's police experience," said Gitlis. "We were the activists that got Cuomo's attention to make this executive order happen. We want a seat at the table."

Print Citations

CMS: Speri, Alice. "Private Company Moves to Profit from New York's Police Reforms." In *The Reference Shelf: Policing in 2020,* edited by Micah L. Issitt, 117-123. Amenia, NY: Grey House Publishing, 2021.

MLA: Speri, Alice. "Private Company Moves to Profit from New York's Police Reforms." *The Reference Shelf: Policing in 2020,* edited by Micah L. Issitt, Grey Housing Publishing, 2021, pp. 117-123.

APA: Speri, A. (2021). Private company moves to profit from New York's police reforms. In Micah L. Issitt (Ed.), *The reference shelf: Policing in 2020* (pp. 117-123). Amenia, NY: Grey Housing Publishing.

Police Reforms Stall around the Country, Despite New Wave of Activism

By Nolan D. McCaskill
Politico, September 23, 2020

Racial justice activists convulsed the country this summer with their protests against police brutality. But as the season shifts to fall, they don't have much to show for it in terms of major policy change.

The announcement Wednesday that Kentucky officials will not charge the police officers for shooting and killing Breonna Taylor, an unarmed Black woman, in her apartment in March just reinforced the feeling that as much as Black Lives Matter and police reform movements may have grabbed the public's attention, they have yet to upend the status quo when it comes to race and public safety.

That's particularly evident at the state and federal level, where Congress and a majority of state legislatures have taken no action, and even states with liberal leadership in governor's mansions and state capitals have failed to move aggressively. Activists tracking bills in state legislatures attribute the inaction to two factors: push back from powerful police unions and poor timing.

At the time that George Floyd, a Black Minnesota man, was killed by a white police officer on Memorial Day, at least 23 state legislatures had already adjourned for the year. And sessions in Arizona and Oklahoma wrapped up shortly thereafter— on May 26 and May 29, respectively. A handful of legislatures, however, have since held special sessions to address issues like the coronavirus and police reform.

Police reform advocates are hopeful that policies that went unaddressed due to time constraints in statehouses will be revisited when legislators reconvene next year, but there is a risk that, by then, the moment sparked by Floyd's death may have passed.

Shortly after a video of Floyd being choked under the knee of a Minneapolis police officer began circulating online, protesters across the country poured into the streets to rally against police brutality. Activists say the reaction, coming in the middle of a deadly pandemic that has disproportionately impacted people of color, felt different than the aftermath of past police shootings, and gave them an opening to push for what they maintain are commonsense demands, even as the most progressive activists seek changes like "defunding the police."

Indeed, a majority of Americans told a Gallup Poll in July that "major changes" to policing were needed, including 88 percent of Black Americans and 51 percent of white Americans. Though only 14 percent of Republicans agreed that major changes were necessary, 72 percent acknowledged the need for "minor changes" to policing.

Public opinion, however, has retrenched since then. After a summer surge in popularity for the Black Lives Matter movement, a *Politico*/Morning Consult poll this month showed that favorable views of BLM had dropped 9 percentage points since June, including a 13-point dip among Republicans.

In interviews, activists who have been involved in state legislative battles this year acknowledged that change won't come any easier in the new year.

Police unions "have pushed back on every single piece of reform pushed" in Massachusetts in 2020, said Jamarhl Crawford, an activist and member of the Boston Police Reform Task Force. But "if we can't win now," he said, "we suck."

Criminal justice organizer Scott Roberts also pointed the finger at the unions. "They, to my knowledge, haven't seen a reform yet that they like," said Roberts, senior director of criminal justice campaigns at Color of Change, a civil rights advocacy group that pushed for murder charges against the officer that shot and killed Breonna Taylor. "The police unions aren't really a group that's going to come to the table and say, 'Hey, let's compromise.' They're real hard-liners. I would classify them as extremists, frankly."

Former Boston Police Commissioner Ed Davis acknowledged: "The unions do carry a lot of sway. But they're not a monolithic power, and there's a lot of legislation that's been passed over the years that police unions have been opposed to. I don't think it's a case of, 'We'll never win this.' I think it's issue by issue."

Indeed, several states have now passed measures restricting how police restrain individuals, and some have mandated the use of body-worn cameras. Minnesota, Floyd's home state, enacted legislation limiting chokeholds and neck restraints and banning warrior-style officer training.

Dave Bicking, a board member of the Minneapolis-based Communities United Against Police Brutality, framed the Minnesota measures that passed as "better than nothing," but expressed hope that lawmakers will return to more substantive legislation next year.

Bicking said Minnesota police unions were a factor in halting more ambitious policy change. "They have a lot of influence at the legislature," Bicking said. "We also have a number of legislators in influential positions, committee chairs, who are themselves police officers or were police officers. Because the legislature is part-time, we even have a current police officer serving in the legislature."

Leslie Rosedahl, a spokesperson for the Minnesota Police and Peace Officers Association, said its staff, lobbyists and allies "worked comprehensively" with Republican and Democratic legislators in both chambers and Democratic Gov. Tim Walz "to help provide our best counsel on the proposals."

"We utilized experts on arbitration, use of force, and more, to educate elected officials on the facts about policing, and our desire to protect and serve," Rosedahl said, adding that thousands of supporters contacted state legislators on behalf of law enforcement. "Our work made a difference."

Even in liberal California, a state where Democrats control all the major levers of government, the most ambitious bills introduced in the wake of Floyd's death failed to make it through the legislative session that ended last month. Two measures ultimately reached Gov. Gavin Newsom's desk: one to ban carotid restraints, which cut off blood flow to the brain, and another to require independent investigations of officer-involved shootings when requested by local law enforcement agencies or district attorneys.

But the highest-profile bills, including those that would have allowed California to decertify problematic officers and established the strictest duty-to-intercede standard in the nation, never even got a vote.

The most contentious fight proved to be over decertification, a process that would prevent officers who've committed serious offenses from returning to departments. California is one of only five states that doesn't have a system for pulling an officer's badge, a fact that both lawmakers and law enforcement groups say must change in order to rebuild public trust.

State Sen. Steve Bradford of Los Angeles County, who authored the bill, said that in spite of a vocal outpouring of support for police reform from lawmakers, the possible political ramifications of voting against law enforcement proved to be a barrier for many.

"This would have been an opportunity for some real profiles in courage," he said. "I understand it's an election year, but I would have been more concerned with the thousands of Californians who have demonstrated over the last five months in the streets wanting police reform, more so than the last-minute opposition of police unions."

> **In spite of a vocal outpouring of support for police reform from lawmakers, the possible political ramifications of voting against law enforcement proved to be a barrier for many.**

Fraternal Order of Police National President Patrick Yoes defended the role police unions are playing in the debate over policing reforms. He cast the FOP, which endorsed President Donald Trump's reelection earlier this month, as a willing partner that wants to be part of conversations around improving policing and the criminal justice system. But he stressed that those conversations have to be fact-based, not knee-jerk reactions based on emotions.

Noting that more than 200 police officers have died from Covid-19 this year, Yoes said that "some 800,000 [officers] are putting their lives in danger every single day to protect communities, and what we're doing is we're focusing on one, two, maybe 10 incidents that happened out of millions and millions and millions of public police contact."

Yoes also noted that the FOP was involved in Trump's executive order on policing, the First Step Act and Senate Republicans' recent JUSTICE Act, and said that he spoke to House Speaker Nancy Pelosi and Congressional Black Caucus Chairwoman Karen Bass about House Democrats' George Floyd Justice In Policing Act after it was introduced. That legislation has not gotten a vote in the Republican-controlled Senate.

Colorado is among the few states that have passed a sweeping reform package this year, with Gov. Jared Polis signing legislation that would, among other things, end qualified immunity, which protects officers from liability for constitutional violations that don't break "clearly established" law. The *Denver Post* reported last month that more than 240 police officers statewide had resigned or retired since the bill was signed in June, though it was unclear how many departures were directly related to the new law.

An effort to end qualified immunity died in Virginia's ongoing special legislative session earlier this month and is currently being debated in Massachusetts.

"That's really, I think, where the battle lines are being drawn," said Carol Rose, executive director of the American Civil Liberties Union of Massachusetts. "The opposition that the police unions have mobilized and the disinformation campaign that the police unions have mobilized around holding police officers accountable by limiting qualified immunity is gonna make it hard to pass in this session, but we remain cautiously optimistic."

Print Citations

CMS: McCaskill, Nolan D. "Police Reforms Staff around the Country, Despite New Wave of Activism." In *The Reference Shelf: Policing in 2020,* edited by Micah L. Issitt, 124-127. Amenia, NY: Grey House Publishing, 2021.

MLA: McCaskill, Nolan D. "Police Reforms Staff around the Country, Despite New Wave of Activism." *The Reference Shelf: Policing in 2020,* edited by Micah L. Issitt, Grey Housing Publishing, 2021, pp. 124-127.

APA: McCaskill, N.D. (2021). Police reform staff around the country, despite new wave of activism. In Micah L. Issitt (Ed.), *The reference shelf: Policing in 2020* (pp. 124-127). Amenia, NY: Grey Housing Publishing.

Could "Insight Policing" Have Saved Sandra Bland, Freddie Gray and Others?

By Megan Price
The Conversation, July 22, 2015

The disturbing video released earlier this week of the stop and arrest of Sandra Bland highlights once again the excessive and inexcusable use of force by police officers in this country. The 28-year-old's death in police custody after a routine traffic stop is currently being investigated as a murder.

Both ordinary citizens and experts have been calling for police departments to ramp up efforts to stop these kinds of abuses, but tragically, they continue.

Why they continue is perplexing and complicated—from history and power to the role of implicit bias. But one answer, as a Memphis cop put it to me in an interview for the Retaliatory Violence Insight Project, is what police officers call the "tricky part": maintaining trust with citizens while enforcing the law.

The Tricky Part

Part of what is tricky, I found talking with police officers, is that traditional policing practice uses deterrence methods—force and the threat of punishment—to motivate compliance.

Most of us are familiar with these methods. Perhaps we have gotten a speeding ticket, or been subject to stop and frisk. The principle is the same—obey the law or face consequences.

Deterrence policies may stop crime in some cases, but they are counter to most people's conception of trust, which depends on the belief that another person will not cause harm.

Because of this trust deficit, deterrence methods can fail to produce compliance; and instead, produce conflict between the public and the police. Just watch Sandra Bland's arrest video, or the public reaction to the high-force police response during last year's Ferguson protests.

Research from the Retaliatory Violence Insight Project into the challenges police departments face curtailing retaliatory violence in high crime communities has produced an alternative: Insight Policing.

Insight Policing is a community-oriented, problem-solving policing practice designed to help officers take control of situations with the public before conflict escalates. By doing so, the police maintain trust and enhance the probability of co-operation in difficult situations of enforcement.

The Role of Insight Policing

Insight Policing helps officers recognize and defuse conflict behavior when they see it—both their own and the public's. Often, conflict behavior resembles such stress-based behaviors as fight, flight and freeze; these are the actions people take when they feel threatened.

The thing about conflict behavior, and what Insight Policing pays particular attention to, is that when we feel threatened, we are reactive, not reflective, in how we respond. We do not take time to think about what we are doing, we simply *do,* in hopes that we will successfully stop the threat.

Sandra Bland refused to get out of her car (conflict behavior), responding to the threat the officer posed when he ordered her to. The officer pulled a taser on Bland (conflict behavior) in response to the threat her refusal posed to him as an agent of the law.

While clearly there are more dramatic instances of conflict behavior in police–citizen encounters—the high speed chase, the standoff—the more mundane conflict interactions are what are undermining police legitimacy.

When conflict behavior manifests as noncompliance, when citizens refuse to cooperate, as was the case with Eric Garner, Mike Brown, Freddie Gray and most recently Sandra Bland, what begins as mundane can become lethal when conflict behavior escalates.

Insight Policing, which has been piloted in two American police departments, Memphis, Tennessee, and Lowell, Massachusetts, is a promising tool for helping officers get a handle on the "tricky part." Eighty percent of officers trained agreed that Insight Policing enhanced their ability to defuse the feelings of threat citizens have about their encounters with police officers.

An Example of Insight Policing

Take an example from Memphis. Three Memphis officers trained in Insight Policing responded to a call for shots fired. They arrived on the scene to find a crowd of young men behind a house. They asked them the kinds of questions they always ask at the scene of a crime: "What happened?" "What did you see?" "Who did this?" The young men refused to cooperate: "We didn't see anything." "Leave us alone." "We don't know what you're talking about."

> **Police officers call [it] the "tricky part": maintaining trust with citizens while enforcing the law.**

The officers suspected otherwise. And ordinarily, they reported, they would have arrested the young men on gang-related charges and questioned them down at the station—to delay any retaliation that might have been brewing as well as to get the information they were after. Instead, having been trained in Insight Policing, they recognized the young men's resistance as conflict behavior. They dropped, for the moment, their crime investigator hats, and put on their conflict investigator hats. They used Insight Policing techniques to become curious about what was motivating the young men's resistance.

What the officers found was not that the young men were protecting somebody or hiding something or breaking the law in some way, but that they had had trouble with police in the past. They did not want to speak because they were afraid of incriminating themselves.

Getting this information allowed the officers to delink the threat they posed by assuring the young men that they were not after them, they were after the shooter. They were able to build enough trust in the moment that the young men gave them the information they needed to catch the shooter later that night.

Had the officers used their power to arrest the young men, just for hanging out together, they would have played into the young men's fear of incrimination. They would have escalated a situation, and who knows how it would have turned out.

By engaging the men in terms of their conflict behavior, the officers were able to build trust, garner cooperation and effectively enforce the law.

What if the officers who stopped Sandra Bland and Freddie Gray and Mike Brown and Eric Garner had been trained to recognize conflict behavior and defuse it? Perhaps history would be different.

Print Citations

CMS: Price, Megan. "Could 'Insight Policing' Have Saved Sandra Bland, Freddie Gray and Others?" In *The Reference Shelf: Policing in 2020,* edited by Micah L. Issitt, 128-130. Amenia, NY: Grey House Publishing, 2021.

MLA: Price, Megan. "Could 'Insight Policing' Have Saved Sandra Bland, Freddie Gray and Others?" *The Reference Shelf: Policing in 2020,* edited by Micah L. Issitt, Grey Housing Publishing, 2021, pp. 128-130.

APA: Price, M. (2021). Could "insight policing" have saved Sandra Bland, Freddie Gray and others? In Micah L. Issitt (Ed.), *The reference shelf: Policing in 2020* (pp. 128-130). Amenia, NY: Grey Housing Publishing.

5
Steps Toward Reform

By Taymaz Valley, via Wikimedia.

Defund the Police Rally in June 2020.

Solving Problems for a Better Policing System

It is difficult to enact effective reform when there are such widely divergent opinions regarding whether reform is even warranted. The federal government, under the Trump administration, provided little support for the idea that any significant police reforms were needed and, in fact, portrayed calls for reform as part of a broad conspiratorial agenda to weaken support for Trump. But calls for serious police reform have been ongoing for decades, and the current movement to call attention to police treatment of African Americans first came to the forefront of the popular debate in 2014. Further, racial prejudice is only one of numerous issues that reform advocates are calling for police departments to address.

The fact that the police reform effort has been ongoing for so long without the changes reform advocates hoped for has helped to politicize the issue. It is not realistic, however, to claim that reform is not necessary. Police in America face a serious public image problem that has seen trust in police plummeting around the country. This has important consequences, as the decline in public trust has led to limitations in funding, a lack of new candidates wanting to join the police force, and a lack of cooperation from citizens.

Funding and Reform

By far the biggest news in the police reform debate has been the "Defund the Police" movement. The basic idea is to remove municipal and state funding from police departments and redistribute that funding to other agencies that might serve similar functions in a different way. Proponents of the movement argue that funding currently allocated to police could be provided to social service organizations that would then expand their activities to address some of the problems that are currently addressed by police. Statistics from emergency centers indicate that 90 percent of calls to police are associated with nonviolent issues. Advocates for the Defund the Police movement argue that social service workers could be more effective than police at addressing calls involving persons with drug addiction or mental illness. Funding could be used to provide safety training for emergency responders from different departments. Police could be utilized in some cases, but the need for police response would be reduced. Writing for Brookings Institution, sociologist Rashawn Ray argues, "Police officers' skill set and training are often out of sync with the social interactions that they have. Police officers are mostly trained in use-of-force tactics and worst-case scenarios to reduce potential threats. However, most of their interactions with civilians start with a conversation."[1]

One of the best explanations of the Defund the Police movement came from New York Representative Alexandria Ocasio-Cortez: "The good news is that it actually doesn't take a ton of imagination. It looks like a suburb. Affluent white communities already live in a world where they choose to fund youth, health, housing, etc more than they fund police. These communities have lower crimes rates not because they have more police, but bc they have more resources to support healthy society in a way that reduces crime."[2]

Representative Ocasio-Cortez went on to explain that, in affluent communities, representatives of both the police and the courts take extra efforts to find solutions that keep children and young people accused of crimes out of the criminal justice system. Social service organizations and alternatives to imprisonment are well funded, utilizing the same funds that, in poorer communities, are dedicated to policing. A less inflammatory way of explaining the movement might therefore be to suggest that investment in alternative methods of addressing problematic behavior should be increased and that investment in police should be decreased, unless it can be shown that further investment in policing is needed or effective. The effort to keep young offenders out of the criminal justice system is important to long-term crime rates, because studies have shown that incarceration limits opportunities for rehabilitation and recovery and thus increases the likelihood of further involvement in crime.[3]

The fact that incarceration is not effective at reducing recidivism is well known, and the data on the issue overwhelmingly shows that incarceration increases crime rates over the longer term. In affluent communities with abundant resources, criminal justice systems have been shaped by research from social science proving that alternatives to incarceration are more effective. Police and courts in these communities therefore support initiatives meant to reduce reliance on aggressive police interventions, arrests, convictions, and imprisonment, and instead invest heavily in more effective alternatives. The idea behind Defund the Police is that the entire criminal justice system should function in this way and that the use of police intervention should be a last resort, rather than the primary method for dealing with any disturbance or legally problematic behavior.

Critics of Defund the Police have argued that reformers should, instead, focus on emphasizing more traditional paths toward reform that would not require extensive reductions in police funding. Some critics of the movement have focused on critiquing the "Defund the Police" slogan, arguing that the slogan is unnecessarily polarizing and too easy to misinterpret. There are some, even among supporters of police reform, who have argued that the movement should adopt new terminology to make the ultimate goals of the movement clearer to the public and to critics. Some of those who criticize the movement demonstrate that they do not understand the movement, arguing, for instance, against eliminating policing, which is not what most supporters of the movement are suggesting. Others have argued that defunding police will lead to an increase in crime, but there is little data to suggest that this is necessarily the case. Less than half of violent crimes are ever solved by police, and police recover property in only 18 percent of cases involving theft and other property crimes. Some critics argue that the current system of policing does not appear to be effective and that there may be little risk in dramatically reallocating funding in an effort to find solutions that are more effective.[4] One of the reasons that police have limited success in combating crime is because of a lack of community support and trust. Research indicates that significantly less than half of violent crimes are even reported to police. In part, this is because members of many communities have little faith that police will improve their situation or will be effective in aiding their recovery.

Some of the resistance to the Defund the Police movement has come from police officers or administrators, who have criticized supporters for discounting the effective work done by police officers around the country and for focusing on the problems associated with a few "bad police." Police administrators and officers may also be reacting to their personal perceptions of being attacked or criticized, or out of concern for their careers. While it is true that police around the country perform admirably and effectively help citizens, well-performing officers are not the intended targets of the reform movement. Rather, supporters of Defund the Police argue that restructuring police funding might help address persistent structural problems in policing and might also be used to provide support for police officers as well, helping to lower stress levels and to improve community relations.

One of the reasons that the current environment surrounding police reform has become so contentious is because police reform methods have been ongoing for years, without sufficient progress. Reform methods often fail because police administrations and political groups resist enacting significant changes to policies or refuse to adopt suggested changes. Police, like members of any group, are sometimes vulnerable to tribalism, defending, excusing, or deemphasizing problems within their own departments out of loyalty to one another. Investigations have found that police officers in many cases face extensive pressure to avoid reporting problems or misbehavior, and investigations have found that officers who do report misconduct may face ostracism or punishment from other officers or administrators.[5]

One of the goals for supporters of police reform is to challenge the perception that police need to remain loyal to one another above their loyalty to the communities and individuals they are sworn to serve and protect. More extreme calls for dramatic reforms, like the Defund the Police movement, are likely to become more common if reformers believe that police are intransigent in their resistance to change and if they believe that police departments cannot be trusted to be transparent with the public. For those who support more moderate reform measures, it is important that the efficacy of these methods can be proven and that members of the public can be convinced that milder reform efforts can improve the current system sufficiently. Those who oppose reform must reckon with the fact that many of the problems facing police departments in America, including lack of funding, problems with recruitment, and the danger of violence directed at police, are in part the result of police having lost the trust and support of the American public. To ensure the future of the American police system, and to ensure that those working as police are treated fairly, are able to perform their jobs safely, and receive the emotional, social, and professional support they need, reform is not an option, but an inevitable necessity.

Works Used

Al-Gharbi, Musa. "Police Punish the 'Good Apples.'" *The Atlantic*. Jul 1, 2020. https://www.theatlantic.com/ideas/archive/2020/07/what-police-departments-do-whistle-blowers/613687/.

Dixon, Emily. "Alexandria Ocasio-Cortez Was Asked About Defunding the Police and Her Answer Went Viral." *Marie Claire*. Jun 12, 2020. https://www.marieclaire.com/politics/a32849383/alexandria-ocasio-cortez-defund-the-police/.

Mark, Michelle. "US Police Don't End Up Solving Most Crimes." *Business Insider*. Jun 18, 2020. https://www.insider.com/police-dont-solve-most-violent-property-crimes-data-2020-6.

Price, Megan, and Jamie Price. "Insights Policing and the Role of the Civilian in Police Accountability." *Clearinghouse Review*. August 2015. https://www.insight-conflictresolution.org/uploads/1/5/5/0/15508726/insight_policing_police_accountability_price_2.pdf.

Ray, Rashawn. "What Does 'Defund the Police' Mean and Does It Have Merit?" *Brookings*. Jun 19, 2020. https://www.brookings.edu/blog/fixgov/2020/06/19/what-does-defund-the-police-mean-and-does-it-have-merit/.

Sangree, Ruth. "Breaking the Cycle of Mass Incarceration." *Brennan Center*. Jan 3, 2020. https://www.brennancenter.org/our-work/analysis-opinion/breaking-cycle-mass-incarceration.

Notes

1. Ray, "What Does 'Defund the Police' Mean and Does It Have Merit?"
2. Dixon, "Alexandria Ocasio-Cortez Was Asked About Defunding the Police and Her Answer Went Viral."
3. Sangree, "Breaking the Cycle of Mass Incarceration."
4. Mark, "US Police Don't End Up Solving Most Crimes."
5. Al-Gharbi, "Police Punish the 'Good Apples.'"

"Perfect Storm": Defund the Police, COVID-19 Lead to Biggest Police Budget Cuts in Decade

By Kevin Johnson and Kristine Phillips
USA Today, July 31, 2020

Facing the dual forces of the coronavirus pandemic and the national movement to "defund the police," law enforcement agencies across the country are bracing for budget reductions not seen in more than a decade.

Nearly half of 258 agencies surveyed this month are reporting that funding has already been slashed or is expected to be reduced, according to a report slated for release this week by the Police Executive Research Forum, a non-partisan research organization.

Much of the funding is being pulled from equipment, hiring and training accounts, even as a number of cities also are tracking abrupt spikes in violent crime, the report concluded.

Few agencies, regardless of size, are being spared. Deep reductions have been ordered or proposed in Los Angeles, New York, Seattle, Baltimore County, Maryland, Tempe, Arizona, and Eureka, California.

Chuck Wexler, executive director of the D.C.-based think tank that authored the report, said police operations have not confronted such a threat since the financial crisis of 2008, when operations and force numbers were cut dramatically to account for the steep decline in available public funds.

"Unfortunately, the situation this time is only certain to get worse because of the pandemic's resurgence and the convergence of the defund police movement," Wexler said. "It's a combustible mixture for police departments, because reform is often achieved by hiring a next generation of officers and acquiring new technology that can assist their work. The unintended consequence of these times is that those reforms will now be held back."

But Scott Roberts, senior director for criminal justice campaigns for the civil rights advocacy group Color of Change, said law enforcement has been "the most out of touch" in recognizing a need for new policing policy.

"The lack of imagination in public safety has only led to continuing down the same path to investing in more law enforcement," Roberts said. "This call for defunding police is not just about taking money from policing, it's about making the investments we need to make in things like health care, including mental illness."

The first shock waves rippled through law enforcement this month when New York municipal officials slashed $1 billion from the largest police force in the country with an operating budget of about $6 billion. The cut effectively canceled a 1,200-person police recruiting class, curtailed overtime spending and shifted school safety deployments and homeless outreach away from the NYPD.

In Minneapolis, where the de-fund movement began following the May 25 death of George Floyd at the hands of police, the fate of the local force remains in doubt. Los Angeles has cut its police budget by $150 million, while Seattle has proposed a 50% reduction to a department that has struggled to contain protests that erupted following Floyd's death.

"There are a lot of pressures dragging down and threatening levels of public safety," Los Angeles Police Chief Michel Moore said. "It's really a perfect storm."

"A Recruiting, Retention Crisis"

Even smaller cities facing less pressure from the social justice movement have not been able to escape an unfolding financial crisis driven by the COVID-19 pandemic.

In Steamboat Springs, a ski-resort town in northwest Colorado largely supported by tourism-driven sales tax dollars, the police department is cutting its budget by 28% or nearly $1.5 million. It means that vacant positions will go unfilled and civilian employees are taking a 10% pay cut, Police Chief Cory Christensen said.

The police department's training and recruiting budgets already have been zeroed out.

"At a time when we're talking police reform and how to make police departments better, one of the strategies is having training. But not having funding for that, we will fall behind in making sure we're up to par with best practices," Christensen said, adding that the department has yet to meet state-mandated training hours.

Christensen was able to hire a few officers in the last three years, but the police force has barely kept pace with the town's growing population—up from 3,000 to 13,000 in

> **More police agencies planned cuts to training, hiring, and technology acquisition this year than during the last economic crisis.**

the last two decades. The police department now has 44 employees, a slight increase over the past 20 years.

At the same time, calls for service are up 23% from last year, the busiest year in Christensen's memory.

"I don't know yet whether I'm going to have to lay off police officers," he said. "I don't have enough police officers as it is to do emergency calls," he said. "Our cuts are going to mean we're going to plow the streets less, water the grass less. We're going to police with less. It's a challenge."

In Eureka, a Northern California town of nearly 27,000 where sales taxes are also the primary source of revenue, the pandemic is responsible for doubling an already projected deficit for the next budget year, Police Chief Steve Watson said.

The police department is cutting its budget by 8%, or nearly $1.2 million. That means losing six positions through a combination of early retirement incentives, resignations and allowing vacant positions to go unfilled, Watson said. The agency currently has about 50 employees, a staffing level that already struggles to keep up with the workload.

"We are already in a recruiting and retention crisis that's been going on for years. I can foresee it's going to get far worse," Watson said.

"It Could Take Years to Recover"

Law enforcement has been at the center of financial and social justice crises in the past, but there is a reason why Wexler and his group believe this storm is different.

Comparing the think tank's 2020 survey—conducted just five months into the pandemic—with similar 2008 research, a year into that recession, the group found that more police agencies planned cuts to training, hiring and technology acquisitions this year than during the last economic crisis.

"If we're just comparing to 2008, the cuts this time could be significantly deeper and it could take years to recover," Wexler said, adding that the social justice movement has yet to take full effect in some communities where local leaders are entirely reassessing public safety operations.

Regardless of the new pressures, Ed Davis, a former police commissioner in Boston who helped oversee the Boston Marathon bombing investigation, cautioned his former colleagues not to sacrifice training to balance a budget.

When forced to decide between training and deploying officers to local neighborhoods, Davis said chiefs often choose the latter.

"Then police don't have the skills they need to do what needs to be done properly, and then something bad happens and everybody wonders why something bad happens," Davis said.

Of the campaign to defund police, Davis called the movement "ill-advised."

"I understand that people are angry. We really have to deal with the kind of system that led to Officer Chauvin being on the police department," Davis said, referring to former Minneapolis police officer Derek Chauvin, now charged with second-degree murder in George Floyd's death. "The problem is if you remove police from the street in large numbers, the very people that have been victimized by racial inequality are going to be the ones suffering the most."

"A Sea Change" in Los Angeles

For the first time in five years, and largely propelled by the recent budget cuts, the police force in Los Angeles will fall below 10,000 officers. Chief Moore said the department had struggled for years to keep its numbers up, and breaking the 10,000-officer mark had been a source of internal pride.

The $150 million moved from the police budget this year, however, will require accepting more than a smaller number. Moore calls it "a new normal."

"We're not just talking about holding on for a few months," Moore said. "There is no immediate exit door from the pandemic. It's likely to go on for some time. With the addition of the social justice movement, there is even more pressure to articulate a path forward that is thoughtful, understanding the challenge before us."

The challenge, Moore said, is "turning the crisis into an opportunity."

Adjusting to the new normal is forcing local leaders to reassess the police department's resource-draining obligation to respond to calls involving people who are mentally ill.

At least one-third of the department's calls for service, Moore said, involve people who are mentally ill or emotionally disturbed. Los Angeles is one of hundreds of police departments struggling to find more meaningful and efficient ways to respond to such calls.

The city also is considering shifting its response to local traffic collisions—about 70,000 last year—to another entity.

"Those calls can tie up officers for hours, and it usually results in reports written for the benefit of insurance companies," Moore said.

Another problem thrown into this year's complicated mix: homicides have been ticking up. There have been 169 murders so far this year, compared to 153 at same time last year in the city. The numbers have prompted Moore to reach out to federal authorities for assistance in gun violence investigations.

"You have to remember, this is a people business; this is not a factory where we make widgets," Moore said. "Where we can shift responsibilities, we will do that. This is a significant sea change for us."

In Seattle, Police Chief Carmen Best said a city council proposal for a 50% cut to the force lacks any plan for how or who would be left to respond to the 800,000 calls for service each year.

"I haven't seen a plan, and I have to deal with legitimate calls for service," Best said. "It's a detriment to public safety; it's reckless and dangerous."

Print Citations

CMS: Johnson, Kevin, and Kristine Phillips. "'Perfect Storm': Defund the Police, COVID-19 Lead to Biggest Police Budget Cuts in Decade." In *The Reference Shelf: Policing in 2020*, edited by Micah L. Issitt, 137-140. Amenia, NY: Grey House Publishing, 2021.

MLA: Johnson, Kevin, and Kristine Phillips. "'Perfect Storm': Defund the Police, COVID-19 Lead to Biggest Police Budget Cuts in Decade." *The Reference Shelf: Policing in 2020*, edited by Micah L. Issitt, Grey Housing Publishing, 2021, pp. 137-140.

APA: Johnson, K., & Phillips, K. (2021). "Perfect storm": Defund the police, COVID-19 lead to biggest police budget cuts in decade. In Micah L. Issitt (Ed.), *The reference shelf: Policing in 2020* (pp. 137-140). Amenia, NY: Grey Housing Publishing.

Los Angeles Cuts LAPD Spending, Taking Police Staffing to Its Lowest Level in 12 Years

By David Zahniser, Dakota Smith, Emily Alpert Reyes
Los Angeles Times, July 1, 2020

The Los Angeles City Council voted Wednesday to cut hiring at the Police Department, pushing the number of sworn officers well below 10,000 and abandoning a budget priority once seen as untouchable by city leaders.

Faced with a grim budget outlook and deluged by demands for reductions in police spending, the council voted 12 to 2 to take the Los Angeles Police Department down to 9,757 officers by next summer—a level of staffing not seen in the city since 2008.

Overall, the council's decision delivered a $150-million hit to the LAPD budget, much of it coming from funds earmarked for police overtime pay. Councilman Curren Price, who pushed for the cuts, said two-thirds of the savings would ultimately be funneled into services for Black, Latino and disenfranchised communities, such as hiring programs and summer youth jobs.

"This is a step forward, supporting minority communities in ways in which they deserve—with respect, dignity and an even playing field," said Price, the only Black member on the council's budget committee.

Councilmen Joe Buscaino and John Lee cast the two opposing votes. Buscaino said afterward that the city should have approved more money for a community policing program, not "a reactive, feel-good budget cut."

Wednesday's actions showed just how much spending policies and views on public safety have shifted at City Hall following mass protests over police brutality. As recently as April, Mayor Eric Garcetti had been pushing for a 7% increase to the LAPD budget, a move he no longer favors.

Reaching and maintaining a 10,000-officer force had been a longtime priority for city leaders. Mayor Antonio Villaraigosa celebrated in 2013 when the LAPD reached that number for the first time. That year, while running for mayor, Garcetti vowed to preserve that staffing level.

The LAPD currently has a sworn deployment of roughly 10,000 officers, according to a recent report by city budget analysts.

The council's decision on Wednesday will allow the LAPD to hire only half the number of officers needed to replace those who resign or retire in the coming year.

The $150-million cut to the LAPD fell far short of demands from Black Lives Matter-Los Angeles and its allies, who had pushed for a "People's Budget" that would effectively eliminate police spending and redirect the savings to housing, mental health services and other needs.

"That is literally pocket change," said Rebecca Kessler, a resident of Van Nuys who called in to the council this week. "It's a slap in the face. You need to defund the police, take way more money, put way more money into these programs."

LAPD spokesman Josh Rubenstein said Wednesday that the department is still reviewing the impact of the approved cuts.

The city spends roughly $3 billion annually on the LAPD, once pensions and other expenses are included. In recent months, progressive activists have called on city leaders to slash that funding and redirect the proceeds to other needs, demanding cuts ranging from 90% to outright abolition of the LAPD.

In response, council members have begun exploring ways of diverting many calls for help—those that involve nonviolent incidents—away from the LAPD and to other city workers. Council members voted this week to direct city staffers to come up with an "unarmed model of crisis response" for further review.

Melina Abdullah, co-founder of Black Lives Matter-Los Angeles praised that step. "Rolling back police functions has the potential to have a far greater impact on advancing the call to defund the police than approving a meager cut of $150 million," she said.

Others questioned whether the LAPD cuts would harm neighborhoods.

Ray Rios, president of the Hillside Village Property Owners Assn. in El Sereno, said his community has been experiencing a spate of car break-ins and illegal fireworks. City leaders should address demands for change at the LAPD by focusing on reforms, not reducing the size of the force, he said.

"Without any enforcement, [crime] is going to get worse," Rios said. "The big question is, who's going to keep order?"

While activists repeatedly delivered the message "defund the police," council members focused much of their deliberations on the city's financial woes. Tax revenues have fallen dramatically below projections since the coronavirus outbreak and the shutdown of an array of businesses.

The city's budget analysts have repeatedly warned that the city could find itself short by $45 million to $409 million. And in recent days they began sounding new alarms about the resurgence in coronavirus cases across Los Angeles County, and what that could mean for city finances.

On Tuesday, council members quickly passed a plan for pushing as many as 2,850 civilian city employees into retirement, by offering them buyout packages of up to $80,000. Employees may begin applying for those payments next week.

If everyone eligible for the retirement program takes part, the city would save $58.7 million this year and an additional $125 million in 2021-22, said City Administrative Officer Rich Llewellyn, the high-level budget analyst.

Both the LAPD cuts and the employee retirement initiative were also billed as ways to delay another budget-cutting measure: putting nearly

City leaders should address demands for change at the LAPD by focusing on reforms, not reducing the size of the force.

16,000 city workers on furloughs. The furloughs, which were proposed by Garcetti but opposed by city employee unions, would have forced civilian city workers to take one out of every 10 days off, cutting salaries by 10%.

Some of this week's decisions by the council could saddle the city with hefty costs in the future.

Of the $150 million in cuts to the LAPD, about $97 million would come from cuts to overtime pay for police officers. Council members and the city's policy analysts cautioned that at least a portion of those overtime hours could still end up being worked by the LAPD, particularly if the city experiences a major emergency.

In those instances, the LAPD could "bank" that overtime, letting officers work the extra hours but delaying payment until a future year, allowing officers to be paid for those hours at higher salaries.

The plan to cut the civilian city workforce could also come with a delayed cost. If every eligible employee takes part in the program, the city will need to spend $28.5 million on buyout packages this year—$10,000 per worker, according to Llewellyn, the budget analyst.

The city would need to spend an additional $128.5 million on those payments the following year, he said.

Llewellyn called the program a "financial winner for the city," but also acknowledged that the mass departure of thousands of city workers would result in a reduction in taxpayer services. To achieve major savings, he said, the city should replace only a small fraction of the positions that become vacant.

"Most of these choices are not choices that any of us would have made in a normal circumstance," said Councilman Paul Krekorian, who heads the budget committee. "But we're not living in a normal circumstance."

Krekorian also said $40 million of the money cut from the LAPD budget will be set aside as an "insurance policy" to help pay for city services if the retirement program does not generate enough savings. Another $90 million will go into a reserve account titled Preservation of City Services, Reinvestment in Disadvantaged Communities and Communities of Color and Reimagining Public Safety Service Delivery.

Craig Lally, president of the Los Angeles Police Protective League, the union that represents LAPD officers, described that account as a "slush fund." He warned that the planned reduction in police officers would result in slower response times.

Over the next 12 months, officers who do end up working overtime won't be paid until years into the future, and at more expensive rates, Lally said.

"They passed a budget by putting everything on the city credit card," he added.

Print Citations

CMS: Zahniser, David, Dakota Smith, and Emily Alpert Reyes. "Los Angeles Cuts LAPD Spending, Taking Police Staffing to Its Lowest Level in 12 Years." In *The Reference Shelf: Policing in 2020,* edited by Micah L. Issitt, 141-144. Amenia, NY: Grey House Publishing, 2021.

MLA: Zahniser, David, Dakota Smith, and Emily Alpert Reyes. "Los Angeles Cuts LAPD Spending, Taking Police Staffing to Its Lowest Level in 12 Years." *The Reference Shelf: Policing in 2020,* edited by Micah L. Issitt, Grey Housing Publishing, 2021, pp. 141-144.

APA: Zahniser, D., Smith, D., & Reyes, E.A. (2021). Los Angeles cuts LAPD spending, taking police staffing to its lowest level in 12 years. In Micah L. Issitt (Ed.), *The reference shelf: Policing in 2020* (pp. 141-144). Amenia, NY: Grey Housing Publishing.

What Exactly Does It Mean to Defund the Police?

By Amanda Arnold
The Cut, June 12, 2020

As thousands of protesters across the country have gathered to demand justice for George Floyd, Breonna Taylor, and other black people killed by the police, a related rallying cry has gained momentum: defund the police. It's an idea that's been popular among activists and critics of the criminal-justice system for decades. In the past two weeks, though, it's gained unprecedented support—and national media attention. Proponents of defunding argue that incremental police reform has failed. A better solution, they argue, would be to more effectively address underlying factors that contribute to crime, like poverty and homelessness; this would be achieved by cutting police forces' often-astronomical budgets on a city level and reallocating those funds toward social services, such as housing and youth services.

Some critics have dismissed defunding the police as a left-wing fantasy, but the concept is quickly gaining mainstream recognition. Perhaps most notably: On June 7, the City Council of Minneapolis announced its intent to disband the city's police department with a vetoproof majority and replace it with "a holistic model of public safety that actually keeps us safe."

So what now? How, exactly, does a city defund the police? Has it ever been done before? Can it be done? Below, here's everything to know about the demand.

What Does It Mean to Defund the Police?

Defunding the police does not necessarily mean getting rid of the police altogether. Rather, it would mean reducing police budgets and reallocating those funds to crucial and oft-neglected areas like education, public health, housing, and youth services. (Some activists want to abolish the police altogether; defunding is a separate but connected cause.) It's predicated on the belief that investing in communities would act as a better deterrent to crime by directly addressing societal problems like poverty, mental illness, and homelessness—issues that advocates say police are poorly equipped to handle, and yet are often tasked with. According to some estimates, law enforcement spends 21 percent of its time responding to and transporting people with mental illnesses. Police are also frequently dispatched to deal with people experiencing homelessness, causing them to be incarcerated at a disproportionate rate.

Even some cops resent society's overreliance on them. "We're just asking us to do too much," said former Dallas police chief David Brown in a 2016 interview. "Every societal failure, we put it off for the cops to solve. That's too much to ask. Policing was never meant to solve all those problems." And the outcome can be deadly: In 2015, the *Washington Post* found that one in four people killed by a police officer suffered from a serious mental illness at the time of their death.

Advocates argue this could be avoided by replacing some police officers with trained social workers or specialized response teams. "Municipalities can begin by changing policies or statutes so police officers never respond to certain kinds of emergencies, including ones that involve substance abuse, domestic violence, homelessness or mental health," Philip V. McHarris and Thenjiwe McHarris argue in an op-ed for the *New York Times*. "So if someone calls 911 to report a drug overdose, health care teams rush to the scene; the police wouldn't get involved. If a person calls 911 to complain about people who are homeless, rapid response social workers would provide them with housing support and other resources. Conflict interrupters and restorative justice teams could mediate situations where no one's safety is being threatened."

The amount of money the United States spends on policing is staggering: According to a recent analysis, the sum is $115 billion, which is bigger than nearly every other country's military budget. In most cities, the police budget dwarfs those for education, housing, and other crucial services. For example, Los Angeles's proposed police budget for 2021 is $1.8 billion—more than half of the city's total spending for the year. New York City's annual police budget is a whopping $6 billion, which is more than the city spends on health, homeless services, youth development, and workforce development combined. Defunding proposals would reallocate a fraction of that—for instance, activists and City Council candidates in New York City have proposed cutting the NYPD budget by $1 billion over the next four years.

But Wouldn't Crime Increase without Police?

One of the main arguments raised by those who oppose defunding: "What will we do about crime if police forces are made to scale back?" Advocates counter that investing in communities and providing them with resources will reduce crime on its own—for example, a 2016 report from the Obama White House's Council of Economic Advisers found that "a 10 percent increase in wages for non-college educated men results in approximately a 10 to 20 percent reduction in crime rates."

But on top of that, those in favor of defunding also point out that police departments across the country consistently have low rates of solving crimes, even as their budgets have increased threefold in the past 40 years. In 2019, for instance, Minneapolis police only cleared 56 percent of cases in which a person was killed. That same year, Baltimore recorded at least 347 homicides, a record-breaking level of violence, but ended the year with a 32 percent clearance rate for homicides; in 2015, the rate was 56 percent. Across the country, rape cases result in a notoriously low number of charges: In 2017, police closed just 32 percent of rape cases, and hundreds of thousands of rape kits have sat untested in police storage for years. According to an FBI database, about 30 percent of robberies and less than 15 percent of burglaries and motor-vehicle thefts result in arrests.

When police investigate a crime involving a black victim, evidence shows that the clearance rate drops significantly: A 2014 *New York Daily News* investigation found that police solved about 86 percent of homicides when the victim was white. When the victim was black, the clearance rate dropped to 45 percent.

Meanwhile, police in the U.S. are killing far more people than law enforcement in other developed countries like the U.K., Japan, and Germany. In the first 24 days of 2015, U.S. police shot and killed more people than police in England and Wales had in the past *24 years*. According to the *Washington Post*, since 2015, police have fatally shot approximately 1,000 people a year, and the rate that police kill black people is more than twice the rate of white people. (Each year, about 50 police officers are shot and killed on the job.)

Why Not Just Reform Police Departments?

Though many politicians argue for reforming police departments using common-sense solutions like installing civilian review boards and banning "warrior style" training, which instructs officers to view all encounters as dangerous and to prioritize their own safety, advocates argue that incremental reform has failed to combat police violence in any meaningful way. After a white officer shot and killed Michael Brown in Ferguson in 2014, for instance, there was a nationwide push for officers to wear body cameras, which advocates predicted would improve police accountability. It has not been successful. An extensive study of more than 2,000 police officers, published in 2017, found that the body cameras had almost zero effect on deterring officers from acting with unnecessary force; and, as evidenced by the recent police shooting of David McAtee, officers can simply turn off their cameras. Another example: The

> **Many politicians argue for reforming police departments using commonsense solutions like installing civilian review boards and banning "warrior style" training.**

NYPD banned choke holds more than two decades ago, which didn't stop Officer Daniel Pantaleo from holding Eric Garner in one until he stopped breathing.

Another reason reforms haven't been tenable, advocates say, is police unions. The purpose of police unions is "to win members better salaries and benefits and to protect their job security—specifically by pushing for safeguards against investigation, discipline, and dismissal," Daniel DiSalvo, a political-science professor at the City College of New York, writes in the *Washington Post*. "These protections can make it difficult for police chiefs to manage their forces effectively and can allow a few bad officers to act with impunity, poisoning an entire organizational culture in the process." As *BuzzFeed News* notes, police collective-bargaining agreements protect even the most violent officers from oversight groups like civilian review boards and police internal-affairs departments, making it nearly impossible to punish officers for serious wrongdoing. While Minneapolis mayor Jacob Frey banned warrior training, the Minneapolis police union has openly defied the ban, and now offers the "fear-based" training—valued at $55,000—to any officer who wants it, for free.

Police unions, which wield great political power, also push back against criminal-justice reform that would promote transparency and accountability. Amid the protests, pressure has mounted within unions that represent police officers—notably, the AFL-CIO—to expel all police affiliates; many of those putting pressure on the unions also support defunding.

Is Defunding Actually Possible?

Another issue advocates of defunding face: Police forces wield an immense amount of power and influence, and, historically, the data shows that many Americans find them trustworthy. As Eric Levitz notes on *Intelligencer*, "There are only three institutions that perennially command a 'great deal' or 'quite a lot' of confidence from Americans in Gallup's polling: the military, small business, and the police." In a Gallup poll from 2018, 54 percent of Americans expressed a "great deal" or "quite a lot" of confidence in the police. (However, a recent Data for Progress report with a similar sample size found that public trust in the institution has fallen amid the ongoing protests against police brutality: Of the 1,352 people surveyed, 37 percent said they are less likely to trust cops.) By supporting the effort to defund police, a prevailing argument goes, elected officials could risk alienating a significant portion of their constituents.

While the call to defund the police has certainly gained momentum, a new *ABC News*–Ipsos poll indicates that many aren't convinced: Out of a random national sample of 686 adults, 64 percent said they oppose the movement, while 34 percent said they support such a move. Among black Americans, support nearly doubled: Fifty-seven percent said they support defunding.

And although a handful of elected officials around the country have vocalized their support of defunding the police—including representative Alexandria Ocasio-Cortez, who said she's actively advocating for a "reduction of our NYPD budget"—most politicians are loath to support the measure. Joe Biden's spokesperson recently said the presidential candidate "supports the urgent need for reform ... so that officers can focus on the job of policing," but not defunding. Even Bernie Sanders does not believe defunding is the answer; instead, he thinks departments should better educate, train, and pay officers.

But this is a change that would take place on a citywide level, not a national one, and some mayors are already heeding their constituents' demands to reconsider how much money they spend on policing. In total, *CityLab* reports, lawmakers in at least 17 U.S. cities—including Minneapolis, Los Angeles, and New York City—have put forward proposals or pledges to divest from the police. Meanwhile, school boards in Minneapolis and Denver have voted to terminate their contracts with local police departments, and a growing list of other cities are similarly considering removing police from their schools.

As of now, the Minneapolis City Council has not released any specifics regarding its approach to defunding the city's $193.3 million police budget, though some members have offered general ideas. "We can invest in cultural competency and mental health training, de-escalation and conflict resolution … We can resolve confusion over a $20 grocery transaction without drawing a weapon or pulling out handcuffs," wrote Councilman Steve Fletcher in an op-ed for *Time*. "The whole world is watching. We can declare policing as we know it a thing of the past, and create a compassionate, non-violent future."

Print Citations

CMS: Arnold, Amanda. "What Exactly Does It Mean to Defund the Police?" In *The Reference Shelf: Policing in 2020,* edited by Micah L. Issitt, 145-149. Amenia, NY: Grey House Publishing, 2021.

MLA: Arnold, Amanda. "What Exactly Does It Mean to Defund the Police?" *The Reference Shelf: Policing in 2020,* edited by Micah L. Issitt, Grey Housing Publishing, 2021, pp. 145-149.

APA: Arnold, A. (2021). What exactly does it mean to defund the police? In Micah L. Issitt (Ed.), *The reference shelf: Policing in 2020* (pp. 145-149). Amenia, NY: Grey Housing Publishing.

The Defunding Debate

By Jack Herrera

Columbia Journalism Review, **Summer 2020**

Prior to May 25—the day Derek Chauvin, a white police officer, killed George Floyd, a Black man, while three other cops looked on—"Defund the Police" was not a message widely repeated in the press. But after that day, it was impossible to ignore. Protesters across the country were painting it onto cardboard signs and boarded-up windows. In march after march, the phrase could be heard in chants and shouts. Reporting from a protest in Oakland, I saw the words scribbled in Sharpie across a skateboard.

By June, "Defund the Police" had spawned an entire genre of coverage. "Defund the police? Here's what that really means," a headline in the *Washington Post* read. "There's a growing call to defund the police. Here's what it means," offered CNN. *The Guardian* asked, "What does 'Defund the Police' mean?" posing the same question that would appear three days later in *New York* magazine as "What Could 'Defund the Police' Mean in Practice?" Similar pieces ran in the *New York Times*, NPR, the *Miami Herald, Esquire*, the *Christian Science Monitor*, MTV.com, *Rolling Stone*, and dozens of other outlets.

By their titles, these explainers may have appeared almost all the same, but in fact they varied dramatically. Journalists discussed "Defund the Police" as a slogan ripe for interpretation. "It's become something of a semantic argument about what that means, exactly," Willie Geist, an MSNBC anchor, told viewers. For some, it was simply a strong call for reform—more body cameras, no choke holds. For others, it was a rallying cry for revolution, including a complete abolition of police departments. A reader could be forgiven for finding the resources hard to parse. Soon, an awkward reality set in: many journalists were trying to explain a concept with which they had little familiarity. As the clumsy reporting continued, arguments over the "real" definition of "Defund the Police" became a battleground, leading to another round of pieces—in *The Atlantic*, the *New Republic*, *The Hill*, and other publications—that provided frustrated-tone correctives on how the media had gotten the protesters' demand wrong.

There was another category of coverage, too, one that performed the maneuver of a matador with a muleta: pieces that simply stepped away from the charging beast of the debate. Instead of actually engaging with any of the demands to defund the police, a large portion of the political press instead focused on the phrase itself and how it would play in the 2020 presidential election. "Is 'Defund the Police' a massive political mistake?" CNN's Chris Cillizza asked, wondering aloud if the broadsides against cops could hurt Democrats trying to pick up middle-of-the-road voters. Like much of the coverage on cable news and in national newspapers, Cillizza's analysis didn't bother to weigh the value—or even the basic details—of police abolition policy, but rather considered how it might affect the chances of Joe Biden, a centrist, as President Donald Trump busied himself painting a picture of a far-left radical. Would the mere existence of the term "Defund the Police" tar Biden as a revolutionary? "The political problem for Democrats is this: They are now being backed into a corner by activists who are demanding radical change," Cillizza wrote. Others chimed in. "Defunding police will lead to Republican victory this year," according to a piece in *The Hill*. Eddie S. Glaude Jr., a professor of African-American studies at Princeton, suggested on MSNBC that Biden "might want to distance himself from the slogan, but he shouldn't distance himself from the substance of the policy."

A couple of months ago, it would have seemed strange, even ridiculous, if a debate moderator had asked the lineup of 2020 Democratic hopefuls, "Do you support defunding police nationwide?" The question of taking money away from cops did not register on the radar of candidates or campaign reporters. Now, suddenly, it had exploded as a central campaign plot point. Journalists asked Biden, his cast of vice-presidential hopefuls, and most other prominent Democrats to offer their views on taking money away from police. The Biden campaign placed op-eds in the *Los Angeles Times* and *USA Today* declaring his allegiance to police departments; he also said as much in an interview on the *CBS Evening News with Norah O'Donnell*. Nancy Pelosi, the Speaker of the House; Jim Clyburn, the House whip; and Sen. Bernie Sanders also came out strongly in opposition to defunding the police.

Alex Vitale, whose book *The End of Policing* was published in 2017, watched with some disappointment as the defunding-as-election-hurdle narrative unfolded. "Now all people are interested in is its relationship to national politics," he told me. "And then the voices that they bring in are people who are a part of *that* world, and who are not a part of the movement, and who have often spent years working *against* it." Defunding the police was never a mainstream Democratic idea, after all. Demands to defund and abolish the police have existed for decades, but in the kinds of places journalists and presidential contenders rarely go and even more rarely come from: overpoliced neighborhoods, underserved Black communities, and Black feminist spaces.

The underinformed takes raged on. Cameras pivoted away from the masses filling the streets and scanned back to the marble halls of the US Capitol: *Here, now, the Democrats are kneeling in honor of George Floyd and—for some ineffable reason—wearing kente cloth; now watch as Kamala Harris, VP hopeful, debates "Defund the Police" with Meghan McCain on* The View. Covering the 2020 presidential election has been no easy task, to be sure; the pandemic turned the standard horse race into a frantic trek across an unfamiliar wilderness. Still, the way political coverage has engaged with the country's anti-racist uprising has often felt inadequate, even hackish, especially when it has assumed that calls to ban police departments must be novel, and can't be literal. ("A three-word slogan is not a detailed policy agenda," Matthew Yglesias wrote, for *Vox.*) "The news media is acting like abolition is a new idea," Samah Sisay, a lawyer and activist, told me. "'Defund the Police' already existed as an abolitionist demand. But it's not being framed that way."

According to Alisa Bierria, a Black feminist philosopher and assistant professor of ethnic studies at the University of California, Riverside, there are two ways to think about the movement that has led to "Defund the Police." One is to look at recent community organizing; the other is to reach back to Angela Davis and other Black feminist radicals of the 1970s. "There's a way in which abolitionist work that's coming from radical Black feminism and radical queer politics gets submerged," Bierria said. "When people see something on a sign at a protest, or see something as a hashtag on Twitter, it's hard for them to understand that it's connected to this broader trajectory and legacy."

In 1971, Davis wrote an essay from inside the Marin County Jail, north of the Golden Gate Bridge. At twenty-seven, she already had a remarkable biography. In 1963, a Ku Klux Klan church bombing had killed four young girls in her hometown of Birmingham, Alabama; two of the victims had been her friends. Within several years, Davis joined the Black Panthers and got fired from a professorship for her communist views; now she was jailed on a dubious charge connecting her to an armed takeover of a courtroom. In her cell, Davis contemplated the role of the police—those who had imprisoned her, and those who had not indicted the Klansmen who killed the girls in Birmingham. "The announced function of the police, 'to protect and serve the people,'" she wrote, "becomes the grotesque caricature of protecting and preserving the interests of our oppressors and serving us nothing but injustice."

In 1997, Davis—along with Ruth Wilson Gilmore and other Black feminists and activists—formed Critical Resistance, a group dedicated to the abolition of police departments and jails, known collectively as the prison-industrial complex. Three years later, a network of feminists of color, joined by the name INCITE!, organized a conference called "The Color of Violence"; Davis was the keynote speaker. Now seventy-six, she has been enshrined by leftists as a luminary; lately, she's been in demand to appear before wider audiences. "Of course, when many of us began to talk about abolishing these institutions, back in the seventies, we were treated as if we were absolutely out of our minds," she told WBUR. Today, she added, "I see myself as witnessing this moment for all of those who lost their lives in the struggle over the decades."

Her comments reflect just how much things have changed in her lifetime. In recent years, the modern abolition movement has grown steadily, as police brutality has been captured more and more on camera and many Americans, especially in majority-Black neighborhoods, have become disillusioned by failed attempts at reform. In 2012, in Florida, a seventeen-year-old Black teenager named Trayvon Martin was shot and killed by George Zimmerman, who was the neighborhood-watch coordinator for a gated community; Zimmerman was acquitted of all charges. In response to the murder, a group of college-age Black, Latinx, and Arab people formed the Dream Defenders, an organization "serious about fighting for a world without prisons and police." In 2013, the Dream

> **The idea of dismantling police departments was to be judged as a set of outlines, not as the result of deep frustration that's built up in the places reporters too frequently ignore. They still didn't get it.**

Defenders staged a thirty-one-day takeover of the Florida state capitol to protest the outcome of Zimmerman's case. The same year—inspired, in part, by the Dream Defenders—the Black Lives Matter movement took to the streets, embarking on the relentless work of forcing Americans to confront police violence. (Patrisse Cullors, one of the founders of Black Lives Matter, affirmed her support for the abolition of police in a June interview with *Newsweek*.)

One of the most ardent fighters in the modern abolition movement has been Mariame Kaba, the activist known on Twitter as @prisonculture. In 2009, she founded Project NIA, an advocacy organization combating the criminalization and incarceration of children and young adults. In the years that followed, Kaba hosted conferences, gave speeches, and traveled widely. She also frequently wrote articles; her children's book *Missing Daddy* is about a girl whose father is in prison. In 2016, Kaba was among a group of lawyers, people in prison, community leaders, and others who established Survived and Punished (S+P), another abolitionist organization, which works to stop sexual violence and the criminalization of survivors.

Efforts such as these, focused on eliminating police departments and replacing them with more compassionate forms of justice, have been developing for years just below the mainstream—quiet and immense and waiting to erupt past the surface, like the dramatic formation of a new island. An observant journalist could see evidence of this. In 2017, Tracey L. Meares, a Yale Law School professor and member of President Barack Obama's Task Force on 21st Century Policing, wrote in the *Boston Review* that "policing as we know it must be abolished before it can be transformed," citing Kaba. In 2019, Critical Resistance was part of a coalition of activists that succeeded in ending a SWAT emergency training expo called Urban Shield. The ongoing campaign to eliminate Immigration and Customs Enforcement has some origins in the abolition movement—the language of "people in cages" comes from abolitionist rhetoric; many immigrant activists and attorneys identify as abolitionists, too. Recently, in Los Angeles, Black Lives Matter helped persuade the city council to advance a proposal that would move as much as $150 million of the police department's operating budget (totaling nearly $2 billion) to health and housing programs.

In Minneapolis, the heart of the latest protests, the demand to defund the police appeared well before this spring. Back in 2007, five high-ranking Black officers sued their department for institutional racism; the case included death threats sent to every Black person on the force, signed "KKK." The American Civil Liberties Union reported in 2015 that Black people in Minneapolis were about nine times more likely than whites to be arrested for low-grade offenses such as disorderly conduct and lurking. That year, in the north of the city, two white police officers, Mark Ringgenberg and Dustin Schwarze, shot and killed a Black twenty-four-year-old named Jamar Clark. In 2016, an officer shot Philando Castile to death. Around that time, the Center for Policing Equity, a think tank, began working with the Minneapolis Police Department to curb burdensome and inequitable police practices. "The Minneapolis police have struggled for a long time with pockets of resistance to those kinds of changes," Phillip Atiba Goff, one of the Center's leaders, recently told the *New York Times Magazine*. "One terrible lesson of George Floyd's death is that we don't have mechanisms to stop terrible officers from doing terrible things on a given shift."

Turning a city's pain into a basis for research, a coalition of local residents reviewed decades of police violence against Black people in Minneapolis. The nominal occasion was the department's 150th anniversary, but the necessity came from the blood in the streets. In 2017, after completing dozens of case studies, the group produced a report. There was a clear conclusion: "Abolition, not reform, is the way forward."

As June wore on, many of the political journalists who had initially covered "Defund the Police" as a breaking news story caught up on their reading. Outlets began to produce pieces that were less reactive, more nuanced. The *New York Times* ran an op-ed by Kaba settling the confusion over "semantics"; its title was "Yes, we mean literally abolish the police." Still, scrutinizing the policy proposals, not everyone was persuaded. The idea of dismantling police departments—according to some writers at *Vox, The Marshall Project*, and other publications—was to be judged as a set of outlines, not as the result of deep frustration that's built up in the places reporters too frequently ignore. They still didn't get it.

"When you see 'Defund the Police' on signs, you have to understand that, for so many of us, it's a placeholder for something much deeper—it has a much bigger spiritual and epistemic commitment behind it," Bierria said. The modern abolition movement, she added, has been guided by Black feminism, which rejects accepted notions of crime and punishment. "As Black women, we exist at the intersections of so many kinds of violence: state violence, sexual violence, racist violence. And that puts us in a unique position to find a politics that responds to that multidimensionality of violence."

The problem with journalists' coverage of police abolition cannot be disentangled from the lack of diversity within newsrooms. Minority groups make up nearly 40 percent of the population of the United States but only about 17 percent of newsroom staff at print and online publications, and only 13 percent of newspaper leadership. This means that the communities most reporters and editors come from do not look like the places where Black Lives Matter activists live. The press also has historically taken the side of police departments in coverage of crime—including cases in which an officer has been at fault. As Jelani Cobb wrote for this magazine, describing a white reporter in a predominantly Black and Latinx neighborhood, "What to the journalist seemed inscrutable was, to many residents, reasonable."

Many non-Black journalists' first personal experience with American police violence came during the protests that erupted after Floyd's death, when hundreds of reporters were arrested, shot with rubber bullets, or gassed with chemical agents.

It's important to recognize that the demand to defund the police is about more than just policy; it's the advent of a new kind of politics, one that breaks the narratives and tropes we have relied on in order to make sense of the country. The movement doesn't work in the same way that journalism, as we know it, expects a movement to work. As reporters, we typically look for leaders to interview and for spokespeople who can explain a rally's demands. But modern abolitionists tend to reject traditional organizing models; instead, they pursue collective, horizontal leadership structures. "We want to let the community lead itself, and we also know that the state surveils and targets leaders," Sisay, who is part of Survived and Punished, told me. Like every other volunteer in the group, Sisay's only title is "member." "No one is trying to be a Martin or Malcolm," she said.

The context of the 2020 campaigns has compounded the challenge to journalists. Other social movements, such as the Tea Party, have thrown their weight behind putting candidates in office, but most abolitionists describe elections as simply one potential—and decidedly limited—tool in pursuit of their goals. More than one abolitionist I spoke to described voting as merely "harm reduction." Elections, they argued, infrequently offer solutions to institutional problems where the government itself is to blame. The race for the White House would seem particularly removed from the organizing modern abolitionists do. "No matter who is president, there is still violence in our communities, and still violence in the prison-industrial complex," Sisay said. And beyond strategy, there's also a deep sense of disillusionment with a system of voting that continually fails Black people, even as they turn out at record levels. If the protesters in the streets don't seem to be pursuing a strategy that prioritizes getting Biden elected president (and if defunding appears to be a "massive political mistake" for Democrats), it is because making Biden president is ultimately not abolitionists' most pressing goal.

The rules of the institutions that non-Black journalists know—the schools, the government buildings, the campaign headquarters—don't apply to the messy cacophony of a passionate protest movement. Anti-police advocates believe that it would be a mistake for political reporters not to understand the energy of this moment as revolutionary in nature. "People are so fed up after the failures of reform, they've embraced what abolitionists have been saying all along: that the systems of policing and imprisonment are, at their core, violent, racist institutions," Mohamed Shehk, the national media and communications director for Critical Resistance, told me.

Then again, the nature of big ideas is that, eventually, they'll be taken up by the masses. Even if it doesn't happen this election cycle, it seems inevitable that politicians will soon pull "Defund the Police" into their campaign platforms. Shehk and others worry that, as their message becomes absorbed into the mainstream, it will be dislodged from its abolitionist roots and transfigured into a call for reform. The gravity of electoral politics is strong, and can be deadly. As time goes on, journalists will have to evaluate different policy proposals to defund the police—starting in Minneapolis, where it seems poised to become a reality. In June, a veto-proof majority of the city council announced their intent to disband the police department and to reinvest the resources into community infrastructure and nonviolent alternatives to policing. Jacob Frey, the mayor, said he was against the plan. He will be up for reelection next year.

Print Citations

CMS: Herrera, Jack. "The Defunding Debate." In *The Reference Shelf: Policing in 2020,* edited by Micah L. Issitt, 150-156. Amenia, NY: Grey House Publishing, 2021.

MLA: Herrera, Jack. "The Defunding Debate." *The Reference Shelf: Policing in 2020,* edited by Micah L. Issitt, Grey Housing Publishing, 2021, pp. 150-156.

APA: Herrera, J. (2021). The defunding debate. In Micah L. Issitt (Ed.), *The reference shelf: Policing in 2020* (pp. 150-156). Amenia, NY: Grey Housing Publishing.

6
Policing the Digital Citizen

By Paul Sableman, via Wikimedia.

Police surveillance cameras and drones, as well as police bodycams, have raised questions of privacy, both for the police and for the public.

Technology in Policing

The "Digital Age," the name that scholars use to describe the era in human history marked by the emergence and spread of digital technology, has forced Americans to adjust to new ways of managing nearly every aspect of their lives. As this change has occurred, the organs of the state have also been forced to change their routines and processes to keep apace. For police departments across America, the shift to the digital age has been transformative, but also controversial. Many of the new technologies that have been adopted, such as facial recognition and remote drones, have raised questions about privacy and personal security. In some cases, digital advances in police tech have been necessary to help police keep ahead of how digital technology has increased the potential for new kinds of crime, but these technologies have also contributed to declining public trust.

High Tech Surveillance

Drones, also called unmanned aerial vehicles (UAVs), are one of the more controversial developments in digital technology. Drones can be either remote-controlled or automated and can be outfitted with cameras and other kinds of surveillance equipment. Drones vary in complexity, from store-bought miniature drones made for recreational and hobbyist use to ultra-advanced multimillion-dollar military and police drones, outfitted with the latest in surveillance technology and, in the case of the military, with deadly weaponry.

Since drone technology evolved to its current state, a variety of different uses for drones have been found. Perhaps the most controversial use of drones has been in the realm of national security. Since the 2000s, military branches and the Central Intelligence Agency (CIA) have been utilizing drones extensively in the ongoing "War on Terror." Semiautomated drones can be used to conduct remote strikes on military targets, and it has been estimated that the United States has killed tens of thousands of people, both combatants and civilians, with drone strikes.[1] In an effort to reduce the potential for unintended casualties, drones can be adapted to utilize facial recognition technology, enabling drones to identify targets before launching attacks. This technology has been used to identify suspected terrorists before military strikes are conducted.

The potential to use drones for long-distance surveillance is the primary reason that police departments around the country began looking into the use of drones in local law enforcement. Long-distance camera and video technology enable police to utilize drones in tracking suspects during police pursuits, while facial recognition technology raises the possibility that police could use drones to search for suspects among crowds or in public places. However, the use of drones for surveillance raises thorny questions about personal privacy.[2] To locate a suspect, police may first engage in widespread surveillance of crowds, potentially filming or photographing hundreds or thousands of citizens without their knowledge. The question is whether the American public is comfortable with potentially being watched and monitored by police, en masse, if doing so means that police might succeed in capturing wanted criminals. As of December 2020, there is no federal framework to establish protocols for the use of drones by police or other state agencies, and so some have argued that enabling police to freely use drones is dangerous until a system of laws is created to regulate the use of drones and to establish when and how police can use them for public surveillance.[3]

The use of facial recognition systems with drones is also part of a broader controversy regarding the overall use of facial recognition systems by police. Facial recognition programs utilize cutting-edge algorithms to map facial features. These maps can then be used to comparatively search through other available photos in an effort to locate suspects. As of 2021, facial recognition technology is not covered by any overarching federal regulations but is governed only by local and municipal law. As a result, police departments around the country have been utilizing facial recognition technology for street-level surveillance. The proliferation of this emerging technology has accelerated due to the involvement of major corporations, including Amazon, which have been developing and are now selling facial recognition tools to police departments.[4]

The problems with the use of facial recognition technology are similar to the problems that activists have identified with the use of drones, and come down to concern about enabling or allowing police to engage in mass surveillance. Proponents of facial recognition technology argue that the tools could allow police to identify and apprehend suspects that might otherwise remain at large, but critics have argued that the potential violations of personal privacy are not worth the potential rewards. Utilizing cameras and drones, police might need to capture and analyze photo or video of hundreds of citizens before identifying a person of interest. Further, studies have shown that "false negatives," in which facial recognition systems mistakenly identify a suspect due to recognition errors, are not uncommon. Data has also shown that African American or darker-skinned individuals are more likely to be misidentified by facial recognition systems, which has raised the concern that the use of the technology may deepen racial bias in policing.[5]

Ultimately, the argument from opponents of facial recognition technology is that researchers and regulatory agencies must establish clear rules for the way that police departments can use this technology that are designed to ensure privacy and to prevent violations of rights. For instance, should police be allowed to conduct mass surveillance looking for any crime that is visible on camera or should the use of facial recognition be limited to situations in which police are searching for an identified suspect and have obtained a warrant to analyze data? Requiring police to file legal notification to analyze surveillance data would ensure that there is oversight and that police use of the technology remains more limited in scope. But as of 2021, only some states have adopted laws regarding how police may use data collected through cameras and other surveillance systems. The central issue that members of the public should consider is whether the potential to arrest suspects is worth allowing police to engage in mass surveillance.

Watching the Detectives

Surveillance, one of the most controversial issues in the modern tech debate, not only concerns whether or not the state has the right to surveil citizens, but also involves a debate over whether or not the state or citizens have the right to surveil the state. The most familiar issue in this debate concerns whether or not police should be required to use body cameras or other tools that provide a legal record of police behavior in the performance of their jobs. Drones figure into this debate as well, as there have been proposals to utilize drones to follow and watch officers as they perform their jobs.

Police organizations and officers who have argued against the use of body cameras and other methods of recording police officers make similar arguments to those critical of police use of mass surveillance. For instance, in an issue of the National Police Foundation blog, Chief Brandon del Pozo of the Burlington Vermont Police Department argued that body cameras would capture private conversations and could capture footage of cops "going to the bathroom, eating lunch, and having cell phone conversations."[6] The argument that police should enjoy privacy in their personal conversations is very similar to the argument that police should not be allowed to use widely available technology, such as public cameras, drones, and other equipment, capable of intruding on the private behaviors and conversations of the public. As the federal government has done little to protect the public from such violations of privacy, it is unclear whether the government has any responsibility to protect police officers, during the course of their jobs, from similar surveillance.

Much of the debate over body cameras and other recording equipment centers on whether the police officers have the ability or permission to turn surveillance equipment off. If police are able to turn off body cameras and other equipment, this effectively eliminates many of the concerns regarding personal privacy, not only for police but the public. For instance, it has been argued that surveillance equipment used to watch police might inadvertently record privileged conversations with lawyers and/or judges and might record citizens providing police with data, inadvertently violating citizen privacy.[7]

Providing police with the ability to turn body cameras off would potentially solve some of the thorniest issues in the body camera debate, but it also makes it less likely that body cameras will have the desired effect, which is to reduce the potential for police misconduct. Providing officers with the ability to decide when and if they are being monitored could allow officers to subvert the system, turning body cameras and other monitoring equipment off when engaged in illegal or inappropriate activities. For officer monitoring to be effective, police would need to be monitored whenever they engage in an interaction with the public.

One overarching question that is still unsettled is whether or not body cameras have done anything to enhance police accountability. Some studies indicate that monitoring systems can, in some cases, improve police interactions with members of the public. Other studies have shown that body cameras and other police surveillance methods may do little to reduce problematic police behavior and have found that police sometimes subvert surveillance systems to avoid being monitored. The best available data suggests that, at best, more data is needed to determine whether or not monitoring systems work in reducing police conflicts and in providing legal records that can be used to investigate allegations of police misconduct.[8]

Beyond the use of equipment like body cameras, dashboard cameras, or drones that would provide data to police administrators on the performance of officers, police are also living in a world in which citizens themselves have become documentarians of police conduct. Most of the controversial instances of alleged police misconduct that fueled the rise of the Black Lives Matter movement and the more recent Defund the Police movement were filmed by citizens using private devices, and the controversy spread as these videos spread through social media and, later, the popular press.

While citizen surveillance of police has uncovered shocking instances of violence and abuse, the spread of data through social media and other channels can be misleading and subverts traditional channels of redress and justice. Officers now face being judged and condemned by the public before or without due process. While this is a new challenge for police, it is the perception that police administrations will not honestly seek to root out racism and the abuse of power that motivates citizens to take alternative routes in seeking what they perceive as justice. Police are under increased scrutiny because citizens no longer trust that they will conduct themselves appropriately without being watched. This too is another example of what happens when the public loses trust in the state, and the increased pressure that police are experiencing is a problem that the police have created for themselves by failing to perform their duties in ways that reinforce public trust.

The Technological Revolution Analyzed

Surveillance, both of the public and of police, is only one of the ways in which policing is changing in the digital world, and new technologies that might assist police, or provide greater transparency or accountability, are always in development. For instance, police departments have recently been experimenting with using video game-like interfaces to train officers in how to de-escalate conflict. Developments like these are at the cutting edge of digital technology and provide a look at the kinds of systems that might be more widespread as policing evolves.

Technology always provides new promise and new perils for citizens and, in many ways, America in 2021 is still a culture in the midst of adjusting to one of the greatest technological revolutions in history, the introduction of personal digital computing. In addition, police technology is controversial in part because America is a country also in the grips of a new civil rights movement aimed at identifying and addressing structural prejudice and inequality. This is a difficult and contentious process that has brought about enormous controversy and has resulted in increasingly polarized views of police officers and their role in society. For this reason alone, some have argued that the adoption of new police technology is a process that should be handled carefully and with serious consideration given to addressing potential civil rights concerns. This has not happened, in part because economic concerns often dominate the adoption of new technology before underlying civil liberties concerns are considered. This moment, then, is one in which Americans are now struggling to determine the civil rights implications of technologies already widely adopted, attempting to determine to what degree police technology needs to be reviewed and regulated as society moves deeper into the new digital world.

Works Used

"Body Cameras and Privacy—Where Do You Draw the Line?" *National Police Foundation*. 2020. https://www.policefoundation.org/body-cameras-and-privacy-where-do-you-draw-the-line/.

Chapman, Brett. "Body-Worn Cameras: What the Evidence Tells Us." *NIJ*. National Institute of Justice. Nov 14, 2018. https://nij.ojp.gov/topics/articles/body-worn-cameras-what-evidence-tells-us.

"Evaluating the Impact of Police Body Cameras." *Urban Institute*. 2020. https://www.urban.org/debates/evaluating-impact-police-body-cameras.

Greenwood, Faine. "How to Regulate Police Use of Drones." *Brookings*. Sep 24, 2020. https://www.brookings.edu/techstream/how-to-regulate-police-use-of-drones/.

Heatherly, Michael C. "Drones: The American Controversy." *Journal of Strategic Security*, vol. 7, no. 4, 2014. https://scholarcommons.usf.edu/cgi/viewcontent.cgi?referer=&httpsredir=1&article=1387&context=jss.

Najibi, Alex. "Racial Discrimination in Face Recognition Technology." *Harvard*. Oct 24, 2020. http://sitn.hms.harvard.edu/flash/2020/racial-discrimination-in-face-recognition-technology/.

"Overview of Drone Technology and Related Controversies." *Lawfare*. 2020. https://www.lawfareblog.com/overview-drone-technology-and-related-controversies.

Schuppe, Jon. "How Facial Recognition Became a Routine Policing Tool in America." *NBC News*. May 11, 2019. https://www.nbcnews.com/news/us-news/how-facial-recognition-became-routine-policing-tool-america-n1004251.

Notes

1. "Overview of Drone Technology and Related Controversies," *Lawfare*.
2. Heatherly, "Drones: The American Controversy."
3. Greenwood, "How to Regulate Police Use of Drones."
4. Schuppe, "How Facial Recognition Became a Routine Policing Tool in America."
5. Najibi, "Racial Discrimination in Face Recognition Technology."
6. "Body Cameras and Privacy—Where Do You Draw the Line?" *National Police Foundation*.
7. "Evaluating the Impact of Police Body Cameras," *Urban Institute*.
8. Chapman, "Body-Worn Cameras: What the Evidence Tells Us."

The Microsoft Police State: Mass Surveillance, Facial Recognition, and the Azure Cloud

By Michael Kwet

The Intercept, July 14, 2020

Nationwide protests against racist policing have brought new scrutiny onto big tech companies like Facebook, which is under boycott by advertisers over hate speech directed at people of color, and Amazon, called out for aiding police surveillance. But Microsoft, which has largely escaped criticism, is knee-deep in services for law enforcement, fostering an ecosystem of companies that provide police with software using Microsoft's cloud and other platforms. The full story of these ties highlights how the tech sector is increasingly entangled in intimate, ongoing relationships with police departments.

Microsoft's links to law enforcement agencies have been obscured by the company, whose public response to the outrage that followed the murder of George Floyd has focused on facial recognition software. This misdirects attention away from Microsoft's own mass surveillance platform for cops, the Domain Awareness System, built for the New York Police Department and later expanded to Atlanta, Brazil, and Singapore. It also obscures that Microsoft has partnered with scores of police surveillance vendors who run their products on a "Government Cloud" supplied by the company's Azure division and that it is pushing platforms to wire police field operations, including drones, robots, and other devices.

With partnership, support, and critical infrastructure provided by Microsoft, a shadow industry of smaller corporations provide mass surveillance to law enforcement agencies. Genetec offers cloud-based CCTV and big data analytics for mass surveillance in major U.S. cities. Veritone provides facial recognition services to law enforcement agencies. And a wide range of partners provide high-tech policing equipment for the Microsoft Advanced Patrol Platform, which turns cop cars into all-seeing surveillance patrols. All of this is conducted together with Microsoft and hosted on the Azure Government Cloud.

Last month, hundreds of Microsoft employees petitioned their CEO, Satya Nadella, to cancel contracts with law enforcement agencies, support Black Lives Matter, and endorse defunding the police. In response, Microsoft ignored the complaint and instead banned sales of *its own* facial recognition software to police in the United States, directing eyes away from Microsoft's other contributions to police surveillance. The strategy worked: The press and activists alike praised the

> **Microsoft is getting paid to run their mass surveillance and facial recognition services on the Azure cloud—services that disproportionately affect people of color.**

move, reinforcing Microsoft's said position as a moral leader in tech.

Yet it's not clear how long Microsoft will escape major scrutiny. Policing is increasingly done with active cooperation from tech companies, and Microsoft, along with Amazon and other cloud providers, is one of the major players in this space.

Because partnerships and services hosting third party vendors on the Azure cloud do not have to be announced to the public, it is impossible to know full extent of Microsoft's involvement in the policing domain, or the status of publicly announced third party services, potentially including some of the previously announced relationships mentioned below.

Microsoft declined to comment.

Microsoft: From Police Intelligence to the Azure Cloud

In the wake of 9/11, Microsoft made major contributions to centralized intelligence centers for law enforcement agencies. Around 2009, it began working on a surveillance platform for the NYPD called the Domain Awareness System, or DAS, which was unveiled to the public in 2012. The system was built with leadership from Microsoft along with NYPD officers.

While some details about the DAS have been disclosed to the public, many are still missing. The most comprehensive account to date appeared in a 2017 paper by NYPD officers.

The DAS integrates disparate sources of information to perform three core functions: real-time alerting, investigations, and police analytics.

Through the DAS, the NYPD watches the personal movements of the entire city. In its early days, the system ingested information from closed-circuit TV cameras, environmental sensors (to detect radiation and dangerous chemicals), and automatic license plate readers, or ALPRs. By 2010, it began adding geocoded NYPD records of complaints, arrests, 911 calls, and warrants "to give context to the sensor data." Thereafter, it added video analytics, automatic pattern recognition, predictive policing, and a mobile app for cops.

By 2016, the system had ingested 2 billion license plate images from ALPR cameras (3 million reads per day, archived for five years), 15 million complaints, more than 33 billion public records, over 9,000 NYPD and privately operated camera feeds, videos from 20,000-plus body cameras, and more. To make sense of it all, analytics algorithms pick out relevant data, including for predictive policing.

The NYPD has a history of police abuse, and civil rights and liberties advocates like Urban Justice Center's Surveillance Technology Oversight Project have protested the system out of constitutional concerns, with little success to date.

While the DAS has received some attention from the press—and is fairly well-known among activists—there is more to the story of Microsoft policing services.

Over the years, Microsoft has grown its business through the expansion of its cloud services, in which storage capacity, servers, and software running on servers are rented out on a metered basis. One of its offerings, Azure Government, provides dedicated data hosting in exclusively domestic cloud centers so that the data never physically leaves the host country. In the U.S., Microsoft has built several Azure Government cloud centers for use by local, state, and federal organizations.

Unbeknownst to most people, Microsoft has a "Public Safety and Justice" division with staff who formerly worked in law enforcement. This is the true heart of the company's policing services, though it has operated for years away from public view.

Microsoft's police surveillance services are often opaque because the company sells little in the way of its own policing products. It instead offers an array of "general purpose" Azure cloud services, such as machine learning and predictive analytics tools like Power BI (business intelligence) and Cognitive Services, which can be used by law enforcement agencies and surveillance vendors to build their own software or solutions.

Microsoft's Surveillance-Based IoT Patrol Car

A rich array of Microsoft's cloud-based offerings is on full display with a concept called "The Connected Officer." Microsoft situates this concept as part of the Internet of Things, or IoT, in which gadgets are connected to online servers and thus made more useful. "The Connected Officer," Microsoft has written, will "bring IoT to policing."

With the Internet of Things, physical objects are assigned unique identifiers and transfer data over networks in an automated fashion. If a police officer draws a gun from its holster, for example, a notification can be sent over the network to alert other officers there may be danger. Real Time Crime Centers could then locate the officer on a map and monitor the situation from a command and control center.

According to this concept, a multitude of surveillance and IoT sensor data is sent onto a "hot path" for fast use in command centers and onto a "cold path" to be used later by intelligence analysts looking for patterns. The data is streamed along through Microsoft's Azure Stream Analytics product, stored on the Azure cloud, and enhanced by Microsoft analytics solutions like Power BI—providing a number of points at which Microsoft can make money.

While the "Connected Officer" was a conceptual exercise, the company's real-world patrol solution is the Microsoft Advanced Patrol Platform, or MAPP. MAPP is an IoT platform for police patrol vehicles that integrates surveillance sensors and database records on the Azure cloud, including "dispatch information, driving directions, suspect history, a voice-activated license plate reader, a missing persons list, location-based crime bulletins, shift reports, and more."

The MAPP vehicle is outfitted with gear from third-party vendors that stream surveillance data into the Azure cloud for law enforcement agencies. Mounted to the roof, a 360-degree high-resolution camera streams live video to Azure and the laptop inside the vehicle, with access also available on a mobile phone or remote computer. The vehicle also sports an automatic license plate reader that can read 5,000 plates per minute—whether the car is stationary or on the move—and cross-check them against a database in Azure and run by Genetec's license plate reader solution, AutoVu. A proximity camera on the vehicle is designed to alert the officers when their vehicle is being approached.

Patrolling the skies is a drone provided by Microsoft partner Aeryon Labs, the SkyRanger, to provide real-time streaming video. (Aeryon Labs is now part of surveillance giant FLIR Systems.) According to Nathan Beckham of Microsoft Public Safety and Justice, the vehicle's drones "follow it around and see a bigger view of it." The drones, writes DroneLife, can "provide aerial views to the integrated data platform, allowing officers to assess ongoing situations in real time, or to gather forensic evidence from a crime scene."

Police robots are also part of the MAPP platform. Products from ReconRobotics, for example, "integrat[ed] with Microsoft's Patrol Car of the Future Program" in 2016. Microsoft says ReconRobotics provides their MAPP vehicle with a "small, lightweight but powerful robot" that "can be easily deployed and remotely controlled by patrol officers to provide real-time information to decision-makers."

Another Microsoft partner, SuperDroid Robots, has also announced they will provide the Microsoft MAPP vehicle with two compact remote-controlled surveillance robots, the MLT "Jack Russell" and the LT2-F "Bloodhound," the latter of which can climb stairs and obstacles.

Although it sports a Microsoft insignia on the hood and door, the physical vehicle the company uses to promote MAPP isn't for sale by Microsoft, and you probably won't see Microsoft-labeled cars driving around. Rather, Microsoft provides MAPP as a platform through which to transform existing cop cars into IoT surveillance vehicles: "It's really about being able to take all this data and put it up in the cloud, being able to source that data with their data, and start making relevant information out of it," said Beckham.

Indeed, Microsoft says "the car is becoming the nerve center for law enforcement." According to Beckham, the information collected and stored in the Azure cloud will help officers "identify bad actors" and "let the officers be aware of the environment that is going on around them." As an example, he said, "We're hoping with machine learning and AI in the future, we can start pattern matching" with MAPP vehicles providing data to help find "bad actors."

Last October, South African police announced Microsoft partnered with the city of Durban for "21st century" smart policing. Durban's version of the the MAPP solution includes a 360-degree ALPR to scan license plates and a facial recognition camera from Chinese video surveillance firm Hikvision for use when the vehicle is stationary (e.g., parked at an event).

According to South African news outlet ITWeb, the metro police will use the MAPP solution "to deter criminal activities based on data analysis through predictive modeling and machine learning algorithms." The vehicle has already been rolled out in Cape Town, where Microsoft recently opened a new Azure data center—an extension of the digital colonialism I wrote about in 2018.

Much like the U.S. (albeit with some different dynamics), South Africa faces the scourge of police brutality that disproportionately impacts people of color. The country had its own George Floyd moment during the recent Covid-19 lockdown when the military and police brutally beat 40-year-old Collins Khosa in the poor Alexandra township, leading to his death—over a cup of beer. (A military inquiry found that Khosa's death was not linked to his injuries at the hands of authorities; Khosa's family and many others in South Africa have rejected the review as a whitewash.)

The MAPP solution will be used for "zero tolerance" policing. For example, Durban Metro Police spokesperson Parboo Sewpersad said the rollout aims to punish "littering, drinking and driving, and drinking and walking" during summer festivities.

It is difficult to determine where else the MAPP vehicle may be deployed. The rollout in South Africa suggests Microsoft sees Africa as a place to experiment with its police surveillance technologies.

Microsoft: Powering CCTV and Police Intelligence in the City

Beyond wiring police vehicles, video surveillance provides another lucrative source of profits for Microsoft, as it is loaded with data packets to transmit, store, and process—earning fees each step of the way.

When building a CCTV network packed with cameras, cities and businesses typically use a video management system, or VMS, to do things like display multiple camera feeds on a video wall or offer the option to search through footage. A leading VMS provider, Genetec, offers the core VMS integrated into Microsoft's Domain Awareness System. A close partner of Microsoft for over 20 years, the two companies work together on integrating surveillance services on the Azure cloud.

Some of the most high-profile city police forces are using Genetec and Microsoft for video surveillance and analytics.

Through a public-private partnership called Operation Shield, Atlanta's camera network has grown from 17 downtown cameras to a wide net of 10,600 cameras that officials hope will soon cover all city quadrants. Genetec and Microsoft Azure power the CCTV network.

On June 14, Atlanta's Chief of Police, Erika Shields, resigned after APD cops shot and killed a 27-year-old Black man, Rayshard Brooks. Last month, six Atlanta police officers were charged for using excessive force against protesters of police violence.

In 2019, Atlanta Police Foundation COO Marshall Freeman told me the foundation had just completed a "department-wide rollout" for Microsoft Aware (Domain Awareness System). Freeman said the Atlanta Police Department uses Microsoft machine learning to correlate data, and plans to add Microsoft's video analytics. "We can always continue to go back to Microsoft and have the builders expand on the technology and continue to build out the platform," he added.

In Chicago, 35,000 cameras cover the city with a plug-in surveillance network. The back-end currently uses Genetec Stratocast and Genetec's Federation service, which manages access to cameras across a federated network of CCTV cameras—a network of camera networks, so to speak.

In 2017, Genetec custom-built their Citigraf platform for the Chicago Police Department—the second-largest police force in the country—as a way to make sense of the department's vast array of data. Powered by Microsoft Azure, Citigraf ingests information from surveillance sensors and database records. Using real-time and historical data, it performs calculations, visualizations, alerts, and other tasks to create "deep situational awareness" for the CPD. Microsoft is partnering with Genetec to build a "correlation engine" to make sense of the surveillance data.

Chicago's police force has a brutal history of racism, corruption, and even two decades' worth of torturing suspects. During police violence protests following Floyd's murder, the CPD attacked and beat protesters, including five Black protesters to the point of hospitalization.

The city of Detroit uses Genetec Stratocast and Microsoft Azure to power their controversial Project Green Light. Launched in 2016 in tandem with a new Real Time Crime Center, the project allows local businesses—or other participating entities, such as churches and public housing—to install video cameras on their premises and stream surveillance feeds to the Detroit Police Department. Participants can place a "green light" next to the cameras to warn the public—which is 80 percent Black—that "you are being watched by the police."

In 2015, the DPD stated, "the day is coming where police will have access to cameras everywhere allowing the police to virtually patrol nearly any area of the city without ever stepping foot."

DPD Assistant Chief David LeValley explained to me that prior to creating the new command center, the department sent a team of people to several other U.S. cities, including New York, Chicago, Atlanta, Boston, and the Drug Enforcement Administration center in El Paso, Texas, to scope out their intel centers. "Our Real Time Crime Center is an all-encompassing intelligence center, it's not just Project Green Light," he explained.

The expansion of police surveillance in Detroit has been swift. Today, Project Green Light has around 2,800 cameras installed across over 700 locations, and two smaller Real Time Crime Centers are being added, a development trending in cities like Chicago. LeValley told me those RTTCs will do things like "pattern recognition" and "reports for critical incidents."

In the wake of George Floyd's murder, activists in Detroit have recharged their efforts to abolish Project Green Light in the fight against police surveillance, which local community advocates like Tawana Petty and Eric Williams deem racist. This year, two Black men, Robert Julian-Borchak Williams and Michael Oliver, were wrongfully arrested after being misidentified by the DPD's facial recognition technology.

Nakia Wallace, a co-organizer of Detroit Will Breathe, told me Project Green Light "pre-criminalizes" people and "gives the police the right to keep tabs on you if they think you are guilty" and "harass Black and brown communities." "Linking together cameras" across wide areas is "hyper-surveillance" and "has to be stopped," she added.

The "function that the [DPD] serve," Wallace said, is "the protection of property and white supremacy." "They're hyper-militarized, and even in the wake of that, people are still dying in the city" because "they have no interest in the livelihood of Detroit citizens." Instead of militarizing, we need to "stop pretending like poor Black people are inherently criminals, and start looking at social services and things that prevent people from going into a life of crime."

In a 2017 blog post, Microsoft boasted about the partnership with Genetec for the DPD, stating that Project Green Light is "a great example of how cities can improve public safety, citizens' quality of life, and economic growth with today's technologies."

Microsoft Actually Does Supply Facial Recognition Technology

While Microsoft has been powering intelligence centers and CCTV networks in the shadows, the company has publicly focused on facial recognition regulations. On June 11, Microsoft joined Amazon and IBM in saying it will not sell its facial recognition technology to police until there are regulations in place.

This is a PR stunt that confused how Microsoft's relationship to policing works technically and ethically, in a number of ways.

First, while the press occasionally criticizes Microsoft's Domain Awareness System, most attention to Microsoft policing focuses on facial recognition. This is mistaken: Microsoft is providing software to power a variety of policing technologies that undermine civil rights and liberties—even without facial recognition.

Second, facial recognition is a notable feature of many video surveillance systems and Real Time Crime Centers that Microsoft powers. The cities of New York, Atlanta, Chicago, and Detroit are among those utilizing Microsoft services to collect, store, and process the visual surveillance data used for facial recognition. Microsoft services are *part and parcel* of many police facial recognition surveillance systems.

Third, at least one facial recognition company, Veritone, has been left out of the conversation. A Microsoft partner, the Southern California artificial intelligence outfit offers cloud-based software called IDentify, which runs on Microsoft's cloud and helps law enforcement agencies flag the faces of potential suspects.

In a 2020 keynote at the Consumer Electronics Show, speaking alongside executives from Microsoft, Deloitte, and Oracle, Veritone CEO Chad Steelberg claimed that thanks to Veritone's IDentify software on Azure, cops have helped catch "hundreds and hundreds of suspects and violent offenders." Veritone's Redact product expedites prosecutions, and Illuminate allows investigators to "cull down evidence" and obtain anomaly "detection insights."

In a recent webinar, Veritone explained how IDentify leverages data police already have, such as arrest records. If a person is detected and has no known match, the IDentify software can profile suspects by creating a "person of interest database" that "will allow you to simply save unknown faces to this database and continuously monitor for those faces over time."

Veritone claims to deploy services in "about 150 locations," but does not name which ones use IDentify. It launched a pilot test with the Anaheim Police Department in 2019.

Microsoft lists Veritone IDentify as a facial recognition law enforcement product offering in its app repository online. The promotional video on the Microsoft website advertises IDentify's ability to:

> … compare your known offender and person of interest databases with video evidence to quickly and automatically identify suspects for investigation. Simply upload evidence from surveillance systems, body cameras, and more. … But best of all, you're not chained to your desk! Snap a picture and identify suspects while out on patrol, to verify statements, and preserve ongoing investigations.

Veritone has been a staunch defender of its facial recognition technology. In May 2019, the company tweeted:

In a promotional video featuring Microsoft, Veritone's Jon Gacek said, "You can see why at Veritone we're excited to be tightly partnered with Microsoft Azure team. Their vision and our vision is very common."

Smoke, Mirrors, and Misdirection

Despite claims to the contrary, Microsoft is providing facial recognition services to law enforcement through partnerships and services to companies like Veritone and Genetec, and through its Domain Awareness System.

Microsoft's public relations strategy is designed to mislead the public by veering attention away from its wide-ranging services to police. Instead, Microsoft president and chief legal officer Brad Smith urges the public to focus on facial recognition *regulation* and the issue of Microsoft's *own* facial recognition software, as if their other software and service offerings, partnerships, concepts, and marketing are not integral to a whole ecosystem of facial recognition and mass surveillance systems offered by smaller companies.

Esteemed Microsoft scholars, such as Kate Crawford, co-founder of the Microsoft-funded think tank, AI Now Institute, have followed this playbook. Crawford recently praised Microsoft's facial recognition PR and criticized companies like Clearview AI and Palantir, while ignoring the Microsoft Domain Awareness System, Microsoft's surveillance partnerships, and Microsoft's role as a cloud provider for facial recognition services.

Crawford and AI Now co-founder Meredith Whittaker have condemned predictive policing but haven't explained the fact that Microsoft plays a central role in predictive policing for police. Crawford did not respond to a request for comment.

Microsoft and its advocates may claim that it is a "neutral" cloud provider and it's up to other companies and police departments to decide how they use Microsoft software. Yet these companies are partnering with Microsoft, and Microsoft is getting paid to run their mass surveillance and facial recognition services on the Azure cloud—services that disproportionately affect people of color.

If these Microsoft clients were offering sex trafficking services on the Azure cloud, Microsoft would surely close their accounts. And because law enforcement agencies purchase surveillance technologies using taxpayer dollars, the public is actually paying Microsoft for its own police surveillance.

If activists force corporations like Microsoft, Amazon, Google, IBM, and Oracle to terminate partnerships and infrastructure services for third parties conducting police surveillance, then cloud providers would have to acknowledge they are accountable for what is done on their clouds. Moving forward, activists could press to replace corporate ownership of digital infrastructure and data with community ownership at the local level.

There is a lot at stake in this moment.

Print Citations

CMS: Kwet, Michael. "The Microsoft Police State: Mass Surveillance, Facial Recognition, and the Azure Cloud." In *The Reference Shelf: Policing in 2020,* edited by Micah L. Issitt, 165-173. Amenia, NY: Grey House Publishing, 2021.

MLA: Kwet, Michael. "The Microsoft Police State: Mass Surveillance, Facial Recognition, and the Azure Cloud." *The Reference Shelf: Policing in 2020,* edited by Micah L. Issitt, Grey Housing Publishing, 2021, pp. 165-173.

APA: Kwet, M. (2021). The Microsoft police state: Mass surveillance, facial recognition, and the Azure cloud. In Micah L. Issitt (Ed.), *The reference shelf: Policing in 2020* (pp. 165-173). Amenia, NY: Grey Housing Publishing.

Cops in Miami, NYC Arrest Protesters from Facial Recognition Matches

By Kate Cox

Ars Technica, **August 19, 2020**

Law enforcement in several cities, including New York and Miami, have reportedly been using controversial facial recognition software to track down and arrest individuals who allegedly participated in criminal activity during Black Lives Matter protests months after the fact.

Miami police used Clearview AI to identify and arrest a woman for allegedly throwing a rock at a police officer during a May protest, local NBC affiliate WTVJ reported this week. The agency has a policy against using facial recognition technology to surveil people exercising "constitutionally protected activities" such as protesting, according to the report.

"If someone is peacefully protesting and not committing a crime, we cannot use it against them," Miami Police Assistant Chief Armando Aguilar told *NBC6*. But, Aguilar added, "We have used the technology to identify violent protesters who assaulted police officers, who damaged police property, who set property on fire. We have made several arrests in those cases, and more arrests are coming in the near future."

An attorney representing the woman said he had no idea how police identified his client until contacted by reporters. "We don't know where they got the image," he told *NBC6*. "So how or where they got her image from begs other privacy rights. Did they dig through her social media? How did they get access to her social media?"

Similar reports have surfaced from around the country in recent weeks. Police in Columbia, South Carolina, and the surrounding county likewise used facial recognition, though from a different vendor, to arrest several protesters after the fact, according to local paper the *State*. Investigators in Philadelphia also used facial recognition software, from a third vendor, to identify protestors from photos posted to Instagram, the *Philadelphia Inquirer* reported.

New York City Mayor Bill de Blasio promised on Monday the NYPD would be "very careful and very limited with our use of anything involving facial recognition," *Gothamist* reported. This statement came on the heels of an incident earlier this month when "dozens of NYPD officers—accompanied by police dogs, drones and helicopters" descended on the apartment of a Manhattan activist who was identified by an "artificial intelligence tool" as a person who allegedly used a megaphone to shout into an officer's ear during a protest in June.

Unclear View

The ongoing nationwide protests, which seek to bring attention to systemic racial disparities in policing, have drawn more attention to the use of facial recognition systems by police in general.

Repeated tests and studies have shown that most facial recognition algorithms in use today are significantly more likely to generate false positives or other errors when trying to match images featuring people of color. Late last year, the National Institute of Standards and Technology (NIST) published research finding that facial recognition systems it tested had the highest accuracy when identifying white men but were 10 to 100 times more likely to make mistakes with Black, Asian, or Native American faces.

There's another, particularly 2020 wrinkle thrown in when it comes to matching photos of civil rights protesters, too: NIST found in July that most facial recognition algorithms perform significantly more poorly when matching masked faces. A significant percentage of the millions of people who have shown up for marches, rallies, and demonstrations around the country this summer have worn masks to mitigate against the risk of COVID-19 transmission in large crowds.

> **Most facial recognition algorithms in use today are significantly more likely to generate false positives or other errors when trying to match images featuring people of color.**

The ACLU in June filed a complaint against the Detroit police, alleging the department arrested the wrong man based on a flawed, incomplete match provided by facial recognition software. In the wake of the ACLU's complaint, Detroit Police Chief James Craig admitted that the software his agency uses misidentifies suspects 96 percent of the time.

IBM walked away from the facial recognition business in June. The company also asked Congress to pass laws requiring vendors and users to test their systems for racial bias and have such tests audited and reported. Amazon echoed the call for Congress to pass a law while asking police to take a year off from using its Rekognition product in the hope that Congress acts by next summer.

Clearview in particular—used in Miami—is highly controversial for reasons beyond the potential for bias. A *New York Times* report from January found that the highly secretive startup was scraping basically the whole Internet for images to populate its database of faces. Facebook, YouTube, Twitter, Microsoft, and other firms nearly all sent Clearview orders to stop within days of the report becoming public, but the company still boasts it has around 3 billion images on hand for partners (mostly but not exclusively law enforcement) to match individuals' pictures against.

The company is facing several lawsuits from states and the ACLU, while individuals are seeking class-action status.

Print Citations

CMS: Cox, Kate. "Cops in Miami, NYC Arrest Protestors from Facial Recognition Matches." In *The Reference Shelf: Policing in 2020,* edited by Micah L. Issitt, 174-176. Amenia, NY: Grey House Publishing, 2021.

MLA: Cox, Kate. "Cops in Miami, NYC Arrest Protestors from Facial Recognition Matches." *The Reference Shelf: Policing in 2020,* edited by Micah L. Issitt, Grey Housing Publishing, 2021, pp. 174-176.

APA: Cox, K. (2021). Cops in Miami, NYC arrest protestors from facial recognition matches. In Micah L. Issitt (Ed.), *The reference shelf: Policing in 2020* (pp. 174-176). Amenia, NY: Grey Housing Publishing.

Police Are Using Facial Recognition for Minor Crimes Because They Can

By Alfred Ng

CNET, October 24, 2020

Cities all across the US have passed bans on facial recognition, with variations in how strong the regulations are. Though Portland, Oregon, banned facial recognition from all government and commercial use, others are only limiting it from police use.

Some cities, like Detroit, have enacted lighter measures, such as allowing facial recognition to be used only when investigating violent crimes, while police in New York have been able to use the technology for crimes like shoplifting.

On Oct. 9, a New York judge decided in a package-theft case that facial recognition identification could be submitted as evidence in the trial, but he noted that lawmakers should set limits on how the technology could be used.

The judge cited concerns about free speech, noting that facial recognition could be used to identify and track protesters—which both the NYPD and the Miami police did in August.

Those sorts of issues, and the intrusiveness of facial recognition generally, have prompted widespread calls for regulation, but there's debate among technology companies, lawmakers and civil rights groups on where to draw the line.

The US has no federal regulations on facial recognition, leaving thousands of police departments to determine their own limits. Advocates say that's a concern for civil liberties. While some members of Congress propose an indefinite nationwide ban on police use, other bills suggest it could still be allowed with a warrant, or they prevent only businesses from using it.

Police often frame facial recognition as a necessary tool to solve the most heinous crimes, like terrorist attacks and violent assaults, but researchers have found that the technology is more frequently used for low-level offenses.

In a recent court filing, the NYPD noted that it's turned to facial recognition in more than 22,000 cases in the last three years.

"Even though the NYPD claims facial recognition is only used for serious crimes, the numbers tell a different story," said Albert Fox Cahn, the executive director of the Surveillance Technology Oversight Project. "As facial recognition continues to grow, it's being routinely deployed for everything from shoplifting to graffiti."

Asked for comment, an NYPD spokeswoman pointed to a 2019 opinion article by police commissioner James O'Neill titled "How Facial Recognition Makes You

Safer." In the piece, O'Neill talked about how facial recognition had been used to make arrests in murder, robbery and rape cases, but he didn't disclose how often it was used for low-level crimes.

The department's facial recognition policy, established in March, allows the technology to be used for any crime, no matter the severity. Without any limits, police have more frequently used the technology for petty thefts than the dangerous crimes, privacy advocates say.

Before Amazon put a moratorium on police use of its Rekognition face-identifying software, the program was used in a $12 shoplifting case in Oregon in 2018. Those cases aren't highlighted in Amazon's marketing material, which plays up how the technology is used to find leads on the victims of human trafficking.

At the *Wall Street Journal*'s Tech Live virtual conference on Oct. 20, Hoan Ton-That, CEO of facial recognition startup Clearview AI, said it isn't the company's responsibility to make sure its technology is being properly used by its thousands of police partners.

Though the company has its own guidelines, Ton-That said Clearview AI wouldn't be enforcing them, saying that "it's not our job to set the policy as a tech company."

Facial Recognition without Limits

Before Detroit established its facial recognition policy, the technology led to the wrongful arrests of at least two Black men in the city—both falsely accused of being involved in theft cases.

Robert Williams was arrested in January and accused of stealing about $3,800 worth of watches after Detroit's facial recognition falsely matched surveillance footage to his driver's license photo. In May 2019, the same facial recognition program wrongly identified Michael Oliver in a larceny case.

Facial recognition is known to have a record of racial bias, with researchers finding that the artificial intelligence frequently misidentifies people of color and women.

When it's able to be used without limits by police departments, the technology increases the chances of mistakes and threatens privacy, said Andrew Guthrie Ferguson, author of *The Rise of Big Data Policing* and a law professor at the University of the District of Columbia.

"Facial recognition should never be used for misdemeanor or low-level felony cases," Ferguson said. "Technology that can destroy privacy in public should be used sparingly and under strict controls."

Without any limits, police can use facial recognition however they please, and in many cases, arrested suspects don't even know that the flawed technology was used.

Williams didn't know that Detroit police used facial recognition to find him, until an investigator mentioned the detail during their conversation. Attorneys representing protesters in Miami didn't know that police used facial recognition in their arrests, according to an NBC Miami report. Police used facial recognition software in a $50 drug dealing case in Florida in 2016 but made no mention of it in the arrest report.

> **The US has no federal regulations on facial recognition, leaving thousands of police departments to determine their own limits.**

In a paper published in October 2019, Ferguson recommended limiting facial recognition to serious felonies, similar to how police restrict the use of wiretapping. He said it's dangerous to assume police should be allowed to use technology as they wish, saying it could damage people's privacy in the long run.

"That assumption is based on valuing the cost of crime higher than the cost to privacy, security and a growing imbalance of police power," Ferguson said. "Prosecuting low-level crimes at the expense of creating an extensive surveillance system may not be the balance society needs."

A Full Ban

Limits would be a welcome start, but privacy advocates argue they're not enough.

Activists in Detroit are still working to get facial recognition banned in the city after the City Council voted to renew its contract in September. The police department's limits on reserving facial recognition for violent crimes came only after months of protests, said Tawana Petty, director of the Data Justice Program for the Detroit Community Technology Project.

Because of the technology's track record for mistakes, she said, any use of it, even under the strictest regulations, leaves the potential for false arrests.

In a City Council meeting in June, Detroit's police chief, James Craig, said the facial recognition software misidentified people 96% of the time without human intervention. By Oct. 12, the police had used facial recognition on Black people about 97% of the time, according to the department's weekly report.

"My stance is that there is potential to lock people up for violent crimes they didn't commit," Petty said. "The technology is a dangerous assault on the civil liberties and privacy rights we all deserve to have protected."

Print Citations

CMS: Ng, Alfred. "Police Are Using Facial Recognition for Minor Crimes Because They Can." In *The Reference Shelf: Policing in 2020,* edited by Micah L. Issitt, 177-179. Amenia, NY: Grey House Publishing, 2021.

MLA: Ng, Alfred. "Police Are Using Facial Recognition for Minor Crimes Because They Can." *The Reference Shelf: Policing in 2020,* edited by Micah L. Issitt, Grey Housing Publishing, 2021, pp. 177-179.

APA: Ng, A. (2021). Police are using facial recognition for minor crimes because they can. In Micah L. Issitt (Ed.), *The reference shelf: Policing in 2020* (pp. 177-179). Amenia, NY: Grey Housing Publishing.

Body Cameras Are Seen as Key to Police Reform: But Do They Increase Accountability?

By Candice Norwood
PBS NewsHour, June 25, 2020

Amid widespread calls for police reform, there's a renewed push from both advocates and lawmakers to require officers to wear body cameras.

This week, New Mexico's legislature approved a bill that would require all officers in the state to wear body cameras. In Congress, House Democrats introduced a bill this month that would, among other things, require federal law enforcement to wear body cameras and provide funding and incentives for municipal law enforcement to do the same. A Republican proposal in the Senate would

> **A number of departments give officers discretion to determine when they turn their cameras on and off, while others provide more guidance.**

also establish grant funding to help police departments purchase body cameras and supporting technology for maintenance and data storage.

For nearly two decades, law enforcement agencies have explored and implemented the use of body cameras as a tool to help hold officers accountable and make departments more transparent—a way to help rebuild trust with their communities and reduce citizen complaints. Video footage can also enable departments to collect evidence during investigations or better defend their actions during a particular encounter.

And reform advocates have long called for all officers to be equipped with the technology that could help document excessive use of force and its disproportionate effect on communities of color.

But despite widespread support for body cameras—from politicians, reform advocates, and police departments—the rules around who wears them, when they are activated and what is done with the footage can still vary widely from state to state, and department to department. And research on whether the devices affect officer behavior and accountability has shown mixed results.

When Did U.S. Police Start to Use Body Cameras?

Police in the United Kingdom began experimenting with body-worn cameras in 2005, after which American police showed a "slow growing interest" in them, said Michael White, who is co-director of training and technical assistance for the Justice Department's body-worn camera policy and implementation program.

By 2013, about one-third of local police departments in the U.S. reported using body cameras, according to the Bureau of Justice Statistics. Around the same time, a study on the Rialto Police Department in California showed a 59 percent reduction in police-reported use of force incidents among officers who used the cameras, said Daniel Lawrence, a principal research associate at the Justice Policy Center with the Urban Institute. Data from that study also showed an 87.5 percent decline in citizen complaints against officers who wore the cameras.

Leaders and other stakeholders used the Rialto study to make a case for the use of body cameras, Lawrence said.

Another catalyst for widespread adoption of cameras came in 2014, after a white police officer killed Michael Brown, an 18-year-old Black man, in Ferguson, Missouri. Brown's death came amid a string of other highly publicized police killings of Black people and gave rise to a national debate over policing practices. Amid that conversation, interest in body cameras for police "exploded," said White, who is also a professor at Arizona State University's School of Criminology and Criminal Justice.

"A lot of departments purchased cameras so they wouldn't be the next Ferguson," White said. "There was a lot of emphasis on transparency, on demonstrating to your community that you're willing to be open and to have some accountability."

In 2015, the federal government under President Barack Obama also provided more than $23 million to 73 local and tribal police agencies to expand the use of body cameras. The BJS reported that by 2016, nearly half of the country's 12,267 local police departments were using body cameras. Among departments with more than 500 full-time officers, 70 percent were using body cameras by that time. Yet only five states have laws specifically requiring at least some officers to use body cameras, according to the National Conference of State Legislatures.

How Does Law Enforcement Feel about Body Cameras?

The initial push for body cameras met some criticism from departments and police unions.

The Boston Police Patrolmen's Association in 2016 sued Boston city administrators in an effort to stop a pilot program mandating body cameras for 100 officers. The union cited "increased risk of harm to officers" based on a study indicating that officers in the U.S. and U.K. who were wearing body cameras were 15 percent more likely to be assaulted.

Three body camera researchers told the *NewsHour* that while they are familiar with this study, they have not found similar results in other research. A Massachusetts judge rejected the union's request to delay the body camera program in Boston.

Other police agencies have resisted body cameras because of the costs, according to BJS reports. The Police Executive Research Forum said in a 2018 report that the Dallas Police Department had deployed about 1,000 cameras to cover 30 percent of its officers. Purchase costs per camera were about $189, but maintenance and storage for the thousands of hours of video footage amounted to $789 per camera for one year. In addition to other administrative staff costs, the annual cost in Dallas was $1,125 per camera, about $1.1 million in total.

Last year, the *Washington Post* reported a number of smaller police departments ended their body camera programs because of the high costs. Despite the costs, police departments are generally accepting of body cameras, experts told the *NewsHour*.

"A lot of chiefs of police want these body cameras, because a lot of times they can also work in the department's favor and the officers' favor in depicting a resident's behavior," said Kami Chavis, a professor with Wake Forest University School of Law.

For civilian complaints, having access to video footage can work in the officer's favor, said Andrea Headley, an assistant professor of public affairs with The Ohio State University who researches police-community relations. Some departments may have civilians review video of an incident before they move forward with a complaint, she said. Upon seeing the video and assessing their own actions, civilians may decide not to pursue the complaint.

What Does the Latest Research Indicate about the Effectiveness of Body Cameras?

Early interest in body cameras stemmed from concern about excessive use of force and how race factored into police encounters, Headley said. However, the research on these areas is limited, she added.

According to Headley, there isn't published research on how body cameras affect racial disparities in policing. "There's nothing that really looks at that race aspect, which to me is almost baffling."

Lawrence of the Justice Policy Center said research indicates overall improvement in civilian satisfaction with officers who wear body cameras, but he has not found specific data comparing that satisfaction among different racial groups.

And when it comes to how cameras affect use of force, recent studies are more mixed than the Rialto report, Lawrence said. Later studies were larger and more rigorous, and indicated that the presence of body-worn cameras has minimal effect as a deterrent.

A 2017 study in Washington, D.C., that examined more than 2,000 officers also found body cameras had a negligible effect on officer behavior. "These results suggest that we should recalibrate our expectations of [body cameras'] ability to induce large-scale behavioral changes in policing," the paper stated.

A 2018 study of 504 officers in the Milwaukee Police Department, conducted by Lawrence and other Urban Institute researchers, found that body cameras had no effect on the likelihood officers would use force in the course of their duties.

However, White of the DOJ's body camera program said he has found that 11 of 19 studies on the subject have shown a reduction in use of force among officers wearing cameras. "I think that's still pretty strong," he said.

Police accountability is another area where body camera research has had mixed outcomes. According to White, 20 out of 26 studies measuring citizen complaints and body cameras show a "sizable reduction" in citizen complaints against officers wearing cameras. Lawrence's research also shows decreases in complaints against officers.

But the presence of body camera does not have much effect on whether disciplinary action is taken, Lawrence said. And the prevalence of video technology on street corners and cell phones means that police officers are already filmed regularly in other ways, he added.

Additionally, whether law enforcement releases dashcam or body camera footage, and how much of the video they choose to release, varies between states and jurisdictions. Police in Minneapolis, for instance, released body camera footage of officers' fatal encounter with Floyd, but it was heavily redacted.

It's very rare for police to face prosecutions generally, White said, even with the use of body cameras. But in a few high-profile cases, body camera footage has been used against officers in trials that led to convictions. In 2018, a former officer in Texas was convicted of killing 15-year-old Jordan Edwards. In the 2014 shooting of Laquan McDonald in Chicago, four officers were fired and one was convicted of second-degree murder and 16 counts of aggravated battery after dash cam video showed McDonald walking away from the officers, conflicting with an officer's claims that he was advancing toward him with a knife.

Much more often, body camera footage is used in the prosecution of civilians. One 2016 study found that 92.6 percent of prosecutors' offices nationally in jurisdictions where police wear body cameras have used that footage as evidence in cases against private citizens, while just 8.3 percent have used it to prosecute police officers.

What Do Researchers Recommend for Police Body Camera Programs?

Despite inconsistencies in their findings, researchers told the *NewsHour* that body cameras can still be an effective tool for police reform and transparency when used properly.

One key challenge is specifying how police body cameras should be used, researchers said. A number of departments give officers discretion to determine when they turn their cameras on and off, while others provide more guidance, Headley said.

White said that getting police officers to activate the cameras can be a challenge. Officers engage in numerous interactions daily, and "an officer may forget; they may decide not to activate because of citizen requests," White said, or they may leave the camera off for more "nefarious" reasons like misconduct.

Chavis said police departments should establish clear criteria for when officers activate cameras, who has access to the video and how often the footage is reviewed. Camera footage may sit for weeks in some cases without review, Headley said.

Police video provides an important opportunity for police departments to train their officers, Chavis and Lawrence said. Police leaders should regularly monitor video to get an understanding of how their officers operate in the field, Lawrence said. Video and audio analytic technology have the potential to help departments flag troubling behavior or language used by officers, he added.

At the federal level, experts said lawmakers can establish clearer standards for agencies while also giving them space to determine how to best use body cameras for their communities. One area to be mindful of, experts said, is civilian privacy and surveillance concerns.

House Democrats' Justice in Policing Act would provide some specific requirements for body camera activation and public access to video footage. But while requiring and encouraging the use of body cameras has bipartisan support, the legislation includes a number of other measures that would struggle to win support from Senate Republicans.

The proposed legislation is a testament to the long push for police reform, Chavis said, and can provide important federal guidance.

"The ideas that are within this federal bill are solutions that for years police reform advocates have been suggesting. They are not new," Chavis said. "I think all police want to be well-trained and seen and viewed as professionals. And I think a lot from this legislation can help them do that."

Print Citations

CMS: Norwood, Candice. "Body Cameras Are Seen as Key to Police Reform: But Do They Increase Accountability?" In *The Reference Shelf: Policing in 2020,* edited by Micah L. Issitt, 180-184. Amenia, NY: Grey House Publishing, 2021.

MLA: Norwood, Candice. "Body Cameras Are Seen as Key to Police Reform: But Do They Increase Accountability?" *The Reference Shelf: Policing in 2020,* edited by Micah L. Issitt, Grey Housing Publishing, 2021, pp. 180-184.

APA: Norwood, C. (2021). Body cameras are seen as key to police reform: But do they increase accountability? In Micah L. Issitt (Ed.), *The reference shelf: Policing in 2020* (pp. 180-184). Amenia, NY: Grey Housing Publishing.

Body Cameras May Not Be the Easy Answer Everyone Was Looking For

By Lindsey Van Ness
The Pew Charitable Trusts, January 14, 2020

When a Maine state senator introduced a bill last year to require all police officers to wear body cameras, she expected some discussion.

But the response that Democratic state Sen. Susan Deschambault got was stronger than she anticipated. Several groups, including police chiefs and municipal and county commissioners, opposed it, citing concerns about cost and questioning the necessity of requiring every officer to wear one. And the American Civil Liberties Union asked for the bill to be amended, saying that requiring the cameras without more study was premature.

The legislature delayed action and instead formed a working group to study the issue—and that was fine with Deschambault.

"If we're going to have it," she said in a recent interview, "let's do it right."

Maine's cautious approach reflects a growing awareness, backed by several new studies, that body cameras don't necessarily have a huge effect on police officers' behavior or how residents view the police.

Daniel Lawrence, a researcher at the Urban Institute in Washington, D.C., who has studied the cameras, said more departments are realizing that just purchasing them isn't enough. "The way I see body-worn camera use being emphasized in the future is really having more of an emphasis on not just deploying and having officers wear body-worn cameras, but a closer examination of how they use those cameras," Lawrence said.

Among other factors, Lawrence said, the effectiveness of the cameras depends on when officers are required to turn them on, whether they must review the video before they write incident reports, and whether videos are released to people involved in an incident or to the public. A camera alone, he said, "isn't going to drastically change how police operate."

The push for police body cameras began about five years ago after several high-profile police shootings, including the 2014 death of Michael Brown in Ferguson, Missouri. The rise of video sharing on social media added to the momentum, and in 2015 the Obama administration handed out more than $23 million in federal grants to help agencies of all sizes purchase them.

By 2016, nearly half of U.S. law enforcement agencies had body-worn cameras, according to a Bureau of Justice Statistics survey. In the same survey, about a third of sheriffs' offices and local police departments that didn't have cameras said they were likely to consider acquiring them within the year.

"We're at the point now where it's just expected. Community members expect that officers will have the cameras on them," Lawrence said.

In addition to Maine, lawmakers in Illinois, Mississippi and North Carolina last year considered making body cameras a requirement for most police, the most proposals in one year since 2015, according to a *Stateline* analysis.

Changing Behavior?

But some recent studies question whether the devices are doing what they've been touted to do.

Although both officers and the public generally support body-worn cameras, or BWCs, the impacts may have been overestimated, according to a study published in March by George Mason University's Center for Evidence-Based Crime Policy. The study, which looked at 70 other body-worn camera studies published through June 2018, found the cameras have not had statistically significant effects on most measures of officer and citizen behavior or citizens' views of police.

The authors noted that studies have found mixed results on body cameras leading to reductions in use of force by police—one of the primary reasons supporters pushed for the cameras. Five studies and experiments showed that officers wearing cameras used force less often than officers not wearing cameras, but eight others showed no statistically significant difference in use of force.

The George Mason study also described an unanticipated result of the cameras: Officers increasingly value them as a tool for evidence collection and protection.

"Officers and citizens both seem to believe that BWCs can protect them from each other," the study said.

Another research article released last year came to similar conclusions.

The article, published in the *South Dakota Law Review*, said that although some studies have shown reductions in use of force and citizen complaints, it is unclear whether the results are worth the cost.

David Erickson, who co-authored the *South Dakota Law Review* study and is a retired police sergeant from Sioux Falls, South Dakota, said government officials are right to be concerned about cost but should be more concerned about setting good policies.

"If we can get that mindset changed," Erickson said of setting policies, "I think the cameras become more useful."

Lawrence shared some of his findings last year at a Washington, D.C., city council roundtable on the D.C. police department's body-worn camera program.

The program began with 400 cameras in 2014 and grew to 2,800 cameras two years later. At the time, it was the largest deployment of body cameras in the country, said Charles Allen, the councilmember who chairs the public safety committee.

"Instead of engendering the type of transparency and trust that we would want this program to have, it has had the complete opposite effect," Allen said after four hours of hearing mostly criticisms of the program.

The main concern was the public's restricted access to video. A person in a video can view the footage at a police station. Others may file open records requests, but the department can withhold or redact video being used for an investigation.

> **About 80% of large departments with 500 or more full-time officers had body cameras in 2016; only about 31% of small police departments with part-time officers did.**

Within a week of the hearing, the council made a change: an emergency resolution to allow close relatives of a person killed by police to access footage of the incident.

Getting It Right

In addition to Maine, lawmakers in at least three other states (Louisiana, Maryland and Massachusetts) proposed task forces last year to study body cameras. An Indiana lawmaker started off the 2020 session with a proposal requiring police to set policies for cameras. Nineteen states and Washington, D.C., require law enforcement to have written policies to use or receive funding for body-worn cameras, according to the National Conference of State Legislatures.

South Dakota state Sen. Reynold Nesiba, a Democrat, plans to introduce a bill in the upcoming session to "start a conversation" about regulating cameras. While Nesiba doesn't anticipate the state funding a camera program, he sees the use of cameras growing and wants to get standards in place, he said in an interview.

The bill includes a requirement for all agencies using cameras to develop a policy on areas including training, discipline, reporting and maintenance.

"We have to figure out a balance between state-mandated rules and local jurisdictions," Nesiba said.

Applicants for federal body-camera grants must include policies with their applications, according to Justice Department spokeswoman Tannyr Watkins. The program awarded $73 million to more than 400 agencies from 2015 to 2019.

The National Institute of Justice and the FBI have published general guidelines on body-worn cameras. So has the International Association of Chiefs of Police, which supports body-worn cameras generally but takes the stance that each agency knows how to craft policy best for its community, according to Julie Parker, spokeswoman for the association.

Cost Concerns

In many places, the cost of body cameras remains the primary concern.

In Kansas, for example, a 2018 bill that would have made body cameras a requirement for most law enforcement officers died in a Senate committee.

State Sen. Rick Wilborn, the Republican chairman of the committee, said in an interview that, like most states, Kansas has a few larger cities but lots of small municipalities with small budgets. "We try to be understanding, especially with smaller counties," Wilborn said. "You can't mandate something that's onerous to the point of breaking a budget."

About 80% of large departments with 500 or more full-time officers had body cameras in 2016, according to the Bureau of Justice Statistics. In comparison, only about 31% of small police departments with part-time officers did.

Among police agencies that did not have the cameras, the primary reason given was cost, including video storage/disposal, hardware costs and ongoing maintenance, according to the Bureau of Justice Statistics.

Cost was on the mind of a chief of a 20-person police department in Salem, Illinois, last year when a city council member asked him to research body-worn cameras.

"We have a good public trust here. We don't have accusations of police misconduct," said Chief Sean Reynolds in an interview.

But he wanted his officers to be able to capture high-profile incidents. Reynolds sought quotes from a retailer, Viridian Weapon Technologies, which estimated that it would cost $5,000 to use and store data from one body camera for five years.

The company provided another option: gun-mounted cameras, which would automatically activate when the weapon was pulled and cost about $800 for five years.

Reynolds chose the second option.

"We wanted something that was cost effective and left no room for error," he said.

Last year Illinois state Rep. Justin Slaughter, a Democrat, introduced a bill to make body-worn cameras a requirement. The bill is still in committee, and Slaughter did not respond to requests for comment.

If the state mandated cameras, Reynolds said he would find a way to comply, but the cost would be difficult for small agencies like his.

Some states don't require cameras but have set aside money for departments that want to purchase them. New Jersey allocated $1 million for cameras in its 2019 budget. New Mexico included $3.1 million for cameras for state police in its 2019 budget, even after a study group led by the attorney general's office was reticent to recommend the program.

A Requirement in Two States

Only two states, Nevada and South Carolina, require all law enforcement agencies to use the cameras. Both states have faced challenges in reaching universal compliance.

In Nevada, former Republican Gov. Brian Sandoval signed measures to mandate body cameras for the state highway patrol in 2015 and all law enforcement agencies in 2017. To help cover the cost, the law allowed county governments to increase 9-1-1 surcharges on phone bills.

But Nevada's use of 9-1-1 fees was criticized in a December report from the Federal Communications Commission. The fees are supposed to be used for 9-1-1 related services, according to the commission.

Law enforcement agencies in Nevada were given a deadline of July 2018 to start using body- worn cameras, but some departments didn't get the equipment until nearly a year later. The law didn't include a penalty for not getting cameras, and it's possible that some departments still don't have them, according to a spokeswoman for the state's public safety department.

In South Carolina, then-Gov. Nikki Haley, a Republican, signed a law to make body cameras a requirement for police in 2015. But the devices aren't everywhere in the state yet.

The law had a caveat: The cameras would be required when the state fully funded the programs.

Since 2016, the state has divvied up $13.4 million to 164 law enforcement agencies, according to the South Carolina Department of Public Safety. There are 180 agencies in the state, according to Scott Slatton, a lobbyist for the South Carolina Municipal Association.

"We supported the idea of body-worn cameras and understood how important they were," Slatton said.

The association pushed for state funding as part of the law and is pushing for more state money to help departments buy body cameras and pay for data storage, he said.

One of the good outcomes of the law, he said, is that it requires agencies that apply for state money to set policies for using cameras.

Print Citations

CMS: Van Ness, Lindsey. "Body Cameras May Not Be the Easy Answer Everyone Was Looking For." In *The Reference Shelf: Policing in 2020*, edited by Micah L. Issitt, 185-189. Amenia, NY: Grey House Publishing, 2021.

MLA: Van Ness, Lindsey. "Body Cameras May Not Be the Easy Answer Everyone Was Looking For." *The Reference Shelf: Policing in 2020*, edited by Micah L. Issitt, Grey Housing Publishing, 2021, pp. 185-189.

APA: Van Ness, L. (2021). Body cameras may not be the easy answer everyone was looking for. In Micah L. Issitt (Ed.), *The reference shelf: Policing in 2020* (pp. 185-189). Amenia, NY: Grey Housing Publishing.

Amazon's Doorbell Camera Ring Is Working with Police—and Controlling What They Say

By Kari Paul

The Guardian, August 30, 2019

Ring, Amazon's camera-connected smart doorbell company, has cameras watching hundreds of thousands of doorsteps across the US. It's also keeping an eye on what local police say online.

Records obtained through an information request show how Ring uses corporate partnerships to shape the communications of police departments it collaborates with, directing the departments' press releases, social media posts and comments on public posts.

Ring, which was acquired by Amazon in 2018, sells smart doorbells that allow users to monitor their doorstep remotely and operates Neighbors by Ring, an accompanying app that lets users view footage uploaded by other Ring owners.

In recent months, Ring has partnered with hundreds of US law enforcement agencies, offering departments access to its platform in exchange for outreach to residents. Ring says the program gives police more resources to solve crimes, while critics fear the company is quietly building up a for-profit private surveillance network. Ring's power over police departments' communications with the citizens they serve is just the latest question about the company's operations.

Andrew Ferguson, a law professor and the author of *The Rise of Big Data Policing* said there has been a rise of tech company influence on police work over the past decade, but shaping marketing language within police departments represents a new level of "distortion of public safety rule".

"Police should not have dual loyalty to a private company and the public—their loyalty should be to the public," he said. "Any sort of blurring of that line causes us to question that loyalty."

How Amazon Controls Social Media of Local Police Departments

Pittsburg, Kansas, a city near the Missouri border with a population of 20,000 people, publicly announced a partnership with Ring on 22 April 2019. Emails obtained by the *Guardian* show Ring first pitched the department in December 2018, offering deals including discounts on devices and sending the police force a free

$200 device for every 20 downloads of the Neighbors app. These types of tit-for-tat agreements were a common practice for the company, reporting from *Motherboard* has showed, and are part of an effort to grow the audience of its app.

On 28 February, once the Pittsburg police green-lighted the program, Ring sent the department a press release template and noted the final communique would have to be approved by Ring before release. The Ring representative also sent Amazon-approved social media assets to be used to promote the Ring program.

"Remember to make sure you highlight your Branch/Text link to try and have your civilians download the Neighbors by Ring App," he said on 12 March. "I recommend reposting these links to your social media pages once a month to re-engage the community to download the app!"

On 25 April, a spokesman from Ring praised social media posts regarding the partnership and encouraged more. "Let's keep this community interaction going strong!" he said. "Hopefully, the department can get a ton of people to download the Neighbors App from your specific link!"

Emails between Ring and police officials in Gwinnett county, Georgia—a county near Atlanta with a population of around 900,000—show a similar script.

Ring first contacted the department in August 2018, and police approved the partnership in May 2019. Ring donated 80 doorbells to police, valued at $15,920. It heavily edited the press release about the program, removing one sentence that said "the company will donate 80 Ring Video Doorbell 2s, valued at $15,920, which the company will give away and help install".

Ring also changed wording from the police department that said the department "will be able to access videos submitted by subscribers of Ring" to say the department will "join existing crime and safety conversations with local residents". Ring also deleted a sentence saying "police cannot access live stream video", changing it to "police will not have access to cameras, live footage, or user data".

> **Advocates fear that the cameras will allow police access to surveillance footage while bypassing the public process to approve more traditional security cameras.**

The Ring representative also offered to cross-promote alerts from Gwinnett county police directly to the Amazon-owned Facebook page, sharing images of people who had not yet been charged with a crime publicly. A spokesman from the Gwinnett county police department said separate from Ring, it often publishes images and videos of suspects in crimes on social media to help identify them for criminal prosecution.

Gizmodo documented similar arrangements between the company and police departments in California, Florida and Texas.

"Ring provides sample social media content for police departments to utilize at their discretion to inform their jurisdictions about their partnerships with Ring," a spokeswoman for the company said. "Ring requests to look at press releases and any messaging prior to distribution to ensure our company and our products and services are accurately represented," she added.

Amazon's Social Media Advising Is Ongoing

Emails between Ring representatives and Pittsburg police show the company continued to shape police rhetoric online, months after the launch of the partnership. In one email the representative encourages officers to tell locals more about crime statistics.

"I just wanted to reach out and say great job with the response you made with neighbors commenting about crime going up etc," the email says. "That's an exact comment residents need to see coming directly from the department to put things into perspective."

In another post, a Ring spokesman tells police to comment more frequently on crime posts to encourage users to report on the Neighbors app when they see crime in the neighborhood. "This is exactly the interaction your community needs to see," he told an officer who commented on a post about a woman whose car had been broken into.

A spokesman for the Pittsburg police said Ring and its Neighbors app represent an extension of its information dissemination and crime reporting efforts in the general community.

"We recognize that social media is a vast and readily accessible public communications mechanism and are trying to openly engage the community through as many platforms as possible to encourage people to become involved and report crime or suspicious activity," a spokesman said. "Ring is another social media platform through which we can communicate and share information with the community and to promote better transparency."

Andrew Ferguson, the law professor, said the language Ring encourages police departments to market Ring products to private citizens, changing the relationship between citizens and the police.

"The purpose for this kind of commentary is to fuel a narrative that these devices are effective in stopping crime, that there is a high rate of crime and thus people need these devices, and police support a particular brand of camera over other brands of camera," he said. "All of those are questionable choices for a public safety organization that should have a primary purpose of serving public safety and not corporate marketing."

These kinds of interactions "undermine public trust in law enforcement", echoed Matt Cagle, a technology and civil liberties attorney for the American Civil Liberties Union said.

"It is shocking to see a private corporation dictating what public officials will say to community members about public safety issues," he said. "Ring answers to Amazon shareholders, and police are supposed to answer to the public. That is the core tension in these relationships."

Privacy Advocates Want Police Surveillance Off Our Doorsteps

Ring had a 97% share of the video doorbell market as of 2018, according to market research firm NPD group. The company had more than one million US customers when it was acquired by Amazon in 2018. A map of existing users in Gwinnett county shared by the company with the police force showed hundreds of cameras in the new area of partnership.

The company has now created partnerships with more than 400 police forces, according to the *Washington Post*, including partnerships with law enforcement agencies across the US in places including Florida, Virginia, Atlanta, California, and Texas.

Ring said police do not automatically have access to Ring video streams. Law enforcement has access to a portal, and then needs to directly request information from Neighbors app users if it wants to watch footage. Ring says it does not share information with law enforcement unless a user consents.

But the company's law enforcement partnerships have faced criticism from privacy and criminal justice activists. Advocates fear that the cameras will allow police access to surveillance footage while bypassing the public process to approve more traditional security cameras. They have pointed out that contracts between police and Ring often face little public scrutiny and experts have raised concerns over requests from Ring to get access to police department's computer-aided dispatch feeds.

Advocates have also questioned how comfortable users feel in denying law enforcement requests. And they have pointed at problems of discrimination that Ring, and the broader industry of neighborhood social networks, have faced.

"What often happens in instances of increased surveillance is that there are more arrests of 'suspicious characters,' which often end up being people of color not breaking any laws," said Caroline Sinders, a machine learning designer in Berlin who studies the intersections between technology and harassment. "This is going to result in more people of color being hassled and arrested for just existing."

Jamie Siminoff, the founder of Ring has said Ring keeps "customers, their privacy, and the security of their information" at the top of its priority list. "Our customers and Neighbors app users place their trust in us to help protect their homes and communities and we take that responsibility incredibly seriously," he said in a blogpost about Neighbors.

Print Citations

CMS: Paul, Kari. "Amazon's Doorbell Camera Ring Is Working with Police—and Controlling What They Say." In *The Reference Shelf: Policing in 2020*, edited by Micah L. Issitt, 190-194. Amenia, NY: Grey House Publishing, 2021.

MLA: Paul, Kari. "Amazon's Doorbell Camera Ring Is Working with Police—and Controlling What They Say." *The Reference Shelf: Policing in 2020*, edited by Micah L. Issitt, Grey Housing Publishing, 2021, pp. 190-194.

APA: Paul, K. (2021). Amazon's doorbell camera Ring is working with police—and controlling what they say. In Micah L. Issitt (Ed.), *The reference shelf: Policing in 2020* (pp. 190-194). Amenia, NY: Grey Housing Publishing.

How to Reform Police Monitoring of Social Media

By Rachel Levinson-Waldman and Angel Diaz
Brookings Institution, July 9, 2020

Civil rights protesters have long been the target of state surveillance. Recent efforts to keep tabs on Black Lives Matter protests and demonstrations against family separation, for instance, echo the FBI's counter-intelligence program used to spy on civil rights leaders from Martin Luther King, Jr. to Huey Newton.

Yet today's surveillance analysts have a new source of information: social media. Consider the recent protests over the police killings of George Floyd and Breonna Taylor. As demonstrations spread across the country, the FBI and local police monitored social media and made arrests based on what people have posted online. In one instance, police in Wichita, Kansas even arrested a teenager on suspicion of incitement to rioting based on a threatening Snapchat screenshot he shared. The teen's post added a note cautioning readers to "stay tf away from" his hometown—rhetoric intended to denounce the call to violence, not to foment it.

Unfortunately, the surveillance of social media is a growing trend. In recent years, social media posts have landed individuals of color in overbroad and unreliable gang databases, and even been used to justify keeping them imprisoned. One New York teen spent more than a year on Rikers Island, based in large part on the district attorney's incorrect assessment that he was a member of a criminal gang. The D.A. relied on Facebook photos of the teen with members of a local crew—a group of kids loosely affiliated by block or housing development—and several posts from crew members that he had "liked." In reality, the teen was simply connected to crew members because they were his neighbors and family members. The extent to which communities of color are viewed with suspicion can create a self-fulfilling prophecy where basic social media etiquette is mistaken for membership in a criminal enterprise. Social media is highly contextual and prone to misinterpretation, magnifying the risk that one person's innocuous post will be taken as something more sinister.

From protests to public housing, social media monitoring raises civil liberties and civil rights concerns that are currently going unaddressed. Establishing a framework that balances public safety and the right to privacy, free expression, and equal protection under the law requires updates to our existing regulatory controls.

How Do Police Monitor Social Media?

To begin with, how do the police watch social media? Most commonly, an officer views publicly available posts by searching for an individual, group, hashtag, or another search vector. Depending on the platform and the search, it may yield all of the content responsive to the query or only a portion. When seeking access to more than is publicly available, police may use an informant (such as a friend of the target) or create an undercover account by posing as a fellow activist or alluring stranger. This allows officers to communicate directly with the target and see content posted by both the target and their contacts that might otherwise be inaccessible to the public.

Police have also used software to monitor people, groups, associations, or locations in a more automated manner. This software included tools that mapped clusters of activity and a platform for linking undercover accounts. This tactic is less common now after the major platforms prohibited app developers from receiving automated access to public content for surveillance.

Dataminr, the prominent social media analytics firm, appears to have found a partial workaround to this prohibition by providing police with "public sector alerts." Dataminr's automated systems analyze public data feeds and deliver automated alerts to law enforcement clients, including the FBI, about shootings and natural disasters. It is unclear whether law enforcement can customize the service to go beyond the types of alerts included in Dataminr's marketing material.

Law enforcement may also request social media data as part of a criminal investigation. By deploying subpoenas and warrants, law enforcement can collect an array of data directly from social media companies. For example, a template warrant drawn up by the Department of Justice to serve on Facebook contemplates collecting an array of data, including contact information, photos, status updates, private messages, friends lists, group affiliations, "friend" requests, future and past event postings, privacy settings, and more.

Social media monitoring is pervasive. According to a 2017 survey by the International Association of Chiefs of Police, 70% of responding police departments use social media for intelligence gathering and to monitor public sentiment. Similarly, Facebook's latest transparency report states that the company received over 50,000 government requests for data between July and December 2019.

What Does the Law Say?

Despite widespread use of social media by police, there are few laws that specifically constrain law enforcement's ability to engage in social media monitoring. In the absence of legislation, the strongest controls over this surveillance tactic are often police departments' individual social media policies and platform restrictions, such as Facebook's real name policy and Twitter's prohibition against using its API for surveillance. While the constitutional landscape is unsettled, constitutional protections for privacy, freedom of speech and association, and equal protection may provide mechanisms for individuals to challenge the government's collection and use of their social media data.

Fourth Amendment Protections

The Fourth Amendment guarantees the right of the people to be free from unreasonable searches and seizures; the inquiry for whether a search was unreasonable, outside of the core protections of the Fourth Amendment for "persons, houses, papers, and effects," generally comes down to whether a person has a "reasonable expectation of privacy" and whether society recognizes that expectation as reasonable. While courts have begun to recognize that privacy doesn't require absolute secrecy, they have nevertheless typically held that individuals do not have a recognized expectation of privacy in data publicly shared online. As one appeals court put it, "If you post a tweet, just like you scream it out the window, there is no reasonable expectation of privacy."

When police want access to information that is not readily available to the public, however, the Supreme Court generally requires law enforcement to meet a higher standard. The Court has held, for instance, that when law enforcement uses digital tools to view information that would otherwise require a warrant to obtain, the use of that tool requires a warrant as well. Nevertheless, courts have generally allowed police to engage in undercover operations (both online and in the real world) without obtaining a warrant—though individual law enforcement agencies may put additional restrictions in place.

This permissive approach largely grows out of a separate legal principle called the "third-party doctrine." Under this doctrine, when people share information with a third party, whether another person or a business, they should expect that the data could be disclosed to the government.

Courts have extended this reasoning to social media. In *United States v. Meregildo* (2012), for instance, a New York district court found that while a person's privacy settings might have signaled an intent to maintain secrecy, any expectation of privacy was "extinguished" when they shared content with Facebook friends because those individuals were free to use that information however they saw fit—including by sharing it with law enforcement.

But the boundaries of the third-party doctrine are becoming murkier, and the Supreme Court is increasingly signaling a need to reconsider the doctrine in light of technological advances. Most recently, in the 2018 case *Carpenter v. United States,* the court ruled that despite the third-party doctrine, the police had to obtain a warrant before it could access historical location information held by cell phone providers. And in the Supreme Court's 2012 decision in *United States v. Jones,* which held that the government had to get a warrant to install a GPS device that enabled constant location tracking, Justice Sonia Sotomayor observed in her concurrence that secrecy might need to stop being treated as a "prerequisite for

> **A single officer can monitor the social media accounts of dozens of people all at once, without having to leave her workstation.**

privacy" in order to account for the volumes of sensitive data shared with third parties on a daily basis.

The application of the Fourth Amendment has been rooted in practical limitations, but the force multiplier effect of social media surveillance calls those limitations into question. If police want to physically trail a car, there are limits to the number of vehicles that can be followed. Having to make determinations about how best to allocate an officer's valuable time provides some rough limits, even if those resource decisions are not always made judiciously. By contrast, a single officer can monitor the social media accounts of dozens of people all at once, without having to leave her workstation. Undercover social media accounts offer greatly expanded power as well. An officer who would have to take care to create and maintain a single undercover persona in real life could have twenty different personas online. And sophisticated software may be able to assist police in monitoring thousands of accounts at the push of a button.

In 1983, the Supreme Court predicted that this kind of wide-scale surveillance could trigger a different legal analysis. "If such dragnet-type law enforcement practices...should eventually occur," it may be time "to determine whether different constitutional principles may be applicable," Justice William Rehnquist wrote in *United States v. Knotts*, in which the court decided that tracking a suspect using a surreptitiously planted beeper device did not constitute a Fourth Amendment search.

Finally, law enforcement can also seek account information directly from social media companies. Under the Stored Communications Act (SCA), law enforcement can serve a warrant or subpoena on a social media company to get access to information about a person's social media profile. The SCA also permits service providers to voluntarily share user data without any legal process if delays in providing the information may lead to death or serious injury.

While numerous defendants have challenged the constitutional validity of warrants to search their social media data, courts have generally upheld the warrants. For example, courts have upheld warrants looking for IP logs to establish a suspect's location, for evidence of communications between suspects, and to establish a connection between co-conspirators.

First and Fourteenth Amendment Protections

The First and Fourteenth Amendments offer protections where surveillance is based on political or religious beliefs, associations, racial and ethnic identities, and other protected categories or activities. Surveillance can have a chilling effect on First Amendment freedoms, and surveillance that disproportionately targets a protected class can give rise to equal protection harms under the Fourteenth Amendment.

Social media monitoring can have serious chilling effects on protected speech and association. When police target individuals for surveillance because of their political viewpoints, people may choose to censor their online activity and associations to reduce the risk of governmental monitoring. Likewise, law enforcement may use social media to compile dossiers on people on the basis of First

Amendment-protected activities and may share them among local, state, and federal agencies—this can increase the risk that protesters later face retaliatory targeting in the form of deportation proceedings or unrelated criminal prosecutions.

The case law on whether these impacts give rise to concrete First Amendment claims continues to evolve. In *Laird v. Tatum* (1972), the Supreme Court adopted a restrictive approach to the First Amendment, ruling that plaintiffs in the case did not have standing to challenge an Army intelligence program stood up in response to 1960s civil rights protests. That program collected information from newspapers and police departments and sent Army intelligence agents to attend public meetings. But, the Court ruled, the mere existence of a surveillance program that may have chilled speech did not cause sufficient harm to give the plaintiffs the right to sue under the First Amendment.

Where the targeting of First Amendment-protected activity leads to a concrete harm, affected individuals may have standing to raise a claim. For example, in *Baird v. State Bar of Arizona*, a lawyer was prevented from joining the state bar because she refused to answer if she had ever been a member of the Communist Party. There, the Supreme Court ruled that the government "may not inquire about a man's views or associations solely for the purpose of withholding a right or benefit because of what he believes." Applying this ruling to the digital era, if a person's social media is surveilled on the basis of her political beliefs or associations, and she is later denied a civil benefit or prosecuted for an unrelated crime in retaliation for the beliefs or associations revealed, she should have standing to bring a First Amendment claim. In a time when social media monitoring allows the government to discover a person's beliefs and associations easily and covertly, there is a particular need to ensure that this information is not misused to target disfavored individuals for adverse government action. Unchecked, discriminatory surveillance can have chilling effects on unpopular but lawful associations.

Fortunately, in *Hassan v. City of New York* (2015), the Third Circuit ruled that where discriminatory government monitoring dissuades individuals from exercising their constitutional rights, they may have standing to challenge the surveillance. The Hassan court evaluated the NYPD's post-9/11 surveillance of Muslim communities in New York and New Jersey. This surveillance program targeted mosques, student groups, businesses, cafes, and more, leading many individuals to limit or withdraw from being active participants in their community. The Third Circuit ruled that where surveillance is racially or religiously biased, or undertaken in retaliation for exercising First Amendment rights, impacted individuals have standing to challenge the practice in court—even if the discrimination is not "motivated by ill will, enmity, or hostility."

Extending Hassan to social media monitoring, surveillance that targets protected speech or disproportionately targets a racial or religious group, and leads to a concrete harm, can give rise to a viable First or Fourteenth Amendment challenge, even if the surveillance was not animated by "overt hostility or prejudice." By intentionally targeting Black Lives Matter activists, police may be engaging in this kind of discriminatory surveillance. The same analysis could also apply to the surveillance of teens and pre-teens of color suspected of gang activity.

These discriminatory surveillance programs, which target their online lives for disparate treatment based on their ethnicity, may stamp them with a badge of inferiority that violates their rights to equal protection under the law. In Boston, a defense attorney recently won a discovery order requiring the police department to produce records related to its surveillance on Snapchat, which will offer an opportunity to determine whether the program disproportionately targets Black and Latino men.

Room for Reform

The availability of social media has dramatically expanded the scope of law enforcement surveillance. At the same time, few departments have publicly available policies governing their use of social media for intelligence, data collection, and criminal investigations. There are a number of practical steps that can be taken to begin to address this gap.

Every jurisdiction should be required to hold public hearings and obtain local government approval before police engage in social media monitoring. Where departments are already engaged in this practice, they should pause the bulk of these operations pending public hearings and evaluate whether existing surveillance programs disproportionately target constitutionally protected groups or associations.

Every law enforcement agency that uses social media for data gathering purposes should have a publicly available policy that describes their use of social media. These policies should detail the restrictions and procedures for social media monitoring and should specify the standards governing collection, use, retention, and sharing of personal information. Social media policies should contain clear prohibitions against surveillance based on race, religion, gender, sexual orientation, immigration status, or a person's exercise of First Amendment freedoms. The policy should also specify the legal processes that must be followed before law enforcement can seek social media data from companies. The restrictions imposed by a department's social media policy should be legally enforceable, such as by state attorneys general or the Department of Justice.

Not every investigation warrants the use of invasive covert accounts. There should be strict controls on the use of this technique, including ongoing monitoring, supervisory approval and oversight, and time limitations. Law enforcement should be banned from impersonating an actual person without that person's permission. Where law enforcement wants to use a covert account, they should be required to document that no less-invasive means are available and to submit the documentation to an external body for oversight and approval. Judicial oversight of online undercover activity would offer the most robust protection.

Police are prevented from interviewing minors without notifying their parent or guardian. This protection should be extended to the online space with a flat prohibition against police connecting with minors via social media.

Social media monitoring should be subject to ongoing reporting and audit requirements. For example, police should have to regularly disclose information such as the number of social media investigations that are open and closed and those that are extended past their original closure date. The reports should also indicate where investigations may impact protected classes of people. Each police department's social media monitoring practices should be audited by an independent entity on an ongoing basis to ensure compliance with constitutional protections and safeguards.

These recommendations are intended as starting points for enacting needed reforms. They represent a regulatory floor, and jurisdictions should be empowered to enact stronger prohibitions against certain types of monitoring. This may prove necessary in jurisdictions where police departments exhibit repeated and consistent practices that violate constitutional rights and freedoms. Establishing the right regulatory controls will require input and action from a number of stakeholders, from communities to civil society to police departments and local government to Congress and the Department of Justice. But this important regulatory action is overdue and should not be put off any longer.

Print Citations

CMS: Levinson-Waldman, Rachel, and Angel Diaz. "How to Reform Police Monitoring of Social Media." In *The Reference Shelf: Policing in 2020,* edited by Micah L. Issitt, 195-201. Amenia, NY: Grey House Publishing, 2021.

MLA: Levinson-Waldman, Rachel, and Angel Diaz. "How to Reform Police Monitoring of Social Media." *The Reference Shelf: Policing in 2020,* edited by Micah L. Issitt, Grey Housing Publishing, 2021, pp. 195-201.

APA: Levinson-Waldman, R., & Diaz, A. (2021). How to reform police monitoring of social media. In Micah L. Issitt (Ed.), *The reference shelf: Policing in 2020* (pp. 195-201). Amenia, NY: Grey Housing Publishing.

Bibliography

Al-Gharbi, Musa. "Police Punish the 'Good Apples.'" *The Atlantic*. Jul 1, 2020. https://www.theatlantic.com/ideas/archive/2020/07/what-police-departments-do-whistle-blowers/613687/.

Andrew, Scottie. "There's a Growing Call to Defund the Police: Here's What It Means." *CNN*. Jun 17, 2020. https://www.cnn.com/2020/06/06/us/what-is-de-fund-police-trnd/index.html.

Bates, Josiah. "'We Cannot Police Our Way Out of a Pandemic.' Experts, Police Union Say NYPD Should Not Be Enforcing Social Distance Rules Amid CO-VID-19." *Time*. May 7, 2020. https://time.com/5832403/nypd-pandemic-police-social-distancing-arrests/.

"Body Cameras and Privacy—Where Do You Draw the Line?" *National Police Foundation*. 2020. https://www.policefoundation.org/body-cameras-and-privacy-where-do-you-draw-the-line/.

Chapman, Brett. "Body-Worn Cameras: What the Evidence Tells Us." *NIJ*. National Institute of Justice. Nov 14, 2018. https://nij.ojp.gov/topics/articles/body-worn-cameras-what-evidence-tells-us.

Clark, Caitlin. "Texas A&M Study: White Police Officers Use Force More Often Than Non-White Colleges." *Texas A&M Today*. Jun 24, 2020. https://today.tamu.edu/2020/06/24/texas-am-study-white-police-officers-use-force-more-often-than-non-white-colleagues/.

Dixon, Emily. "Alexandria Ocasio-Cortez Was Asked About Defunding the Police and Her Answer Went Viral." *Marie Claire*. Jun 12, 2020. https://www.marieclaire.com/politics/a32849383/alexandria-ocasio-cortez-defund-the-police/.

"Evaluating the Impact of Police Body Cameras." *Urban Institute*. 2020. https://www.urban.org/debates/evaluating-impact-police-body-cameras.

Fan, Andrew. "Chicago Police are 14 Times More Likely to Use Force Against Young Black Men Than Against Whites." *The Intercept*. Aug 16, 2018. https://theintercept.com/2018/08/16/chicago-police-misconduct-racial-disparity/.

Greenberg, Jon. "PolitiFact: Has Coronavirus Killed More Cops Than All Other Causes?" *Tampa Bay Times*. Sep 6, 2020. https://www.tampabay.com/news/health/2020/09/06/politifact-has-coronavirus-killed-more-cops-than-all-other-causes/.

Greenwood, Faine. "How to Regulate Police Use of Drones." *Brookings*. Sep 24, 2020. https://www.brookings.edu/techstream/how-to-regulate-police-use-of-drones/.

Gross, Elana Lyn. "New York City Civil Rights Organizations Sue NYPD and City Officials for Alleged 'Police Brutality' at Protests." *Forbes*. Oct 26, 2020.

https://www.forbes.com/sites/elanagross/2020/10/26/new-york-city-civil-rights-organizations-sue-nypd-and-city-officials-for-alleged-police-brutality-at-protests/?sh=4aebb6ba6810.

Gross, Terry. "Militarization of Police Means U.S. Protesters Face Weapons Designed for War." *NPR*. Jul 1, 2020. https://www.npr.org/2020/07/01/885942130/militarization-of-police-means-u-s-protesters-face-weapons-designed-for-war.

Heatherly, Michael C. "Drones: The American Controversy." *Journal of Strategic Security*, vol. 7, no. 4, 2014. https://scholarcommons.usf.edu/cgi/viewcontent.cgi?referer=&httpsredir=1&article=1387&context=jss.

"Impact of Stress on Police Officers' Physical and Mental Health." *Science Daily*. Sep 29, 2008. https://www.sciencedaily.com/releases/2008/09/080926105029.htm.

Ingraham, Christopher. "Two Charts Demolish the Notion That Immigrants Here Illegally Commit More Crime." *Washington Post*. Jun 19, 2018. https://www.washingtonpost.com/news/wonk/wp/2018/06/19/two-charts-demolish-the-notion-that-immigrants-here-illegally-commit-more-crime/.

Ingraham, Christopher. "White People Are More Likely to Deal Drugs, but Black People Are More Likely to Get Arrested for It." *Washington Post*. Sep 30, 2014. https://www.washingtonpost.com/news/wonk/wp/2014/09/30/white-people-are-more-likely-to-deal-drugs-but-black-people-are-more-likely-to-get-arrested-for-it/.

Jennings, Wesley G., and Nicholas M. Perez. "The Immediate Impact of COVID-19 on Law Enforcement in the United States." *American Journal of Criminal Justice*. Jun 6, 2020. https://www.ncbi.nlm.nih.gov/pmc/articles/PMC7275851/.

Johnson, Kevin, and Kristine Phillips. "'Perfect Storm': Defund the Police, COVID-19 Lead to Biggest Police Budget Cuts in Decade." *USA Today*. Jul 31, 2020. https://www.usatoday.com/story/news/politics/2020/07/31/defund-police-covid-19-force-deepest-cop-budget-cuts-decade/5538397002/.

"Judiciary Committee Releases Report on Trump Administration Family Separation Policy." *House Committee on the Judiciary*. Oct 29, 2020. https://judiciary.house.gov/news/documentsingle.aspx?DocumentID=3442.

Koerth, Maggie, and Amelia Thomson-DeVeaux. "Many Americans Are Convinced Crime Is Rising in the U.S.: They're Wrong." *FiveThirtyEight*. Aug 3, 2020. https://fivethirtyeight.com/features/many-americans-are-convinced-crime-is-rising-in-the-u-s-theyre-wrong/.

Lally, Robin. "Police Use of Fatal Force Identified as a Leading Cause of Death in Young Men." *Rutgers*. Aug 8, 2019. https://www.rutgers.edu/news/police-use-fatal-force-identified-leading-cause-death-young-men.

Lartey, Jamiles. "By the Numbers: US Police Kill More in Days Than Other Countries Do in Years." *The Guardian*. Jun 9, 2015. https://www.theguardian.com/us-news/2015/jun/09/the-counted-police-killings-us-vs-other-countries.

Maciag, Mike. "Where Police Don't Mirror Communities and Why It Matters." *Governing*. Aug 28, 2015. https://www.governing.com/topics/public-justice-safety/gov-police-department-diversity.html.

Mark, Michelle. "US Police Don't End Up Solving Most Crimes." *Business Insider.* Jun 18, 2020. https://www.insider.com/police-dont-solve-most-violent-property-crimes-data-2020-6.

Miller, Brian. "The Militarization of America's Police: A Brief History." *FEE.* May 24, 2019. https://fee.org/articles/the-militarization-of-americas-police-a-brief-history/.

Mummolo, Jonathan. "Militarization Fails to Enhance Police Safety or Reduce Crime but May Harm Police Reputation." *PNAS.* Sep 11, 2018. https://www.pnas.org/content/115/37/9181.

Najibi, Alex. "Racial Discrimination in Face Recognition Technology." *Harvard.* Oct 24, 2020. http://sitn.hms.harvard.edu/flash/2020/racial-discrimination-in-face-recognition-technology/.

Netherland, Julie, and Helena B. Hansen. "The War on Drugs That Wasn't: Wasted Whiteness, 'Dirty Doctors,' and Race in Media Coverage of Prescription Opioid Misuse." *Culture, Medicine, and Psychiatry*, vol. 40, no. 4, 2016.

Ortiz, Aimee. "Confidence in Police Is at Record Low, Gallup Survey Finds." *New York Times.* Aug 12, 2020. https://www.nytimes.com/2020/08/12/us/gallup-poll-police.html.

"Overview of Drone Technology and Related Controversies." *Lawfare.* 2020. https://www.lawfareblog.com/overview-drone-technology-and-related-controversies.

Peeples, Lynne. "What the Data Say about Police Shootings." *Nature.* Sep 04, 2019. https://www.nature.com/articles/d41586-019-02601-9.

Phillips, Kristine. "Many Face Mask Mandates Go Unenforced as Police Feel Political, Economic Pressure." *USA Today.* Sep 16, 2020. https://www.usatoday.com/story/news/politics/2020/09/16/covid-19-face-mask-mandates-go-unenforced-police-under-pressure/5714736002/.

"Police Responses to COVID-19." *Brennan Center.* Jul 8, 2020. https://www.brennancenter.org/our-work/research-reports/police-responses-covid-19.

Price, Megan, and Jamie Price. "Insights Policing and the Role of the Civilian in Police Accountability." *Clearinghouse Review.* Aug. 2015. file:///Users/Adrienne/Downloads/InsightPolicingPoliceAccountability_Price.pdf.

Ray, Rashawn. "What Does 'Defund the Police' Mean and Does It Have Merit?" *Brookings.* Jun 19, 2020. https://www.brookings.edu/blog/fixgov/2020/06/19/what-does-defund-the-police-mean-and-does-it-have-merit/.

Rice, Johnny II. "Why We Must Improve Police Responses to Mental Illness." *NAMI.* National Alliance on Mental Health. Mar 2, 2020. https://www.nami.org/Blogs/NAMI-Blog/March-2020/Why-We-Must-Improve-Police-Responses-to-Mental-Illness.

Sangree, Ruth. "Breaking the Cycle of Mass Incarceration." *Brennan Center.* Jan 3, 2020. https://www.brennancenter.org/our-work/analysis-opinion/breaking-cycle-mass-incarceration.

Sauter, Michael B., and Charles Stockdale. "The Most Dangerous Jobs in the US Include Electricians, Firefighters and Police Officers." *USA Today.* Jan 8, 2019.

https://www.usatoday.com/story/money/2019/01/08/most-dangerous-jobs-us-where-fatal-injuries-happen-most-often/38832907/.

Schultz, David. "A Long, Powerful History: How We Militarized the Police." *Minnpost.* https://www.minnpost.com/community-voices/2014/08/long-powerful-history-how-we-militarized-police/.

Schumaker, Erin. "Police Reformers Push for De-Escalation Training, but the Jury Is Out on Its Effectiveness." *ABC News.* Jul 5, 2020. https://abcnews.go.com/Health/police-reformers-push-de-escalation-training-jury-effectiveness/story?id=71262003.

Schuppe, Jon. "How Facial Recognition Became a Routine Policing Tool in America." *NBC News.* May 11, 2019. https://www.nbcnews.com/news/us-news/how-facial-recognition-became-routine-policing-tool-america-n1004251.

Siegel, Michael. "Racial Disparities in Fatal Police Shootings: An Empirical Analysis Informed by Critical Race Theory." *Boston University Law Review*, vol. 100, no. 1069. https://www.bu.edu/bulawreview/files/2020/05/10-SIEGEL.pdf.

Solomon, Danyelle, Tom Jawetz, and Sanam Malik. "The Negative Consequences of Entangling Local Policing and Immigration Enforcement." *Center for American Progress.* Mar 21, 2017. https://www.americanprogress.org/issues/immigration/reports/2017/03/21/428776/negative-consequences-entangling-local-policing-immigration-enforcement/.

Thomas, Tobi, Adam Gabbatt, and Caelainn Barr. "Nearly 1,000 Instances of Police Brutality Recorded in US Anti-Racism Protests." *The Guardian.* Oct 29, 2020. https://www.theguardian.com/us-news/2020/oct/29/us-police-brutality-protest.

Tuccille, J.D. "U.S. Cops Are Facing a Recruitment Crisis: Will It Force Them to Change Their Ways?" *Reason.* Jun 25, 2019. https://reason.com/2019/06/25/us-cops-are-facing-a-recruitment-crisis-will-it-force-them-to-change-their-ways/.

"Understanding Community Policing." *NCJRS.* Office of Justice Programs. 1994. https://www.ncjrs.gov/pdffiles/commp.pdf.

"U.S. Criticized for Police Brutality, Racism at U.N. Rights Review." *NBC News.* Nov 10, 2020. https://www.nbcnews.com/news/nbcblk/u-s-criticized-police-brutality-racism-u-n-rights-review-n1247256.

Valdez, Jonah. "Some Police Agencies Won't Enforce New Stay-at-Home Coronavirus Orders, Others Will as a 'Last Resort.'" *OC Register.* Nov 19, 2020. https://www.ocregister.com/2020/11/19/some-police-agencies-will-not-enforce-new-stay-at-home-orders-is-a-last-resort-for-others/.

"Why Americans Don't Fully Trust Many Who Hold Positions of Power and Responsibility." *Pew Research Center.* Sep 19, 2019. https://www.pewresearch.org/politics/2019/09/19/why-americans-dont-fully-trust-many-who-hold-positions-of-power-and-responsibility/.

Williams, Timothy. "Study Supports Suspicion That Police Are More Likely to Use Force on Blacks." *New York Times.* Jul 7, 2016. https://www.nytimes.com/2016/07/08/us/study-supports-suspicion-that-police-use-of-force-is-more-likely-for-blacks.html.

Websites

Black Lives Matter Network
www.blacklivesmatter.com

The Black Lives Matter movement is a decentralized political action movement focused on calling attention to police abuse of African Americans. The movement became one of the most controversial of the 2010s when critics mistakenly alleged that the BLM movement was a violent or radical leftist movement or that members of the movement were involved in destructive looting following high-profile controversies like the George Floyd killing. There is no evidence that BLM members or organizers have been involved in any violent activities or property destruction, but local chapters of the organization have been active in organizing protests and demonstrations across the country.

International Association of Chiefs of Police
www.IACP.org

The International Association of Chiefs of Police supports research into outreach, education, and advocacy programs aimed at addressing problems faced by police. The IACP also funds and publishes research on police methods and strategies and on police culture. The IACP has supported some of the reform proposals put forward by organizations like Black Lives Matter, but has opposed the Defund the Police movement. The IACP does support moderate police reform and also funds and provides training and educational materials for regional police departments.

International Association of Women Police
www.iawp.org

The International Association of Women Police (IAWP) is an outreach and research organization focusing on women in law enforcement. The organization supports local and national lobbying to combat sex discrimination and to promote equal treatment of officers; supports research into issues surrounding female participation in police departments; and publishes research on challenges facing women in law enforcement around the world.

Movement for Black Lives

https://m4bl.org/

The Movement for Black Lives, stylized M4BL, is not a single group, but a coalition of associated groups working to bring attention to police abuse and, racial injustice in the criminal justice system. The organization includes the famous Black Lives Matter Network, in addition to smaller groups like the Color of Change and the ONE DC movements. The National Conference of Black Lawyers also works with the organization. M4BL has issued policy recommendations and has helped to author several bills addressing police violence or calling for greater oversight. Since the killing of George Floyd, M4BL has been one of the primary groups promoting the idea of defunding the police and redistributing funds currently used for police to other community and social welfare and groups.

National Association of Police Organizations (NAPO)

www.napo.org

The National Association of Police Organizations is a lobbyist group that represents regional and local police networks and officers and lobbies in Washington to increase funding and for other efforts aimed at providing additional support or resources for police officers. NAPO provides a resource on the political issues important to law enforcement officers and departments and helps officers determine what initiatives or proposals to support when elections are held.

National Black Police Association (NBPA)

www.blackpolice.org

The National Black Police Association (NBPA) is a national organization that seeks to represent regional and local black police officers' organizations and also provides political advocacy for the national population of black police officers across the country. In addition to chartered chapters across the United States, the NBPA has international members groups in Canada, the United Kingdom, and the U.S. territories. The NBPA provides scholarships, funding, and advocacy for African Americans seeking careers in law enforcement, and supports lobbies on political issues facing black law enforcement workers in America.

National Police Association

www.nationalpolice.org

The National Police Association is an activist organization that states its purpose is to highlight "abuses by anti-police elected officials," and to protect police against "powerful special interests." The organization provides assistance, resources, and legal aid for officers accused of violence or cases where officers have been injured or attacked while performing their duties. The organization is a proponent of the controversial "broken windows" policing policy, expanding public surveillance, and expanding the availability of military equipment to local police departments.

Index

1963 March on Washington, 9
287(g) program, 53-54, 56, 60
2020 presidential election, 52, 151
9/11, 76, 166, 199
911 calls, 69, 166

Abdullah, Melina, 142
Aeryon Labs, 168
aggressive policing, 14
Aguilar, Armando, 174
Akbar Nurid-Din Shaba, zz101
Allen, Charles, 186
Amazon, 160, 165-166, 171, 173, 175, 178, 190-194
ambush killings, 15
Amdur, Spencer, 64
American Civil Liberties Union (ACLU), 61, 65, 119-120, 175-176
Anaheim Police Department, 172
anti-bias training, 19
anti-police bias, 32
Arpaio, Joe, 56
arrest, 13, 16, 21, 39, 56, 64, 76-77, 82, 85, 93, 128, 130, 161, 172, 174-176, 179
Asian, 29, 175
Atlanta Police Department, 114, 169
audio analytic technology, 184
Austin Police Department, 99-100
automatic license plate readers, 166
automatic pattern recognition, 166
Azure cloud, 165-169, 171, 173

bail, 37, 57
Balko, Radley, 18
Baltimore Police Department, 22
Bannon, Stephen, 58
Beckham, Nathan, 168
behavioral health crisis, 111
Best, Carmen, 140
bias, ix, xi, 3-4, 19-20, 24, 32, 37-40, 115, 128, 160, 175, 178

Bicking, Dave, 125
Biden, Joe, 52, 67, 148, 151
Bierria, Alisa, 152
Black Americans, ix, xiii, 4-5, 7, 9-11, 13-14, 17-21, 23-24, 26-30, 32, 34-35, 37-39, 44, 50, 68, 70-71, 98, 111, 114, 124-126, 141-142, 145, 147-148, 150-155, 162, 165, 169-171, 174-175, 178-179, 181, 195, 199-200
Black communities, 9, 11, 14, 20-21, 30, 68, 151
Black Lives Matter, ix, 9-10, 18, 44, 124-125, 142, 153-154, 162, 165, 174, 195, 199
Black officers, 30
Black Panthers, 152
Bland, Sandra, 128-130
Blasio, Bill de, 174
"Blue wall of silence", 50
body armor, 11
body cameras, 15-16, 120, 125, 147, 150, 161-163, 166, 172, 180-189
Boston Marathon bombing, 139
Boston Police, 125, 181
Bradford, Steve, 126
Brannan, Andrew Howard, 14
Bratton, William, 59
broken windows theory, 24, 68
Brooks, Rayshard, 111, 169
Brown, David, 146
Brown, Michael, 147, 181, 185
Brown, Mike, 129-130
Brown, Peter, 65
budget reductions, 77, 137
burglaries, 76, 91, 147
Burlington Vermont Police Department, 161
Buscaino, Joe, 141
Bush, George W., 54, 93
Buttigieg, Pete, 120

Cabrera, Jorge, 98
Cagle, Matt, 192
Cahn, Albert Fox, 177
camera, 120, 152, 159-161, 166, 168-170, 181-188, 190-194
Capone, Al, 10
CARES Act, 81
Castile, Philando, 9, 11, 15, 154
Cattani, Robert, 18
cellphones, 15-16, 161, 183, 197
Centers for Disease Control and Prevention (CDC), 84, 88
Chacon, Joseph, 99
Chauvin, Derek, 16, 139, 150
Chavis, Kami, 182
Chicago Police Department, 170
chokeholds, 117, 124, 125, 147, 150
Christensen, Cory, 138
Cillizza, Chris, 151
civil liberties, xi, 3, 44, 61, 64, 119, 127, 153, 163, 177, 179, 185, 192, 195
civil rights, xi, 10, 44, 46-47, 49-50, 54, 67, 106, 119, 125, 137, 162-163, 166, 171, 175, 177, 195, 199
Civil Rights Era, 10, 49-50
Civil War, 18, 23, 94-95
civilian review boards, 147-148
Clark, Jamar, 154
Clearview AI, 172, 174, 178
Clinton, Bill, 52
closed-circuit TV, 166
Clyburn, Jim, 151
Cobb, Jelani, 154
Collaborative Reform Initiative (CRI), 68
collider bias, 37-39
communities, xi-xii, 4-5, 9-10, 13-14, 17, 21, 23-24, 44-47, 53-56, 58, 60, 67-68, 71, 77-78, 82, 93-94, 96, 105-106, 117-118, 125-126, 128, 134-135, 139, 141, 143, 145-146, 151, 154-155, 171, 180, 184, 193, 195, 199, 201

community, xii, 11, 14, 17, 19-20, 30, 34, 41, 43, 45-47, 55, 58-60, 67-72, 77, 81-84, 86, 92-93, 98-101, 105-110, 113, 117-122, 128, 135, 141-142, 152-153, 155-156, 170, 173, 179, 181-182, 186-187, 191-192, 199
community contacts, 70
community outreach, 41, 99, 107
community policing, 17, 43, 45-47, 55, 60, 67-72, 77, 98-99, 101, 107, 109-110, 141
community relations, 34, 135, 182
community trust, 55, 58, 67, 69
complaints, 83, 99, 166, 180-183, 186
contact information, 196
Conwall, Jason, 119
cooperation, 44, 46, 57, 64-65, 119, 129-130, 133, 166
cop killers, 15
coronavirus, 78-79, 81, 83-87, 91-94, 96, 100-101, 113, 124, 137, 142
corruption, xii, 106, 170
COVID-19, ix-x, 73, 75-79, 81-85, 88-93, 95-101, 126, 137-140, 169, 175
Craig, James, 175, 179
Crawford, Jamarhl, 125
Crawford, Kate, 172
crime reduction, 67, 115
crime scene, 168
crime statistics, 192
criminal justice system, 23-24, 26, 28, 37-38, 53, 81, 126, 134
crisis intervention training, 111, 113-114
Cullors, Patrisse, 153
Cuomo, Andrew, 117
Dallas Police Department, 182
dashcam, 9, 14, 15, 183
data collection, 200
data storage, 180, 189
Dataminr, 196
Davis, Angela, 152
Davis, Ed, 125, 139

Davis, Ron, 76, 81
de-escalation, 6, 107-116, 120, 149
decentralization, 68, 120
defendants, 37, 198
Defund the Police, ix, xii-xiii, 44, 49, 51, 72, 77-79, 117, 124, 131, 133-136, 137-140, 142, 145-149, 150-156, 162, 165
dehumanizing behaviors, 68
Democrats, 28, 50-51, 111, 126, 151, 155, 180, 184
demonstrators, 37
deportation force, 53, 59
Deschambault, Susan, 185
detainer request, 55, 57, 64-65
deterrence methods, 128
digital data, xii
Dinkheller, Kyle, 14
DiSalvo, Daniel, 147
discrimination, 21, 23-24, 38-39, 72, 106, 163, 193, 199
dispersion tactics, 10
diversity, 20, 45-46, 154
Domain Awareness System, 165-166, 169, 171-172
domestic violence, 15, 53, 83, 87, 91, 146
Dominguez, Robert, 98
drone, 159, 163, 168
drug-related offenses, 23

education, 39, 51, 105, 107, 109, 145-146
Edwards, Jordan, 183
Egerton, Samuel, 9
Elgin Police Department, 69
emergency calls, 138
emergency medical services (EMS), 84
encounter denominator, 37-38
Engel, Robin, 113
equal protection, 195-196, 198, 200
equal rights, 32
Erickson, David, 186
ethnicity, 27, 29, 56, 200

evidence collection, 83, 186
excessive force, xi, 3, 17, 50, 72, 169

face masks, 86, 99
Facebook, 11, 19, 95-96, 165, 175, 191, 195-197
facial recognition, xi, 159-160, 163, 165-179
Fagan, Jeffrey, 20
Federal Bureau of Investigation (FBI), 15, 96, 147, 187, 195-196
Ferguson, Missouri, 128, 147, 181, 185
Ferguson, Andrew Guthrie, 178, 190, 192
First Amendment, 198-200
Fletcher, Steve, 149
Floyd, George, 1, 9, 16-17, 23-26, 49-50, 67, 111, 114, 117-118, 124, 126, 138-139, 145, 150-151, 154, 165, 169-170, 195
Fourteenth Amendment, 198-199
Fourth Amendment, 57, 65, 197-198
Fraternal Order of Police, 100, 126
free expression, 195
free speech, 177, 196
Freeman, Marshall, 169
Fryer, Roland, 38

Gacek, Jon, 172
gang activity, 91-92, 94, 96, 129, 195, 200
Garner, Eric, 129-130, 147
Gaston, Shytierra, 23
Geist, Willie, 150
gender, 200
Genetec, 165, 168-172
Germany, 147
Gilmore, Ruth Wilson, 152
Gitlis, Zohar, 118
Glaude, Eddie S., Jr., 151
Goff, Phillip Atiba, 19, 154
goggles, 84, 99
Gonzalez, Ed, 56
Google, 173

GPS, 197
Grand Rapid Police Department, 70
Gray, Freddie, 128-130
gun crimes, 53
gun violence, 92, 140
guns, 95, 112
Gwinnet County Police, 191, 193

Haley, Nikki, 189
handcuff, 114
harassment, 193
Harris, Allison P., 38
Harris, Christopher, 70
Harris, Kamala, 151
Headley, Andrea, 182
helicopters, 174
high speed chase, 129
Hispanic, 5, 20, 29-30, 37-39, 68
Hispanic officers, 30
hit rate, 38
Ho, Angela, 113
Holmes, Malcolm D., 10
homeless, 138, 146
homicides, 91-92, 140, 146-147
Hoover, Herbert, 10
housing, 11-12, 22, 25, 36, 40, 51-52,
    56, 63, 66, 72, 84, 87, 90, 97-98,
    101, 116, 123, 127, 130, 134, 140,
    142, 144-146, 149, 153, 156, 170,
    173, 176, 179, 184, 189, 193-195,
    201
Houston Police Department, 69, 99,
    101
hyper-masculine traits, 112

IBM, 171, 173, 175
illegal detention, 65
immigrants, 10, 46, 53, 55, 58, 60, 62-
    63, 93-94
immigration, 43-44, 47, 53-64, 76, 93-
    94, 119, 153, 200
Immigration and Customs Enforcement
    (ICE), 54, 59, 64, 93, 119, 153

Immigration and Nationality Act, 54,
    59-60
implicit bias, 21, 24, 69, 128
incarceration, 68, 82, 134, 136, 153
inequality, 19, 68, 72, 78, 139, 162
Insight Policing, 107, 109, 128-130
Instagram, 174
intelligence, 107, 159, 166-167, 169-
    171, 175, 178, 195-196, 199-200
internal culture, 14
internal-affairs departments, 148
International Association of Chiefs of
    Police, 187, 196
International Association of Fire Fight-
    ers, 100
Internet, 167, 175
Internet of Things, 167
investigation, 10, 19, 44, 55, 83, 96,
    139, 147, 172, 187, 196, 200

jail, 37, 54-56, 61, 64-65, 81, 152
Japan, 147
Jennings, Wesley G., 98
Jim Crow laws, 10
Johnson, Eddie Bernice, 116
Johnson, Lyndon B., 11, 52

Kaba, Mariame, 153
Kanbay, Renan, 114
Karen Bass, 126
Kelling, George, 68
Kessler, Rebecca, 142
Khosa, Collins, 169
King, Martin Luther, Jr., 10, 50, 195
King, Rodney, 11
Knox, Dean, 38
Kobach, Kris, 58
Kraska, Peter, 17
Krekorian, Paul, 143
Ku Klux Klan, 23, 152

Lally, Craig, 143
Latino, 24, 60, 71, 141, 153-154, 200
law and order, 6, 52, 69, 105

law enforcement agencies, 53, 57, 65, 67, 81, 85, 87, 96, 118, 120, 126, 137, 165-167, 171, 173, 180, 185, 188-190, 193, 197

Lawn, Joey, 18

Lawrence, Daniel, 68, 71, 181, 185

lawsuits, 57, 65, 119-120, 176

Lee, John, 141

Legewie, Joscha, 20

LeValley, David, 170

Levitz, Eric, 148

Lewis, Latonya, 101

Lexipol, 117-122

LGBTQ, 14

liability protection, 65

Llewellyn, Rich, 142

local government, 44, 51, 200-201

local law enforcement, 53-54, 58-59, 64-65, 76, 83, 119, 126, 159

lockdown, 87, 91-93, 95-96, 169

Logan, Eric, 120

Lori Lightfoot, 83

Los Angeles Police Department, 59, 77, 84, 137-140, 141-144, 146, 148, 153

Lowe, Will, 38

mainstream media, 11

Martin, Trayvon, 152

mask mandate, 77

masking, 88-89

Mata, Mike, 99

McDonald, Laquan, 183

McHarris, Philip V., 146

McHarris, Thenjiwe, 146

Meares, Tracey L., 153

Medina, Jason, 99

Memphis, Tennessee, 128-129

mental health, xiii, 20-21, 51, 53, 72, 82, 107-109, 121, 142, 146, 149

mental health services, 72, 82, 142

mental health training, 149

mental illness, xii, 13, 107-110, 113-114, 133, 138, 145-146

Microsoft, 165-173, 175

militarization, xi-xiii, 11, 103, 106, 109-110

military equipment, xi, 69

Milwaukee Police Department, 182

Minneapolis Police Department, 16, 23, 26, 49, 71, 111, 114, 117, 124-125, 138-139, 145-146, 148-149, 153-154, 156, 183

minorities, xi, 4, 23, 50

minority communities, 23-24, 45, 141

misconduct, x, xii, 3, 7, 13, 30, 43, 50, 106, 135, 161-162, 183, 188

Moore, Mark, 68

Moore, Michel, 138

Moskos, Peter, 15

Mueller, John, 100

Mummolo, Jonathan, 38

murder, 9, 24, 117-118, 125, 128, 139, 153, 165, 170, 178, 183

Nadella, Satya, 165

Nagel, Michael, 19

National Institute of Standards and Technology (NIST), 175

Native American, 175

neck restraints, 125

Neighbors app, 191-193

Nesiba, Reynold, 187

New York City Police Department, 18, 38, 44, 46-47, 49, 78-79, 81, 113-114, 117-123, 137-138, 146-148, 165-166, 170-171, 174-177, 199

Newsham, Peter, 82

Newsom, Gavin, 126

Newton, Huey, 195

Nixon, 52

nonviolent crimes, 82

nonviolent incidents, 142

O'Neill, James, 177

Obama, Barack, 54, 68, 71, 153, 181, 185

Ocasio-Cortez, Alexandria, 134, 136, 148
officer behavior, 182
Oliver, Michael, 170, 178
oppression, 9-10
Oracle, 171, 173
Outlaw, Danielle, 82

Palantir, 172
pandemic, ix, 73, 75-76, 78-79, 81-84, 88-89, 91-94, 96, 98-100, 113, 124, 137-140, 151
Pantaleo, Daniel, 147
Paoline, Eugene III, 15
Parker, Julie, 187
patrols, 18, 23, 68, 86, 165
Peel, Robert, 106
Pelosi, Nancy, 126, 151
people of color, 14, 57, 124, 165-166, 169, 173, 175, 178, 193
Perez, Rosie, 100
Petty, Tawana, 170, 179
Philadelphia Police Department, 82
physical danger, 16
physical force, 111
Pieper, Shannon, 118
Pimentel, Mark, 19
Piner, Kevin, 18
Pittsburgh Police Department, 190-194
planting evidence, 13
police abolitionists, 14
police academy, 15, 69, 113
police brutality, xi, xiii, 3, 5, 7, 9-12, 18, 20, 23, 25, 46-47, 49-51, 69, 98, 100, 124-125, 141, 148, 152, 169
police chiefs, 56, 60, 93, 147, 185
police custody, 128
police dogs, 10, 174
police ideology, 14, 18-20
police killings, 10, 15, 70, 181, 195
police leadership, 116
police legitimacy, 70-71, 129
police misconduct, x, xii, 3, 13, 43, 161-162, 188

police reform, ix, 3, 6, 51, 77, 111, 117-118, 124-127, 133-135, 138, 145, 180-181, 183-184
police spending, 141-142
police stations, 68-69, 99
police surveillance, 157, 162, 165, 167, 169-170, 173, 193
police training, xii, 45, 107
police unions, 20, 51, 124-127, 147-148, 181
police violence, 3-4, 13, 16-17, 24, 44, 49, 147, 153-155, 169-170
Polis, Jared, 127
population denominator, 37, 39
Portillo, Shannon, 20
poverty, 11, 76, 106, 145
Pozo, Brandon del, 161
PPE, 83-84, 99
predictive policing, 166, 172
prejudice, x-xii, 4-5, 20, 43, 78, 105, 133, 162, 199
Pretzer, William, 10
Price, Curren, 141
prison, 68, 81, 101, 152-153, 155
privacy, xii, 157, 159-161, 163, 174, 178-179, 184, 193, 195-198
private messages, 196
privatization, 118, 121
Project Green Light, 170-171
prosecution, 92, 96, 183, 191
protesters, xii-xiii, 9, 13, 17-18, 20, 26, 32, 37, 49, 50-52, 67, 117, 124, 145, 150, 155, 169-170, 174-175, 177-178, 195, 199
protests, xi, 1, 6, 9-11, 14, 17-18, 21, 23-24, 26, 32, 44, 46-47, 49-50, 52, 67, 69, 93, 99, 101, 103, 106, 117-118, 120, 124, 128, 138, 141, 148, 153, 155, 165, 170, 174-175, 179, 195, 199
psychological stressors, 19
PTSD, 14, 21
public health, 77, 81, 85, 89, 121, 145
public housing, 98, 170, 195

public safety, 3, 51, 53-62, 69-71, 76, 82-84, 86-87, 96, 119, 124, 137-141, 143, 145, 167-168, 171, 186, 189-190, 192, 195

public sector alerts, 196

public services, 51

public trust, x, 6, 45-46, 53, 126, 133, 148, 159, 162, 188, 192

punishment, x, 128, 135, 154

Purnell, Derecka, 71

quarantine, 81, 85, 89

Rabideau, Clyde, 117

race, x-xi, 4-5, 7-8, 18, 23-24, 26-27, 29-33, 35-36, 56, 94-95, 124, 151, 155, 182, 200

racial bias, ix, xi, 3-4, 19-20, 37-39, 114-115, 160, 175, 178, 199

racial discrimination, 23-24, 106, 163

racial disparities, 4, 7-8, 10, 37-39, 71, 116, 175, 182

racial equality, 69

racial hierarchy, 19

racial inequality, 139

racial injustice, 24, 49-50, 67, 99, 124

racial prejudice, x-xii, 4-5, 43, 133

racial profiling, 56

racial slur, 18

racial superiority, 23

racial violence, 18, 154

racism, xi, xiii, 4-6, 13, 18-20, 23-24, 37, 39, 47, 50, 72, 98, 100, 121, 153, 162, 170

racist policing, 118, 165

Ralph, Laurence, 17

Ramsay, Rick, 65

rape, 147, 178

Reagan, Ronald, 52

ReconRobotics, 168

recruiting, 138-139

reform, ix-x, xii, 3, 5-6, 43, 49, 51, 67-72, 77, 103, 107-109, 111, 117-118, 124-127, 131, 133-138, 140, 142, 144-148, 150, 152, 154-156, 180-181, 183-184, 195, 197, 199-201

Rehnquist, William, 198

Rekognition, 175, 178

religion, 56, 200

Republicans, 14, 28, 50-52, 58, 111, 125-126, 184

retention, 138-139, 200

retirement, ix, 139, 142-143

Reynolds, Diamond, 11

Reynolds, Sean, 188

Reynolds-Stenson, Heidi, 18

Rialto Police Department, 181

right to privacy, 195

Ring, 9, 190-194

Ringgenberg, Mark, 154

Rios, Ray, 142

riots, 10-11, 44, 50, 94, 195

Rizer, Arthur, 13

robbery, 178

Roberts, Scott, 125, 137

robots, 165, 168

Rodriguez, Nicole, 101

Rolfe, Garrett, 114

Rose, Carol, 127

Rosedahl, Leslie, 125

Rubenstein, Josh, 142

Rushing, Jessica, 100

Sanctuary Cities, 43, 53-63, 64-66, 93

Sanders, Bernie, 148, 151

Sandoval, Brian, 188

school safety, 138

Schuessler, Adam, 69

Schwartz, Joanna, 119

Schwarze, Dustin, 154

science, xiii, 38, 88, 116, 134, 147, 150

Scotland, 112

Scott, Phil, 89

Scott, Tim, 111

searche and seizure, 55, 197

secrecy, 197

security cameras, 191, 193

segregation, 11

self-quarantining, 88
serious crime, 24, 55, 93
"serve and protect," xii, 67, 135
Sewpersad, Parboo, 169
sexual orientation, 200
sexual violence, 153-154
San Francisco Police Department, 19
Shehk, Mohamed, 155
sheriffs, 61, 65, 186
Shields, Erika, 169
shootings, 7-8, 14, 51, 71, 124, 126, 185, 196
shoplifting, 177-178
siege mentality, 16-17
Sierra-Arèvalo, Michael, 15, 70
Siminoff, Jamie, 193
Sinders, Caroline, 193
Sisay, Samah, 152
Slatton, Scott, 189
Slaughter, Justin, 188
slave patrols, 18, 23
slaves, 5, 18, 23, 105
Smith, Brad, 172
Smith, John, 10
Snapchat, 195, 200
social distancing, 75, 82, 89, 99
social dominance orientation, 19
social justice, 121, 138-140
social media, 3, 50, 92, 95-96, 162, 174, 185, 190-192, 195-201
social media monitoring, 195-196, 198-201
socialization, 15
Sotomayor, Sonia, 197
South Africa, 92, 169
state surveillance, 195
stay-at-home orders, 78, 83
Steelberg, Chad, 171
stereotype, 11
stop and frisk, 24, 128
Stored Communications Act (SCA), 198
subpoena, 198
substance abuse, 53, 121, 146

super spreader events, 89
SuperDroid Robots, 168
surveillance, xi, 157, 159-162, 165-173, 177-179, 184, 190-191, 193, 195-196, 198-200
Special Weapons and Tactics (SWAT), x, 106, 153
systemic racism, 37, 39, 72

tactical training, 69, 106
Tait, Dr. Lewis, Jr., 99
Takei, Carl, 119
Taylor, Breonna, 124-125, 145, 195
tear gas, x, 103
technology, xi, 11, 23, 56, 82, 137-139, 159-163, 166, 169-172, 174-175, 177-180, 183-184, 192-193
Tenth Amendment, 64
terrorist attacks, 54, 76, 96, 120, 177
thefts, 147, 178
"thin blue line," 17
third-party doctrine, 197
three-strike sentencing rule, 68
torture, 17
torturing suspects, 170
training, xii, 6, 15, 19, 45-46, 53-54, 56-58, 64-65, 68-69, 77, 103, 106-116, 118, 120, 122, 125-126, 130, 133, 137-139, 147-149, 153, 181, 187
transparency, 71, 118-120, 148, 162, 181, 183, 186, 192, 196
Trejo, Lisa, 101
Trejo, Marvin Wayne, 101
Trump, Donald, ix, 43-44, 47, 49, 52-55, 57-59, 62-63, 67, 69, 92-94, 115, 126, 133, 151
trust, ix-x, xii, 3, 6, 43, 45-46, 53-56, 58, 67, 69-70, 98-101, 106-107, 109-110, 117, 126, 128-130, 133, 135, 148, 159, 162, 180, 186, 188, 192-193
trust-building measures, 67, 69, 98, 100

Twitter, 152-153, 175, 196
Tyler, Tom, 71

U. S. Congress, 62, 81, 124, 175, 177, 180, 201
U.S. Constitution, 21, 44, 62
U.S. Department of Homeland Security, 54, 59, 61
U.S. Department of Justice, 56, 59, 68, 81, 110, 114, 181, 187
U. S. Drug Enforcement Administration (DEA), 170
U.S. Supreme Court, 58, 89, 197-199
United Kingdom (UK), 4, 86, 112, 181
undercover operations, 196-198, 200
unnecessary force, x, 147
urban renewal, 11
use of force, x, 3, 6, 13, 23, 38-39, 45, 51, 67, 70-71, 107, 111, 113-116, 120, 125, 128, 180-183, 186

vaccine, 89
vandalism, 24, 82
Veritone, 165, 171-172
victims, 5, 10, 55, 58, 68, 91, 152, 178
Victorian, Sheryl, 101
video, 11, 15, 23, 95, 124, 128, 159-160, 162, 166, 168-172, 180, 182-185, 187-188, 191, 193
video analytics, 166, 169
Villaraigosa, Antonio, 141
violence, ix-xi, 3-6, 9, 11, 13, 15-19, 23-24, 43-44, 49-50, 52-53, 83, 87, 91-92, 94-96, 98, 106-107, 128, 135, 140, 146-147, 152-155, 162, 169-170, 195
violent crime, x, 4, 71, 92, 93, 106, 113, 135, 137, 177, 179

Violent Crime Control and Law Enforcement Act, 50, 68
violent death, 15
violent offenders, 51, 171
Vitale, Alex, 121, 151

Wallace, Nakia, 171
Walz, Tim, 125
War on Drugs, 7-8, 68, 106
warrant, 64-65, 160, 177, 196-198
warrior training, 148
Watkins, Tannyr, 187
Watson, Steve, 139
Weaver, Vesla, 21
Wexler, Chuck, 55, 60, 112, 137
whistleblower, 17
white officers, 30, 32
White, Michael, 181
Whittaker, Meredith, 172
Wilborn, Rick, 188
Williams, Eric, 170
Williams, Robert Julian-Borchak, 170, 178
wiretapping, 179
Wittkowski, John, 70
Worden, William, 122
workplace pressure, ix

Yanez, Jeronimo, 9, 15
Yglesias, Matthew, 152
Yoes, Patrick, 126
YouTube, 95, 175

Zhao, Jihong, 69
Zimmerman, George, 152
Zoom, 99